To my Ph[...]
Dr. B[...] —

Whose "techne" is superb
and his integrity even better.

Janet Giddings
2017

Beware the Evil Eye

BEWARE
THE EVIL EYE

The Evil Eye in the Bible and the Ancient World

—Volume 1—

Introduction, Mesopotamia, and Egypt

JOHN H. ELLIOTT

 CASCADE *Books* • Eugene, Oregon

BEWARE THE EVIL EYE
The Evil Eye in the Bible and the Ancient World
Volume 1: Introduction, Mesopotamia, and Egypt

Cascade Books
An Imprint of Wipf and Stock Publishers
199 W. 8th Ave., Suite 3
Eugene, OR 97401

www.wipfandstock.com

ISBN 13: 978–1-62032–147-8

Cataloging-in-Publication data:

Elliott, John Hall.

Beware the evil eye : the evil eye in the Bible and the ancient world / John H. Elliiott.

xiv + 210 p.; 23 cm. Includes bibliographical references and indexes.

ISBN 13: 978-1-62032-147-8

Vol. 1: Introduction, Mesopotamia, and Egypt

1. Evil eye. 2. Evil eye—Mesopotamia. 3. Evil eye—Egypt. 4. Envy. I. Title.

GN475.6 E45 2015

Manufactured in the U.S.A.   11/06/2015

For Dick Rohrbaugh
Context Group colleague, dear friend, expert himself in Evil Eye lore,
and
Madison River angler *sans pareil*.
in gratitude
for years of creative collaboration
and for generous assistance on this project in particular.
Abaskantos!

"The Eye is Evil, the most Evil thing"
(Sumerian incantation against the Evil Eye, YOS 11,71)

CONTENTS

ILLUSTRATIONS

PREFACE

This four volume study traces evidence of Evil Eye belief and practice in the ancient world from Mesopotamia (c. 3000 BCE) to Late Roman Antiquity (c. 600 CE), with particular attention to the Bible and post-biblical traditions of Israel and early Christianity.

Belief in the Evil Eye is a long-standing and widespread folk concept that some persons are enabled by nature to injure others, cause illness and loss, and destroy any person, animal or thing through a powerful noxious glance emanating from the eye. Also known as "fascination" (Greek: *baskania*; Latin: *fascinatio*), this belief holds that the eye is an active organ that emits destructive emanations charged by negative dispositions (especially malevolence, envy, miserliness, and withheld generosity). These emanations arise in the heart or soul, and are projected outward against both animate and inanimate objects. The full constellation of notions comprising the Evil Eye complex includes the expectation that various prophylactic words, gestures, images, and amulets have the power to counter and avert the damaging power of the Evil Eye.

From its likely origin in ancient Sumer (3000 BCE) and its early spread to Egypt and the Circum-Mediterranean region, to its later movement eastward to India and westward and northward to Europe, the belief eventually made its way from "old worlds" to "new." It now constitutes a cultural phenomenon with personal, social, and moral implications that has spanned the centuries and encircled the globe.

This multi-volume study concentrates on the Evil Eye phenomenon in the ancient world, with new and extensive attention to mention of it in the Bible and the biblical communities of Israel and early Christianity. It is an up-to-date, comprehensive account of the extant ancient texts, amulets, and the modern research on this perennial topic. It is the first book-length study of all the biblical and related texts mentioning the Evil Eye. The study consists of four volumes, with the material on the Evil Eye treated in roughly historical sequence from ancient Mesopotamia to Late Roman antiquity. This is the context within which Evil Eye belief and practice mentioned in the Bible is best understood.

Volume One opens with an introductory overview of references to, and research on, the Evil Eye from the ancient past to the modern present (Chapter One). Chapter Two of Volume One examines Evil Eye belief and practice in ancient Mesopotamia and Egypt. Volume Two is devoted to evidence on the subject from ancient Greece and Rome. Within the geographical and cultural matrix detailed in these first two volumes, the evidence of Evil Eye belief and practice in the Bible is then examined (Volume Three). A final volume considers post-biblical evidence of Evil Eye belief and practice in Rabbinic Israel (Chapter One) and early Christianity (Chapter Two) through Late Antiquity (c. 600 CE). Concluding reflections on the import and implications of our study (Chapter Three) close this final volume.

The fulsome footnotes in these four volumes intend to register the abundance of the ancient sources relevant to our topic, the pertinent information on the physical, social, and cultural contexts of these sources, and the wide extent of modern research on the topic of Evil Eye belief and practice. It is hoped that this updated overview of research since the early years of the twentieth century will provide the basis and stimulus for future studies of this fascinating topic.

ACKNOWLEGMENTS

This has been a research project like no other in my professional experience. The extensive ramifications of the topic –Evil Eye belief and practice from antiquity to the present—have required research in a diversity of fields and disciplines (history, archaeology, ancient languages, the social sciences, biblical exegesis, folklore and cultural studies, among others). From colleagues, students, audience members, and readers over the course of almost three decades I have been graced with a constant flow of information consisting of bibliographical references, newspaper clippings, photographs, personal experiences and anecdotes, and even amulets acquired by my wanderlusting friends. Your names are legion and too numerous to acknowledge individually, but you are held in gratitude, each and every one. To one and all I am most grateful for your interest and your assistance in this project.

Members of the Context Group, in particular, have been especially generous with their information, photos, and feedback (Dick Rohrbaugh, Dennis Duling, K. C. Hanson, John Pilch, Bruce Malina, Jerry Neyrey, Carolyn Osiek, Dietmar Neufeld, Doug Oakman, Zeba Crook; Anselm Hagedorn, Ray Hobbs, Gary Stansell, Alicia Batten). Other colleagues have also generously provided support and information: David Balch, George Bohigian, M.D. Eugene Botha, Fred Brenk, Bob Coote, Jan Giddings, Ray Humphreys, Mark Jesenko, Petri Luomenon, Vijaya Nagarajan, Peter Oakes, Romano Penna, Chris Seeman, Brenda Schildgen, Phil Stevens, among scores of others. Special thanks to Rev. Dr. Anselm Hagedorn for his assistance in acquiring some vital Mesopotamian materials. More thanks to particular colleagues for their critical reading of drafts of one or more of the volumes: Bob Coote, Norman Gottwald, Gary Stansell, Dennis Duling, Stephen Black, and Richard Rohrbaugh, to whom this first volume is gratefully dedicated.

Thanks likewise to my generous hosts at various universities where I delivered lectures on this topic: Professor Andries van Aarde at the

University of Pretoria, South Africa; for collaboration with Eugene Botha at UNISA, South Africa; to professors Adriana Destro and Mauro Pesce at the University of Bologna; to Professor Alexander Negrov, rector of St. Petersburg Christian University, St. Petersburg, Russia; Professor Santiago Guijarro Oporto at Salamanca University, Spain; and Professor Philip Esler, St. Andrews University, Scotland.

I am grateful to the National Endowment for the Humanities for the Summer Stipend (FT-34963-91) of $3,750 awarded 6-8/1991 for research on the Evil Eye, eventually published as "The Evil Eye and the Sermon on the Mount: Contours of a Pervasive Belief in Social Scientific Perspective." *Biblical Interpretation* 2/1 (1994) 51–84.

Warm thanks go also to Dr. K. C. Hanson for his keen interest in the topic and his generous editorial aid and counsel over all these years. Thanks too to Ian Creeger, patient and expert typesetter. For the errors that remain. I have only myself and some nasty Evil Eye to blame.

A special thanks to my sweet Linde for your patience with your much-too- preoccupied *Ehemann*, especially in the concluding years of this project, and for your assistance with this publication in so many loving ways. Jetzt, Suesse, endlich Schluss mit dem Schreiben und ein frischer Anfang des Zusammenlebens!

May each and every one be and remain *abaskantos*—safe from the Evil Eye!

ABBREVIATIONS FOR
CHAPTER 1: INTRODUCTION

ABD *The Anchor Bible Dictionary.* 6 vols. Edited by David Noel Freedman. New York: Doubleday, 1992

ET English translation

HWDA *Handwörterbuch des deutschen Aberglaubens.* 10 vols. Edited by H. Bächtold-Stäubli and E. Hoffmann-Krayer. Berlin: de Gruyter, 1927–1942; Reprinted, 1987

HERE *Encyclopaedia of Religion and Ethics.* 13 vols. Edited by James Hasting, James, et al. Edinburgh: T. & T. Clark, 1908–1927. 4th ed. Reprinted, 1958

IDB *Interpreter's Dictionary of the Bible.* 4 vols. Edited by G. W. Buttrick. Nashville: Abingdon, 1962

JSNTSup Journal for the Study of the New Testament Supplements

LCL Loeb Classical Library

RAC *Reallexikon für Antike und Christentum.* Sachwörterbuch zur Auseinandersetzung des Christentums mit der antiken Welt. 25+ vols. Edited by Theodore Klauser et al. Stuttgart: Hiersemann, 1950–

REB *Revue des études Byzantines,* successor of *Échos d'Orient.* Paris, 1897–1942

ABBREVIATIONS FOR CHAPTER 2: MESOPOTAMIA AND EGYPT

A. ANCIENT PRIMARY SOURCES

Mesopotamian and Ugaritic Sources

ALASP(M) Abhandlungen zur Literatur Alt-Syrien-Palästinas (und Mesopotamiens)

ArOr *Archiv Orientální*

AO Antiquités orientales. Tablets in the collection of the Louvre Museum, Paris

BAM *Die babylonisch-assyrische Medizin in Texten und Untersuchungen.* Edited by Franz Köcher. 6 vols. Berlin: de Gruyter, 1963–1980

BL *Babylonian Liturgies.* Edited by Stephen H. Langdon. Paris: Geuthner, 1913

BM Tablets, Objects of the British Museum

CAT *Canaanite in the Amarna Tablets.* Edited by A. F. Rainey. Handbuch der Orientalistik I 25,1–4, Leiden: Brill, 1996

CT Cuneiform Texts from Babylonian Tablets in the British Museum. 58 Volumes.

IM Museum siglum of the Iraq Museum in Baghdad

KTU *Die keil-alphabetischen Texte aus Ugarit.* Edited by M. Dietrich, O. Loretz and J. Sanmartín. AOAT 24.1. Neukirchen-Vluyn: Neukirchener, 1976

KTU²   *Die keil-alphabetischen Texte aus Ugarit.* Edited by M. Dietrich, O. Loretz and J. Sanmartín. 2nd ed. ALASP(M) 8. Munster: *Ugarit*-Verlag, 1995

MDP   Mémoires de la Délégation en Perse. Paris 1900–

PT   Pyramid Text

RS   Ras Shamra. Museum siglum of the Louvre and Damascus Museums

SEL   *Studi Epigrafici e Linguistici sul Vicino Oriente Antico.* Verona: Essedue, 1984–

STT   *The Sultantepe Tablets.* Volume 1. Edited by O. R. Gurney and J. J. Finkelstein. Occasional Publications of the BritishInstitute of Archaeology at Ankara no. 3. London: British Institute of Archaeology at Ankara, 1957

        The Sultantepe Tablets. Volume 2. Edited by O. R. Gurney and P. Hulin. Occasional Publications of the British Institute of Archaeology at Ankara no. 7. London: British Institute of Archaeology at Ankara, 1964

TCL   Textes Cunéiforms, Musées du Louvre. Paris 1910–

UDB   Ugaritic Databank (electronic) Madrid 2003–

VAT   Tablets in the Collections of the Staatliches Museum, Berlin, Vorderasiatische Abteilung, Tontafeln

YOS   Yale Oriental Series, Babylonian Texts. New Haven, 1915–

YOS 11   *Early Mesopotamian Incantations and Rituals.* Edited by J. van Dijk, M. I. Hussey, and Albrecht Götze. YOS 11. New Haven: Yale University Press, 1985

Papyri, Inscriptions, Epigrapha, Ostraca

BGU   *Ägyptische Urkunden aus den staatlichen Museen zu Berlin.* Griechische Urkunden. 15 vols. Berlin: Weidmann, 1895–1983

CIG   Corpus inscriptionum graecarum. Edited by A. Boeckh. 4 vols. Berlin, 1825–1877

CIL   Corpus inscriptionum latinarum

CIL   Corpus inscriptionum latinarum. Begun by T. Mommsen. 17 vols. Berlin: Reimer, 1862–

Epigr. Gr.   See Kaibel, *Epigr. Gr.*

GVI   *Griechische Vers-inschriften.* I: *Die Grabepigramma.* Edited by
W. Peek. Berlin: Akademie, 1955

Kaibel, *Epigr. Gr. Epigrammata Graeca ex lapidibus conlecta.* Edited by G.
Kaibel. Berlin: Reimer, 1878

GMPT   *The Greek Magical Papyri in Translation, Including the Demotic
Texts.* Edited by H. D. Betz et al. Chicago: University of Chicago Press, 1986. See PGM

IG   *Inscriptiones Graecae.* Berlin, 1873- 1903

IG²   *Inscriptiones Graecae, editio minor.* Berlin, 1913–

IGLS   *Inscriptions grecques et latines de la Syrie,* edited by L. Jalabert,
R. Mouterde, et al. Paris: Geuthner, 1929

IGRRP   *Inscriptiones Graecae ad res romanas pertinentes.* Vol. 1. Paris:
E. Leroux, 1901

ILS   Inscriptiones Latinae Selectae. Edited by H. Dessau. 3 vols. In
5 parts. Berlin: Weidmann, 1892–1916

O.Amst.   *Ostraka in Amsterdam Collections,* edited by R. S. Bagnall P. J.,
Sijpestein P. J. et al. Studia Amstelodamensia ad epigraphicam,
ius antiquum et papyrologicam pertinentia, 9. Zutphen, 1976

O.Flor.   *The Florida Ostraka: Documents from the Roman Army in Upper Egypt,* edited by R .S. Bagnall. Greek, Roman and Byzantine Monographs 7. Durham, N.C. 1976. Nos. 1–31

OGIS   *Orientis Graeci Inscriptiones Selectae.* Edited by W. Ditten-
berger, 2 vols. Leipzig: Hirzel, 1903–1905

PAES   Première Année des Etudes de Santé

PDM   *Papyri Demoticae Magicae.* Translated in *The Greek Magical
Papyri in Translation Including the Demotic Spells.* Edited by
H. D. Betz. Chicago: University of Chicago Press, 1986.

PGM   *Papyri Graece Magicae: Die griechischen Zauberpapyri.* 2 vols.
Vol. 1 (1928), Vol. 2 (1931). Edited by K. Preisendanz. Berlin:
Teubner, 1928–1931. Vol. 3 (1942), edited by K. Preisendanz
et al. 1941. 2d. rev. ed. by A. Heinrichs. 2 vols. Stuttgart: Teu-
bner, 1973–74. cf. ET: *Greek Magical Papyri in Translation,* ed.
H. D. Betz

Papyrus Leiden   *The Demotic Magical Papyrus of London and Leiden.*
Edited by F. L. Griffith and Herbert Thompson. London:
Grevel, 1904

P.Leid.   *Papyri Graeci Musei Antiquarii Publici.* 2 vols. Edited by C.
Leemans. Leiden: Brill. Vol. 1 (1843); vol. 2 (1885)

P.Lond.   *Greek Papyri in the British Museum.* 7 vols. Edited by F. G. Kenyon et al. Vols.1 and 2 edited by F. G. Kenyon; Vol. 3 edited by F. G. Kenyon and H. I. Bell; Vols. 4 and 5 edited by. H. I. Bell. London: British Museum, 1893–1974. =P.Mag.Lond.

P.Mag. Leid.W.   Leiden Magical Papyrus W. Edited by A. Dieterich

P.Mag.Par.   C. Wessley, "Griechische Zauberpapyrus von Paris und London." *Denkschrift der kaiserlichen Akademie der Wissenschaft, Philosoph.-Historische Klasse* 36/2 (1888) 27–108; "Die Pariser Papyri des Fundes von El-Faijûm." *Denkschrift der kaiserlichen Akademie der Wissenschaft, Philosoph.-Historische Klasse* 37/2 Vienna (1889) 97–256.

P.Mich   University of Michigan Papyri, various editors. 1931—

P.Oxy.   *The Oxyrhynchus Papyri.* Edited by B. P. Grenfell and A. S. Hunt et al. 72 vols. London: Egypt Exploration Society, 1898–1972

P.Petr.   *The Flinders Petrie Papyri.* 3 vols. Edited by J. Mahaffy and J. Smyly. Dublin: Acamemy House, 1891–1905

P.Rein.   *Papyrus grecs et démotiques recueilles en Égypte.* Edited by T. Rienach, W. Spiegelberg, and S. de Ricci. París: Leroux, 1905 [Milan 1972]

PSI   *Papiri greci e latini.* Pubblicazioni della Società italiana per la ricerca dei papyri greci e latini in Egítto., Florence: Arini, 1912–

P.Thead.   *Papyrus de Théadelphie.* Edited by P. Jourget. Paris: Fontemoing, 1911

P.Turner   *Papyri Greek and Egyptian Edited by Various Hands in Honour of E.G. Turner on the Occasion of his Seventieth Birthday.* London 1981

Rev.Ég.   *Revue égyptologique*

SB   *Sammelbuch griechischer Urkinden aus Ägypten.* Edited by Friedrich Preisigke et al. 13 vols. Berlin: de Gruyter, 1915–1979

SEG   *Supplementum Epigraphicum Graecum.* Leiden, 1923–1971. Edited by H. W. Pleket and R. S. Stroud et al. Amsterdam: Gieben, 1972–

van Haelst, *Catalogue*   J. van Haelst, *Catalogue des papyrus littéraires juifs et chrétiens.*Université de Paris IV. Série Papyrologie 1. Paris: Publications de la Sorbonne, 1976

2. MODERN ENCYCLOPEDIAS, JOURNALS, SERIES

ALASP(M)	Abhandlungen zur Literatur Alt-Syrien-Palastinas (und Mesopotamiens)
AO	*Archiv Orientalni*
AOAT	Alter Orient und Altes Testament
AOS	American Oriental Series (New Haven 1925–)
ASJ	Acta Sumerologica (Hiroshima 1979–)
BIFAO	Bulletin de l'Institut Francais d'Archéologie Orientale au Caire, Le Caire
CBQ	*Catholic Biblical Quarterly*
CRAIBL	Comptes rendus des séances de l'Académie des Inscriptions et Belles-Lettres. Paris: Picard, 1857–
Daremberg-Saglio	Daremberg, Charles and Edmond Saglio, eds. *Dictionnaire des antiquités grecques et romaines*. 10 vols. Paris: Hachette, 1877–1919
HERE	*Encyclopaedia of Religion and Ethics*. 13 vols. Edited by James Hastings et al. 13 vols. Edinburgh: T. & T. Clark, 1908–1926
IDB	*The Interpreter's Dictionary of the Bible*. 4 vols. Edited by George Arthur Buttrick. Nashville: Abingdon, 1962
IDBSup	*The Interpreter's Dictionary of the Bible Supplementary Volume*. Edited by K. Crim. Nashville: Abingdon, 1976
ISBE	*The International Standard Bible Encyclopaedia*. 4 vols. Edited by James Orr, et al. Revised ed. by M. G. Kyle. Chicago: Howard–Severance, 1929; revised and reedited by Geoffrey W. Bromiley. Grand Rapids: Eerdmans, 1979–1988
JESHO	*Journal of the Economic and Social History of the Orient*
JNES	*Journal of Near Eastern Studies*
JRAS	*Journal of the Royal Asiatic Society of Great Britain and Ireland*
LCL	Loeb Classical Library
NABU	Nouvelles Assyriologiques Bréves et Utilitaires
NISABA	Studi Assiriologici Messinesi
ÖAW	Die Österreichische Akademie der Wissenschaften
OBO	Orbis biblicus et orientalis
PSBA	*Proceedings of the Society of Biblical Archaeology*
TWAT	*Theologisches Wörterbuch zum Alten Testament.*
UF	*Ugarit-Forschungen 1969–*

ZA	*Zeitschrift für Assyrologie und vorderasiatische Archäologie*
ZÄS	*Zeitschrift für ägyptische Sprache und Altertumskunde*
ZPE	*Zeitschrift für Papyrologie und Epigraphik*

OTHER ABBREVIATIONS AND SIGLA

adj.	adjective
adv.	adverb
a.k.a.	also known as, alias
act.	active
AMB	Aramaic Magic Bowl
anon.	anonymous
aor.	aorist
BCE, CE	Before the Common Era; Common Era (replacing B.C. / A.D.)
c.	*circa* (about)
cent.	century
cf.	confer, see
ch(s).	chapter(s)
col.	column
cp.	compare, contrast
fl.	*floruit* (flourished, was active at a certain time)
fig.	figure
FS	Festschrift
gen.	genitive
HT	Hebrew Text, a.k.a. MT (Massoretic Text)
ill.	illustration
JHE	John H. Elliott (as translator)
l(l)	line(s)
lit.	literally
MT	Hebrew Massoretic Text a.k.a HT (Hebrew Text)
no(s)	number(s)
P.	Papyrus
part.	participle
pass.	passive
per.	person

Pl.	Plate
pl.	plural
p(p)	page(s)
Prol.	*Prologus* (prologue)
Ps.-	pseudo- (inaccurately ascribed to)
Q	Qumran
SBL	Society of Biblical Literature
s.v.	*sub voce* (under the [listed] word)
v.l.	*varia lectio* (variant reading)
[ ]	Square brackets identify textual material supplied by the translator of the original source or by the present author (JHE)

I

INTRODUCTION

In his celebrated "Sermon on the Mount," Jesus of Nazareth makes reference to one of the oldest beliefs in the ancient world—the malignity of an Evil Eye (Matt 6:22–23): "If, however, your Eye is Evil, your entire body will be full of darkness." Another of Jesus's references to the Evil Eye appears in his parable concerning workers in a vineyard and an eruption of Evil-Eyed envy (Matt 20:1–16). At the parable's conclusion, a generous vineyard owner chides disgruntled workers envious of their fellow laborers: "Is your Eye Evil because I am good?" (Matt 20:15). The apostle Paul also mentions the Evil Eye in his emotional letter to the Galatians. As he struggles with rival authorities for winning the hearts and minds of a vacillating mission outpost in Galatia, Asia Minor, he writes impatiently and asks rhetorically: "O you uncomprehending Galatians, who has injured you with an Evil Eye?" (Gal 3:1).

Jesus and Paul are only some of the biblical persons commenting on the Evil Eye. The Holy Scriptures in their original languages contain no less than twenty-four and possibly more references to the Evil Eye, although this is obscured by most modern Bible translations. Nor is this belief in any way restricted to the biblical communities. Quite the contrary. Written and material evidence attests to the existence of this belief across the Mediterranean and Near Eastern worlds of antiquity. From Mesopotamian incantations and the amuletic Egyptian Eyes of Horus to the *baskania* of the Greeks and the *fascinatio* of the Romans, the *'ayin harah* of the Hebrews and the *ophthalmos ponêros* of the Christians, belief in the Evil Eye haunted the ancient world, prompted the production of vast arsenals of amulets, and engendered an array of spoken expressions, gestures, and social customs, many of which are with us to the present day.

The story of the Evil Eye is a theme of the human drama that weaves its way through history from a fictional New Jersey crime family ("The Sopranos") and international rock stars (Madonna), from deposed heads of state (Manuel Noriega) and the menacing look of American football linebackers (Ronnie Lott) to calamity-causing Italian popes to medieval witch trials to Jewish Talmudic wisdom, death-dealing rabbis, and the apotropaic practices of Jews and Christians of late antiquity to the sermons and biblical commentaries of the Christian church fathers to the words of Jesus, Paul and Israelite sages of the Bible, to the Greco-Roman, Egyptian and Mesopotamian worlds of myths of petrifying glances, restored eyes of gods, and Sumerian incantations against the roving Evil Eye.

Our study describes this belief and associated practices, its history, its voluminous appearances in ancient cultures, and the extensive research devoted to it over the centuries. The study's chief focus, and its novel contribution, is a full-scale examination of the numerous references to the Evil Eye in the Bible and their meaning within the context of Mesopotamian, Egyptian, Greek, and Roman Evil Eye belief and practice. The study in other words is a contextual analysis of the Evil Eye in the Bible shaped by the conviction that traces of biblical Evil Eye can only be understood in relation to ancient Evil Eye belief and practice in general. The chapters on Mesopotamia and Egypt (chap. 2) and Greece and Rome (Vol. 2) are prelude to and context for Volume 3 on the Evil Eye in the Old and New Testaments. Volume 4, chaps. 1 and 2 trace the continued dread of the Evil Eye in the cultures of both post-biblical Israel and post-biblical Christianity down through Late Antiquity (sixth century CE). This concentration on the Evil Eye belief and practice in the ancient world, however, will be accompanied by constant comment on Medieval, Reformation, Enlightenment, and modern traces of the belief in the diverse realms of philosophical and theological commentary, art, literature, and popular culture.

DEFINITION AND DESCRIPTION

What is this phenomenon called the Evil Eye? One recent writer opens his study with the astute observation, "the evil eye is perhaps the most widespread complex system of beliefs in the world and in history, yet, to anybody who is not part of an Evil Eye culture, the Evil Eye is an enigma."[1] This book intends to unravel this enigma for readers who have never heard of the Evil Eye and its presence in the Bible. It also aims at providing more information to those who know a bit but want to know more.

1. Gravel 1995:3.

The concept of the Evil Eye is a millennia old and geographically wide-spread folk belief complex and one of the most widespread and behaviorally influential beliefs in the ancient world. This belief holds that certain individuals (humans, gods, demons, animals, and mythological figures) possess an eye whose powerful glance or gaze can harm or destroy any object, animate or inanimate, on which it falls. Through the power of their eye, which can operate involuntarily as well as intentionally, such Evil Eye possessors (also known as "fascinators")[2] are thought capable of injuring, withering, or obliterating the health and life, means of sustenance and livelihood, familial honor, and personal well-being of their hapless victims.[3] The Evil Eye is believed to harm nursing mothers and their babies, breast milk, fruit bearing trees, crops in the field, milking animals, and the sperm of men. All persons, things, and sound states of being, however, are deemed vulnerable, but especially children, the beautiful and successful, and what is most prized and essential to survival. The more attractive, beautiful, flourishing and outstanding the object, the more likely an attack from an Evil Eye.

All persons and creatures of all classes and social ranks are deemed potential Evil Eye possessors, but especially those with unusual ocular features or physical deformity, those manifesting anti-social behavior, or strangers and foreign peoples. Dangerous occasions include birth, marriage, and encounters with strangers. Thought to be animated by some malevolent disposition such as envy, miserliness, greed, or malice, an Evil Eye is believed to convey, project, and cast forth particles of energy that damage or destroy the object struck. In some cases, it has been believed, an Evil Eye is inherited and can work involuntarily, injuring even loved ones and the Evil-Eyed person her/himself. When exercised voluntarily, an Evil Eye directs malice arising in the heart through the eye against external objects with the intent to harm others and destroy what makes them stand out or gives them pleasure. It can be the cause of illness or death to humans (especially children) or animals, damage to crops or means of livelihood, loss of battles or contests, and ruin of reputation and honor.

Persistent anxiety concerning the omnipresent danger posed by the Evil Eye has led to a variety of efforts to ward off or counteract its power through the extensive use of apotropaic charms and amulets, words and gestures, the

2. From the Latin *fascinare*, "to cast, to harm with, an Evil Eye." This and other ancient terms for "Evil Eye" are discussed in chap. 2 below and Vols. 2–4.

3. For definitions and descriptions see also Jahn 1855:31–32; Elworthy 1912:608; Seligmann 1910 1:2–9; Maloney 1976:v–vii, 3. Seligmann (1910 1:3) notes that when an admiring eye is accompanied by words of praise, this action is known in German as "berufen" or "beschreien," utterance by which the object of admiration is exposed to harm and damage; cf. also Perkmann 1927.

great majority of which are common to numerous cultures and periods from past to present. An *apotropaic* is that which is thought to possess the power to repel and "drive away" threatening evil forces (from the Greek *apotropein*, "to drive away"). Amulets, words, and gestures are various forms of apotropaics. These will be itemized and discussed at various points in our study. Many of these apotropaics have been thought to operate according to the ancient (and later homeopathic) principle of *similia similibus*, "like influences like."

Evil Eye belief and practice is a vivid indicator of social relations and interpersonal dynamics. "The evil eye," Blum and Blum have noted,

> symbolizes the intensity of community interaction; it indicates that each person is under observation by others. Everyone is measured from moment to moment and regarded with admiration or envy, with approbation or censure. Implicit awareness of the consequences of the opinions and action of others towards oneself emerges in the evil eye concept which attributes ones' own health and welfare to the judgments made and feelings held about one by others. Community-wide interdependency and sensitivity to the feelings of others is demonstrated. There is evidence for the very considerable importance attached to interpersonal relations and the interplay of pride and envy as a source of disaster. The feelings of humans towards one another are understood as a source of illness, disability, anxiety, injury, and death . . . Good fortune is a dangerous blessing and its enjoyment, for the most part visibly through its flaunting, is an invitation to destruction. Those who have or achieve that which is valued (having a child, getting married, enjoying the sexual favours of another, acquiring property or reputation), must expect the congratulations of the neighbours to be but a mask for jealousy.[4] Success is the forbidden fruit: to taste it is to know joy at the certain risk of alienation oneself from one's fellows.[5]

Fear of the Evil Eye and its devastating effects was intense and pervasive in antiquity. Dread of the malevolent eye still lingers today.[6] From

4. Envy, not jealousy, is the salient emotion; on this point see below, pp. 21–23.

5. Blum and Blum 1970:221.

6. Descriptions of the phenomenon in general, its suspected origin and dissemination, and selective documentation are offered by Smedley et al. 1855:205; Story 1860; 1877; Andrée 1878:35–45; Pitré 1884; 1889; 1913; Anonymous, *The Celtic Magazine* (1887); Potts 1890; Elworthy, 1895/1958, 1912; Blau 1898:152–56; 1907b; Vigouroux 1899; O'Neil 1908; Kuhnert 1909; Brown 1909–1910; Mather 1910; Seligmann 1910; 1912–13; 1914; 1922; 1927a; 1927b; Anonymous, *Encyclopaedia Brittanica*, 11th ed., (1911) 10:21–22; Ranke 1911; Park 1912:9–31; Anonymous, *Encyclopaedia Britannica*,

antiquity onward, it has remained a powerful belief with powerful social and personal consequences. "One may conclude that present evil eye beliefs have survived without important changes over several thousands of years."[7] Over the centuries, the Evil Eye has played a significant role in conceptualizing evil, identifying sources of hostility, explaining causes of illness and disaster, interpreting emotions and moral dispositions, regulating social relations, and reinforcing norms of moral conduct.

References to the Evil Eye occur in Old and New Testaments of the Bible and in fact appear in cuneiform texts of the Sumerians as early as 3000 BCE.[8] From its origin in the ancient Near East and Circum-Mediterranean area, Evil Eye belief spread eastward to India, European Russia, and Asia and westward to Spain, Portugal, and Britain, northward to continental Europe and southward into North Africa. Eventually it traveled the seas from Old World to New World. European colonists brought the belief to North, Central, and South America. Islam carried it to Indonesia and the East.

Evil Eye belief and practice over the centuries is represented by an astounding range of evidence. Antiquity has given us Mesopotamian/Sumerian art and incantations (3000 BCE), myths of Horus and his restored eye with anti-Evil Eye power, the *baskania* of the Greeks, the *oculus malus* of the Romans along with Greek and Roman poetry, drama, literature and amulets; the *ra' 'ayin* of the Hebrews and biblical stories of the patriarchs, matriarchs, and kings, advice of the sages; the *ophthalmos ponêros* condemned by Jesus and the *baskainein* deplored by the apostle Paul; the anti-Evil Eye theological treatises and homiletical warnings of the Christian

---

14th ed. (1929) 8:915; Waterman 1929, 2006; *Enciclopedia universal ilustrada. Europeo-Americana* 1907–1930, 32:408–12; Taylor 1933; Vijaya-Tunga 1935; Probst-Biraben 1936; Servadio 1936; B. L. Gordon 1937; Rolleston 1942; Schoeck 1955/1992; Deichgraeber 1957; Anonymous, *Dizionario Enciclopedico Italiano* 1957 6:24; Gifford 1957, 1958; Robbins 1959; Baroja 1965:38, 142, 234–35; Sanders 1967; Edwards 1971; Noy 1971; Steinbach 1973; Rush 1974:33–34, 57–77, 137–44 (healing ritual); Maloney 1976 passim; Moss and Cappannari 1976; Morris 1977, 1985:57–60; Morris et al. 1977; Stephenson 1979; Izzi 1980; Muthu Cidambaram 1980; Bronzini 1981; Lykiardopoulos 1981; Potts 1982:5–16; Bourguignon 1983; Lauer 1983; Maple 1983; L. Sachs 1983; Shimizu 1983; Cavendish-Deutsch 1983 4:885–894; *Encyclopedia of Occultism & Parapsychology* 1984 1:454–56; Morris 1985:57–60; Perdiguero Gil 1986; Berke 1988:35–56; Djéribi 1988; Dundes 1992 passim; Gravel 1995; Pavesi 1995:43–51; Racokzy 1996; Stevens 1996; Morris 1997b:120–60; Elliott 1988 etc.; Kunesh 1998 (eye in hand amulet); Salmon and Cabre 1998; Ribichini 1999; Elsie 2001; Centini 2002; Vanel 2004; Greenfield 2006; Spence 2006; Campo 2009; Avar Nuño 2012a, 2012b.

7. Blum and Blum 1970:310.

8. On the Evil Eye in antiquity, beside the general studies (listed in n. 6), see Jahn 1855; Story 1877; Budge 1978/1930:354–65; Racokzy 1996; and the works listed in Vols. 2–4.

church fathers; Israel's Hand of Miriam (*Hamesh*), Islam's protective Hand of Fatima (*Hamsa*, lit. "five" [fingers]), and the vast body of amulets employed by all the populations of the ancient Circum-Mediterranean and Near East. Throughout the Middle Ages, Renaissance, and Reformation eras, Evil Eye belief and practice continued unabated.

In the Middle Ages and beyond, many luminaries, including Thomas Aquinas, Dante Alighieri, Leonardo da Vinci, Martin Luther, and Francis Bacon spoke of the Evil Eye.[9] The sublime *Commedia Divina* of Dante Alighieri tells of a thief, Vanno Fucci of Pistoia, in the bowels of hell defying the Almighty by holding out both hands toward heaven and making a double *mano fica*—a potent gesture generally employed against the Evil Eye: "When he had finished with his words, the thief /raised high his fists with both figs cocked [*le mani alzò con amendue de fiche*] and cried: 'Take that, O God; I square them off for you'" (*Inferno*, Canto 25.1–3).[10]

In the medieval period, Jews were held to be wielders of the Evil Eye. In fourteenth-century Spain, Jews were forbidden by canon law from standing among ripening crops in order to keep the fields safe from their Evil Eyes.[11] Germans designated the Evil Eye not only as *böser Blick* ("evil glance") but as *Judenblick* ("Jews' glance").

The famous *Malleus Maleficarum*, or "Witches' Hammer," authored by the Dominicans Heinrich Kramer and James Sprenger,[12] discusses the *fascinatio* of the Evil Eye and the deadly gaze, references to it by Aristotle, Avicenna, Al-Gazali, and Thomas Aquinas, its link with witches and old women, and its threat to children (Part One, Question Two). The comments of church reformer Martin Luther on the Evil Eye in the Bible and in his own day are discussed in Vol. 3, chap. 2 in connection with Paul's letter to the Galatians.

Francis Bacon, philosopher and essayist, includes among his fifty-eight learned *Essays of Counsels, Civil and Moral* (3rd ed., 1625) a ninth one "On Envy," the longest of them all. It begins by reflecting on the relation of envy and the Evil Eye (and witchcraft) and illustrates the striking stability of this belief complex from antiquity to his own time, including the presumed extramission theory of vision:

---

9. See Story 1877:183–205 and the list in Seligmann 1910 2:472 n. 1.

10. Translation by Allen Mandelbaum, vol. 1, *Inferno*, 1982. I am grateful to Prof. Romano Penna (personal communication, 11/17/98) for directing me to this famous instance in the *Commedia*. My thanks also to Dante expert, Prof. Brenda Dean Schildgen, for guidance on this text and Dante's thought about envy.

11. Maloney 1976:5–8.

12. Kramer and Sprenger 1487/1948.

There be none of the affections which have been noted to fascinate or bewitch, but love and envy. They both have vehement wishes; they frame themselves readily into imaginations and suggestions, and they come easily into the eye, especially upon the presence of the objects, which are the points that conduce to fascination, if any such thing there be. We see, likewise, the Scripture calleth envy an evil eye, and the astrologers call the evil influences of the stars evil aspects, so that there seemeth to be acknowledged, in the act of envy, an ejaculation or irradiation of the eye; nay, some have been so curious as to note, that the times when the stroke or percussion of an envious eye doth most hurt, are when the party envied is beheld in glory or triumph, for that sets an edge upon envy; and besides, at such times, the spirits of the person envied do come forth most into the outward parts, and so meet the blow.[13]

In the realm of art, an aspect of Evil Eye practice appears in the famous Brera Madonna (the Montefeltro or Brera Altarpiece), by early Renaissance Italian master Piero della Francesca.[14] It depicts a Madonna surrounded by saints and angels. On her lap is the infant Christ child with a necklace of red coral hanging from his neck. Both coral and the color red are traditional media used for warding off the Evil Eye, which targets infants in particular.[15] A painting of the Dutch artist, Gerard Terborch, *The Suitor's Visit* (c. 1658), portrays an elegant suitor bowing before a young lady, who, however, is making a covert gesture of a *mano fica*, presumably in self-defense.[16] From the French artist Jean Louis Géricault has come the portrait of the "Mad Woman with the Mania of Envy" (and an Evil Eye). From the Russian painter Ilya Yefimovich Repin we have the portrait of "A Peasant with an Evil Eye" (1877), depicting the artist's godfather, Ivan Fyodorovich Radov. In 2009, an art exhibition in Braunschweig, Germany, of the work of German artist Armin Bohem was devoted to the subject of the Evil Eye.[17] A far more mundane trace of painted eyes repelling the Evil Eye are those adorning the prows of innumerable Mediterranean boats, a practice in place for over 2000 years.

13. Quoted in Walcot 1978:77.

14. Painted in 1472–1474, it is now housed in the Pinacoteca di Brera of Milan, Italy. I am grateful to my colleague Dr. Brenda Schildgen for calling this piece of art to my attention.

15. On the Evil Eye in Italian art, see also Callisen 1937.

16. Roodenburg 1991:154–55 and fig. 7.1. The painting is now in the National Gallery of Art, Washington, DC, Andrew W. Mellon Collection.

17. Boehm 2009. For the Evil Eye in contemporary art see also Frisch 1995.

Characters of William Shakespeare also allude to the Evil Eye and being "overlooked":

> "Beshrew your eyes/They have o'erlooked me and divided me. One half of me is yours, the other half yours." (Portia to Bassanio in *Merchant of Venice*, Act 3, Scene 2)

> "Vile worm, thou wast o'erlook'd even in thy birth." (Pistol, of Falstaff in *Merry Lives of Windsor*, Act 5, scene 5)

> ". . . then lend the eye a terrible aspect" (King Henry before battle, rousing his warriors to frenzy in *Henry V*, Act 3, Scene 1).

> "A largess universal, like the sun/His liberal eye doth give to every one/ thawing cold fear." (The Chorus, regarding King Henry in *Henry V*, Act 4, Prologue)[18]

> "Hath Romeo slain himself? say thou but 'I,' And that bare vowel 'I' shall poison more than the death-darting eye of cockatrice" (Juliet to the nurse who told her of Romeo's suicide in *Romeo and Juliet*, Act 3, Scene 2).[19]

The Evil Eye makes a brief appearance in Samuel Taylor Coleridge's, "The Rime of the Ancient Mariner" (1798):

> Each turned his face with a ghastly pang,
> And cursed me with his eye.[20]

The Irish novelist William Carleton, in his short story on "The Evil Eye or The Black Spectre," gives an extensive description of Evil Eye belief and practice in the Irish culture in his own day,[21] although his story is cast in an earlier period when the Evil Eye was deemed the most formidable of evils.[22] One possessor of the Evil Eye, Harry Woodward, had a "baleful and demoniacal glance," a "dreadful eye," an "annihilating glance" that caused withering and death.[23] A female character, hideously ugly, with nearly blood-red

---

18. Jesus speaks of a generous or "liberal" eye as the antithesis of an Evil Eye (Matt 6:22–23/Luke 11:34. [**X-ref**]

19. The cockatrice is a legendary creature: a two-legged dragon with a rooster's head, which, like Medusa, was ascribed the ability to turn people to stone or killing them by either looking at them or touching them or breathing on them.

20. "The Ancient Mariner," part 1, published in the first edition of Coleridge's *Lyrical Ballads* (1798).

21. Carleton 1882 1:613–775. See also Price 2001.

22. Ibid., 694, 702.

23. Ibid., 696, 702, 769.

hair, knit eyebrows, and wild wiry hair injured a child and killed a cow with her withering glance.[24]

Edgar Allan Poe's lament "Lenore" (1843–1849) attributes the all too early death of "sweet Lenore" to an Evil Eye and a slanderous tongue:

> Wretches! ye loved her for her wealth and hated her for her pride,
> And when she fell in feeble health, ye blessed her—that she died!
> How shall the ritual, then, be read? —the requiem how be sung
> *By you,—by yours, the evil eye,—by yours, the slanderous tongue,*
> That did to death the innocence that died, and died so young?[25]

Since antiquity, Evil Eye and Evil tongue have been paired as conveyers of injury and death, as we shall see, but rarely so poetically.

Theophile Gautier, prompted by the Neopolitan belief in the Evil Eye, *jettatura*, wrote a short story at whose center was a *jettatore* whose demonic gift gradually became known to him and his circle.[26]

Then there are appearances of the sinister Evil Eye in Herman Melville's *Billy Budd*, which turns on innocent Billy enviously Evil-Eyed by John Claggart, master-at-arms of the HMA Bellepoint.[27] It features also in Mark Twain's story, "Life on the Mississippi" (1883). One of the burly characters on the raft leaps into the air and declares:

> I'm the man they call Sudden Death and General Desolation!
> Sired by a hurricane, dam'd by an earthquake, half-brother to
> the cholera, nearly related to the smallpox on my mother's side!
> Look at me! I take nineteen alligators and a bar'l of whiskey for
> breakfast when I'm in robust health, and a bushel of rattlesnakes
> and a dead body when I'm ailing. *I split the everlasting rocks with
> my glance* and I squench the thunder when I speak![28]

Mariano Azuela's *The Underdogs: A Novel of the Mexican Revolution* (1915/2008) tells of Senora Agapita lamenting that, "They've cast an evil eye on my daughter!"[29] reminding us of the *mal de ojo* dreaded by Latin American peasants.[30]

---

24. Ibid., 629.

25. Poe 1969:330–39, esp. 337.

26. Gautier 1863.

27. The novella *Billy Budd* by Melville was published posthumously in 1924. On the Evil Eye theme in Melville's work see the analysis of Adamson (1997), esp. chap. 7, "The Evil Eye," 257–93; also 215, 226–27.

28. Twain, *Life on the Mississippi*, ch. 3 (italics added).

29. Azuela, *The Underdogs*, 2008[1915]:36.

30. Kearney 1976, 1982:86, 197–202; Cosminsky 1976.

Roger Vailland's novel, *The Law* (*La Loi*),[31] is set in the ficticious town of Porto Manacore, Apulia, Southern Italy, in the aftermath of World War II. The story illustrates several conventional features of Evil Eye practice. Don Cesare, the ailing town padrone, is treated by his wife for suspected injury from the Evil Eye. The ritual is a traditional one using oil and water. Brigante, another character, "hastily brought his hand to his groin; that was how you warded off the evil eye. He was trying to convince himself that the Judge's wife [with whom Francesco was having an affair] had cast a spell on Francesco."[32] "Hurriedly Marietta made a pair of horns with her index finger and thumb. Don Cesare realized that she was casting a spell for him . . . she was defending him [as he lay dying]."[33] A short story on "The Evil Eye" (*Jettatura*) appears in Cesare Pavesi's collection, *Summer Storm*.[34]

The Manor, a novel about a Polish family of Hasidic Jews (c. 1863–1900) by the Yiddish novelist Isaac Bashevis Singer (1967) has characters making numerous anti-Evil Eye remarks: "A beautiful girl . . . may she escape the Evil Eye"; "you are—may the Evil Eye spare you—a beautiful girl," etc.

More recently, the historical novel of Umberto Eco, *Baudolino* (2002), concerns political and social upheavals of the city of Constantinople in 1204. Residents of Constantinople encountered Genoese of Italy in their city and took steps to protect themselves against the strangers' Evil Eyes: "some made the sign of the cross, some made the horns sign to ward off the evil eye, and some touched their balls."[35]

Jonathan Franzen's *The Corrections* describes Alfred hallucinating about a "big black bastard circling the two of them with her evil eye."[36]

A short story by Paul Theroux, "The Furies" (2013), describes the mother of one of the main characters, Angie, as sounding "like her mother, Gilda—Emenegilda—sour, mustached, habitually in black, pedantically superstitious, Sicilian, always threatening the evil eye."[37]

Recent fiction in English with "Evil Eye" in the title includes: *The Evil Eye*, a mystery novel by Pierre Boileau and Thomas Narcejac (1959); *Minnie Santangelo and the Evil Eye*, a detective novel by Anthony Mancini (1977); *Evil Eye* by Ehren Ehly (1989); *Evil Eye* by Ann Diamond (1994); *Evil Eye* by Michael Slade (1997); *Evil Eye* by Veronica Di Grigoli (2008); *Malocchio:*

31. Vailland 1958.
32. Ibid., 266.
33. Ibid., 302.
34. Pavese 1966.
35. Eco 2000:37.
36. Franzen 2001:555.
37. Theroux 2005:67.

The Evil Eye Murders by Michael Chiardona and James T. Vance, the first volume of the Evil Eye Murders series (2011); *Stalking the Evil Eye* by Richard Jay (2010); *An Evil Eye: A Novel* by Jason Goodwin (2011); and the new offering of best-selling author Joyce Carol Oates, *Evil Eye: Four Novellas of Love Gone Wrong* (2013).

Then there is the autobiographical account of North American journalist David St. Clair living in Rio de Janiero. Having fallen ill and landing on bad financial times, he was told by the locals that he had been struck by his housekeeper's envious Evil Eye. When healed by a priestess *curandera*, he turned from adamant skeptic to nonplused questioner.[38]

Best-selling physician-author, Larry Dossey, writing from his medical practice on the power of prayer to harm as well as heal, devotes an entire chapter to belief in the injurious power of the Evil Eye and its roots in folk medical systems.[39]

Patricia Storace's account, *Dinner with Persephone*, describes her encounter with Evil Eye belief and practice in Greek society today as she traveled around the country.[40] A businessman explains that the eye is active and projects energy that can injure and destroy. Association of the Evil Eye with envy was pronounced. Scores of anti-Evil Eye amulets (mostly blue glass eyes) were on view in shops and on vehicles. Descriptions are given of suspected fascinators (persons with blue eyes, knit eyebrows and fair skin), of victims (children, prized possessions, young woman with flashy clothes) and of calamities caused by the Evil Eye (dead animals, ruined vineyard). Measures taken to counteract the Evil Eye are also recounted (saying the word "spit" thrice when complimenting, avoiding compliments and praise altogether, the rituals of old women, and offering prayers, including those of a priest).

On the political front, Manuel Noriega, former military dictator of Panama (1983–1990), was deposed by the United States, and in April 9, 1992, he was convicted on eight counts of drug smuggling and racketeering.

---

38. St. Clair 1971:271–304.

39. Dossey 1997:115–24; see also 60, 202. For publications on the Evil Eye by ophthalmologists, psychologists, and representatives of medicine and healthcare systems see, e.g., Seligmann 1910, 1922, 1927; McDaniel 1918; McKenzie 1927:225–62; Gordon 1937; Friedenwald 1939; Pazzini 1948; Gifford 1957, 1958, 1960, 1971; Harfouche 1965; Meerloo 1971; Glenn 1978; Potts 1982; Hand 1992; Oyler 1992; Parsons 1984; Parsons and Wakeley 1991; Coss 1992; Pavesi 1995; Prioreschi 1995:56–59; Bohigian 1997, 1998; Dossey 1997; Salmon and Cabre 1998:53–84; Pilch 2000a, 2000b; Hedarot and Pirzadeh 2001.

40. Storace 1997; see especially "The Blue Glass Eye" (22–27); see also pp. 162, 176, 179, 220, 374–75.

In the course of his public degradation in the U.S. press, he was accused of wearing red underwear for protection against the Evil Eye.[41]

On the stage, a play by Charles H. Yale and Sidney R. Ellis was performed in Washington, DC, 1896, and titled, *The Evil Eye and the Many Merry Mishaps of Nid and the Weird, Wonderful Wandering of Nod: A Fantastical Spectacular Trick Comedy in Three Acts.*[42] A later reference to the Evil Eye occurs in the hit Broadway play, "The Rose Tattoo," by Tennessee Williams (1951; film adaptation, 1955). Seraphina delle Rose, a Sicilian woman living on the Lousiana Gulf coast and a main character of the story, believes firmly in the Evil Eye. She steers clear of an old woman with rheumatism in her hands and cataracts in her eyes, who is held by her neighbors to be a witch, a *strega*. As Serafina and this witch chase the witch's goat running about Seraphina's yard, Serafina warns her daughter Rosa not to make eye contact with the strega's "evil eye."

In the one-act play *La Patente*, or *The License* (1919), of Sicilian author Luigi Pirandello, winner of the Nobel Prize for literature, the Evil Eye functions as a central feature. A key character, Rosario Chiàrchiaro, is regarded as an outsider by other members of his community and as capable of injuring others with an Evil Eye. A victim of injustice, he fails to win his libel suit and ends up as a tragic figure.[43] *Non è vero . . . ma ci credo* ("It's not true . . . but I believe it") is the title of a comedy by the Italian actor and playwright, Peppino De Filippo. It was staged for the first time in 1942. The narrated events take place in the early twentieth century and concern Gervasio Savastano, a Neapolitan businessman who is tormented by the fear of *jettatura*.[44]

For fans of the cinema there instances of Evil Eye belief and practice in Clint Eastwood films ("Unforgiven," "True Crime") and other movies ("High Sierra," "Clash of the Titans," "Matewan," "The Evil Eye," "Manhattan Baby," "Broadway Danny Rose," "My Big Fat Greek Wedding," "Ciao Professore," "Malocchio," and scenes with characters referring to the Evil Eye. A documentary film, "Kypseli," of everyday life in a Greek village of the island of Thera/Santorini off the coast of Athens in the Aegean Sea was made by anthropologist Susannah M. Hoffmann of the University of San Francisco's Department of Sociology in 1972. This highly informative ethnographic study includes the image of an anti-Evil Eye *cornuto* (horn) on one of the

41. BBC News, Latine America and Caribbean, 12/11/2011.

42. Yale and Ellis 1898. For stage plays see also Peake 1831; and Phillips and Jones 1831.

43. Pirandello 1964:119–38.

44. See De Ceglia 2011.

village walls.[45] A cinematic review magazine bears the title, "The Evil Eye Review."

A 2012 interview with the Oscar-winning film actress Merle Streep and actor Tommy Lee Jones[46] reports that when Streep was asked "Of all your accomplishments, what is it tht makes you most proud?" she responded, "My kids." To the follow-up questions, "Is it that they're happy that makes you proud?" she answered, "Yeah, *kineahora*. You don't want to say what you're grateful for. It's enough to say I'm happy for them. I'm happy." The published version of the interview mistakenly explains in brackets that *kineahora* is "a Yiddish version of 'knock on wood.'" It actually means "no Evil Eye (intended)" or, in this case, "may no Evil Eye (strike them)."

The television series "The Sopranos" (HBO, 1999–2007), hailed the greatest TV series of all time, made repeated reference to the Evil Eye. Mafiosi characters repeatedly attribute illness and other harm to "*maluucch*" (one of several Italian expressions for "Evil Eye"—a Neapolitan variation on *malocchio*). Pussy's bad back was blamed on *maluucch*. Furio, Tony Soprano's Italian driver, on returning from Italy, brings a gobbo (anti-Evil Eye hunchback amulet) as a present for one of Tony's kids. A newspaper advertisement for this series shows an ensemble photograph of the cast, with one character, Silvio Dante, Tony Soprano's *consigliere*, making the protective gesture, the *mano cornuta*.

Television actress Stana Katic is asked in an interview about her name "Stana" and she replies, "I was named for my grandmother. It's an evil eye name, to protect you from bad things."[47]

The Evil Eye has also featured in the world of music. Playing at Le Hot Club in France in the 1930s, the legendary Gypsy guitarist Django Reinhardt is said once to have been so picqued by members of his own Le Hot band that he cast a *mauvais oeil*, an Evil Eye, on them one evening.[48]

The American poet and singer Bob Dylan makes repeated reference to the Evil Eye in his songs. His song, "Disease of Conceit," speaks of the aggression of an Evil Eye:

> Whole lot of people seeing double tonight /
> From the disease of conceit
> Give ya delusions of grandeur / and a evil eye /
> Give you the idea that / you're too good to die

45. See Hoffman 1972; also Hoffman 1976, 1988.
46. Grant 2012, esp. 84.
47. *Parade Magazine* (18 March 2012) 2.
48. Dregni 2004:152, 162.

His song, "My Wife's Home Town," contains the lines,

> State gone broke, the county's dry /
> Don't be lookin' at me with that evil eye.

Still another Dylan song, "Need a Woman," warns,

> Well, believing is all right;
> just don't let the wrong people know what it's all about.
> They might put the evil eye on you,
> use their hidden powers to try to turn you out.

The album "Meltdown" by the rock band Ash (2005) has a track titled "Evil Eye." It contains the backward message "She's giving me the Evil Eye."

An article about pop singer Gladys Knight in MIX (Professional Audio and Musical Production, 95/2003) reported her appearance at the Flamingo Showroom in Las Vegas. As she tried out a pair of new loudspeakers, she declared, "I haven't been the recipient of a single Evil Eye from the stage." "Evil Eye" is the name of a jazz quartet led by drummer Mike Pride and saxophonist Jonathan Mortiz with Nate Wooley on trumpet and Ken Filiano on bass.

Acclaimed Canadian poet, songwriter and singer, Leonard Cohen, in his poem, "I See You on a Greek Mattress," mentions a common practice for protecting children and others from the Evil Eye: "I see the plastic Evil Eye pinned to your underwear."[49]

The vocalist Madonna was reported wearing a Hamesh (Hand of Miriam) and a red string on a flight to Israel in the late 1990s—both to repel the Evil Eye. Under her influence, wearing a red string for warding off the Evil Eye became popular with many celebrities in the United States, including many non-Jews.

In an interview on television show "60 Minutes" (CBS 9/9/2007), the world-renown opera singer Luciano Pavarotti made the gesture of the *mano cornuta* in self-defense against his critics.

The Evil Eye also takes a bow in Ingwie Malmsteen's track "Evil Eye" on his album "Rising Force."

In the world of sports, Ronnie Lott, former feared linebacker for the San Francisco Forty-Niners football team, was described in the *San Francisco Chronicle* as staring down his opponents with an Evil Eye.

Elsewhere on the cultural scene, *The New York Times* reports in its section on "Style"[50] on a piece of jewelry created by an Italian-born jewelry

---

49. Cohen 1994:86.
50. *New York Times*, November 12, 2006, Style, p. 12.

designer Amadeo Scognamiglo for Olivia Chantecaille, director of a beauty line. The piece is intended to protect against the Evil Eye, "that creepy eye of envy." It looks like a *corno* [horn] in gold and is called "the cornicello, an Italian charm in the shape of an eland's [African antelope] twisted horn." An *Oakland Tribune* article has reported that an Evil Eye is now also aroused in the classroom by cell-phoners: "Yoga teacher gives cell-phoning student the Evil Eye."[51] In Germany, Franca Magnani reported on the Evil Eye on German radio: "Der böse Blick" in "Römische Skizzen."[52]

The Evil Eye also has made its way into the cartoons and comic strips of our daily newspapers. The popular comic strip of mid-twentieth century USA, "Li'l Abner" of Dogpatch, featured a character named Evil-Eye Fleegle and his triple whammy. His destructive eye was said to be so powerful it could challenge the sun. The strip's creator, Al Capp, included in his comic strip traditions reflecting his Russian Jewish heritage.[53] In the popular cartoon strip "Hagar the Horrible" by Dik Browne, one sequence shows a scribe asking the fictional Viking warrior Hagar, "For my records, what illnesses have you had?" Hagar ponders, "Lemme see, Black Plague . . . Evil Eye . . . Demon Possession . . . Spells." The scribe responds, "I'll just put down, 'regular childhood diseases.'"[54] Another cartoon depicts a man examined by an oculist with the latter declaring, "Evil Eye, Mr. Gruenfeld, Evil Eye." A humorous treatment of the topic in Jewish folklore by Brenda Rosenbaum has even made its way to the practical "how to" section of the local bookstore. Complete with illustrations, it bears the appropriate title *How to Avoid the Evil Eye*.[55] In a similar practical vein, the American magician, Henri Gamache, said to be an expert on the Evil Eye, dispensed practical advice on protecting oneself against the Evil Eye.[56]

Finally there are the omnipresent anti-Evil Eye amulets that have made their way around the world. From the wrist bracelet of Madonna and those red or blue ribbons attached to newborns in countless hospitals, Manuel Noriega's anti-Evil Eye underwear, to the Brazilian *mano figa* amulets, to the miniature protective blue eyes on Greek and Turkish buses and taxis, the glass blue eye amulets of a million Greek and Turkish tourist shops, and the middle-finger "high sign" (the ancient *digitus infamis* against the Evil Eye)

51. *Oakland Tribune*, July 7, 2012, pp. 1, 8.

52. Magnani, "Der böse Blick."

53. On the Evil Eye and Evil Eye Fleegle see Elliott 1988:42–43. On Al Capp and the comic strip "Li'l Abner," see Berger 1978.

54. Dik Browne, "Hägar the Horrible," *The Sun* (9/9/1983) 32.

55. Rosenbaum 1985.

56. Gamache 1946/1969.

of auto drivers everywhere, the lore of the Evil Eye has traveled across the continents and down through the ages.

In myriad ways the Evil Eye continues to haunt our everyday lives and imagination, whether we are aware of it or not. Looks can insult; glances can threaten; Evil Eyes can wreck havoc in families and communities. The serious Evil Eye is no laughing matter. "The evil eye," folklorist Alan Dundes reminds us, "is not some old-fashion superstitious belief of interest only to antiquarians. The evil eye continues to be a powerful factor affecting the behavior of countless *millions* of people throughout the Indo-European and Semitic world."[57] Over the centuries the Evil Eye has haunted our dreams and spooked our imaginations. Our present study will focus on one chapter of the long history of Evil Eye belief and practice, namely the biblical record in its historical, social, and cultural contexts. This will entail a look at Evil Eye belief and practice in the ancient Near East and Circum-Mediterranean world in general—the cultural contexts of biblical Evil Eye belief. Even with this focus will come a sense of the long shadow cast by this belief over the human story.

TERMINOLOGY FOR "EVIL EYE" IN VARIOUS LANGUAGES

The linguistic evidence indicates particular and ongoing aspects of the Evil Eye concept. One major study, the classic by Siegfried Seligmann (*Der böse Blick*, 1910), lists terms for Evil Eye in thirty-nine languages.[58] Some languages speak of an *eye* that is evil; e.g., *raʿ ʿayin* (Hebrew); *ophthalmos ponêros* (Greek; also *baskania* etc.; modern Greek, *vaskania, matiasma*); *oculus malus* (Latin; also *fascinatio* etc.]); *malocchio* (Italian); *mal de ojo* (Spanish); *mauvais oeil* (French); *mau olhado* (Portuguese); *ayn al-ḥasūd* (Arabic); *ʿainat* (Ethiopian); *cheshme nazar* (Persian); *droch shuil* (Celtic, Irish); *cronachadt* (Scottish) *zte oko* (Polish); *ondt ojel* (Danish); *paha simlä* (Finnish); "Evil Eye" (English).[59] Others speak of a *gaze, glance* or *look*: e.g., *böser Blick* (German; also *Scheel, Scheelsucht*); *booze blik* (Dutch); *mauvais regard* (French); *onde blik* (Norwegian); *baleful gaze* (English); *nazar* (Turkish); *squardo invidioso* (Italian, also *jettatura*, "casting an Evil Eye"). This is only a selection of terms, which, of course, indicates some of the

57. Dundes (1992) and Maloney (1976) present collections of scholarly case studies of Evil Eye belief and practice from antiquity to the present and from East to West.

58. Seligmann 1910 1:48–63 (nine categories); see also Seligmann 1922:15–93; Budge 1930/1978:363.

59. In antiquity, also Sumerian, Akkadian, Ugaritic, Egyptian, Aramaic, and Syriac.

cultures where the Evil Eye belief is present. Beside Europe and the Americas, the belief has also been found in Thailand, Burma, Tibet, Korea, Malay, Malacca, Sumatra, Tahiti, Samoa, Greenland, Alaska, Nicaragua, Mexico, British Guyana, Brazil, Peru, Bantu peoples, Busmen, Pygmies, and parts of Australia and New Guinea.[60]

SALIENT FEATURES OF EVIL EYE
BELIEF AND PRACTICE

Ideas and practices associated with the Evil Eye over five millennia and across the globe of course include features that are culturally and temporally specific. A core of common features, nevertheless, has been found among the Evil Eye cultures of the twelve world regions (or ethnic groups). Clarence Maloney, introducing an anthology of anthropological essays on the Evil Eye that he edited and published in 1976, lists seven features:[61]

(1) power emanates from the eye (or mouth) and strikes some object or person;

(2) the stricken object is of value, and its destruction or injury is sudden;

(3) the one casting the evil eye may not know he has the power;

(4) the one affected may not be able to identify the source of power;

(5) the evil eye can be deflected or its effects modified or cured by particular devices, rituals, and symbols;

(6) the belief helps to explain or rationalize sickness, misfortune, or loss of possessions such as animals or crops;

(7) in at least some functioning of the belief everywhere, envy is a factor.

Our study of the phenomenon in antiquity will present evidence of these and additional common features among the ancient cultures. Heading our list of salient features is a complex of associated beliefs or concepts that over the centuries have lent Evil Eye belief and practice their plausibility and power.

60. See Roberts 1976:230–33, Table 1; and Maloney 1976:xii–xiii (global map of Evil Eye belief distribution).

61. Maloney 1976:vii–viii.

Evil Eye Belief Complex

A number of interrelated folk ideas together form an *Evil Eye belief complex*; that is, a web of ideas, beliefs, attitudes, emotions, symbols, and actions that recurs and appears to have remained relatively stable over time. This belief complex includes the notion of the eye as an active organ that projects energy capable of harming, withering or destroying; the eye as conveyor of emotions or dispositions arising in the heart, especially the disposition of envy aroused by the sight of the good fortune of others and fueled by the notion that all goods of life are scarce and in limited supply (the notion of "limited good") so that one person's gain occurs only at another's loss; the notion that certain individuals and groups possess an Evil Eye and can be identified as such; the notion that certain victims are particularly vulnerable such as nursing mothers, newborn babies, and children; the involuntary as well as voluntary operation of an Evil Eye; the association of the eyes with the genitals as symbols of power and vitality; the resort to Evil Eye accusations to discredit rivals; the odium of wielding an Evil Eye; the fear of being struck by an Evil Eye, and the belief that attack from an Evil Eye can be prevented or repelled by a variety of words, gestures, and amulets; and the notion that the Evil Eye was among the most dangerous and deadly forces of evil in existence and therefore a power that is to be greatly feared, dreaded, and guarded against. These features form a cluster of ideas, emotions, and actions that are repeatedly associated with Evil Eye belief and practice in the ancient sources. Not all elements of the complex are always mentioned, but each reappears enough in conjunction with mention of an Evil Eye to suggest a constantly implied latent presence. It is this web of ideas, beliefs, attitudes, emotions, symbols, and actions that sustains belief in the Evil Eye and lends it plausibility and power. Our study discusses each of these features in detail in our examination of the ancient biblical and extra-biblical evidence.

It is important to keep in mind that Evil Eye belief and its complex of associated concepts is an instance of folk belief and folklore[62] and is best analyzed as such, similar to ethnology in its focus, aims, and methods. Folklore has been defined as "traditional knowledge, customs, oral and artistic traditions among any community (or sector of the community) united by some common factor such as a common occupation, co-residence, or a common language or ethnic identity . . . The essence of folklore is its spontaneous or organic nature; that is to say, it is the result of the experiences and interpretations of experience of persons engaged in social interaction."[63] Since this

---

62. Ibid., 258 and passim.
63. Seymour-Smith 1986a:120. On folklore see also Dundes 1965.

implies that the belief will likely undergo modification as it travels from one culture to another, it is remarkable how consistent certain features of this belief complex remain across cultures and down through time. James Russell, writing on Evil Eye in the Byzantine period and the Circum-Mediterranean region, underscores the "homogeneity of practice and belief," which is especially evident in the iconography of devices to ward off the Evil Eye.[64]

The questioning of these folk beliefs by modern science has led to a demise of Evil Eye belief in many so-called advanced societies but not to its complete disappearance. The persistence of this folk belief in modern time in the face of countervailing scientific evidence is a fascinating phenomenon that begs for closer examination. Such an investigation is beyond the limit of this study, which focuses on the Evil Eye in antiquity, but is surely an important topic for a future agenda. The issue, moreover, does present a problem that all readers of the Bible must be prepared to address: what am I, a reader enlightened by modern science, to make of these several biblical passages assuming the existence and danger of an Evil Eye? How does this affect my understanding and use of these sacred Scriptures? Here too is a worthy subject for future study. We will revisit this issue in our concluding Volume 4, chap. 3.

The Eye as Vital Organ

"The eyes," the renowned zoologist and ethnologist Desmond Morris tells us, "are the dominant sense organs of the body," supplying an estimated eighty percent of our information about the outside world.[65] At the same time, "[t]he eyes themselves are the center of facial expression, appearing to convey love and hate, joy and sorrow," ophthalmologist Edward Gifford observes.[66] The eyes have also been viewed for millennia as windows of the mind and soul. Since they are the chief means of apprehending reality, Plato and the Christian church fathers spoke of paradise and eternal life as a (beatific) *vision* of God. In discussing aspects of belief concerning the eye and the Evil Eye, we will be considering a web of biological, psychological, social, cultural, religious, and moral factors.[67]

64. Russell 1995:36.

65. Morris 1985:49; on the eyes, see 45–64, including 57–60 on the Evil Eye and its aversion; for Evil Eye aversion also 105 (spitting) and 200 (baring buttocks).

66. Gifford 1958:3.

67. On the eye in general as organ of perception, medium of sexual attraction, symbol of enlightenment but also of evil see Ferenczi 1913/1956; Leclercq *DALC* 12, 2 (1936):cols. 1936–43; Wilpert 1950; Gifford 1958:163–93; Déonna 1965; Jaeger 1979; Potts 1982; Cavendish-Deutsch 1983 4:885–94; Morris 1985:45–64; Huxley 1990;

The Eye as Active Organ

The eye, until the 1500s and later, was thought to be an *active*, rather than a passive organ (as held today). It was deemed to project particles of energy or light. This understanding of the eye and vision is known as the "extramission theory of vision," which prevailed in the ancient world and through the Middle Ages and beyond.[68] In the seventeenth century, the English philosopher Francis Bacon was still describing envy as "an ejaculation, or irradiation of the eye."[69] It stands in contrast to an "intromission theory of vision," which is the current prevailing scientific theory holding that the eye is a passive organ and recipient, not projector, of light and sensation. Under the presumption of an active eye and an extramission theory of vision, the ancients described the eyes of humans and the gods as "fiery," "gleaming," and "flashing," projecting particles of energy similar to the rays of the sun, a lighthouse, or a lamp. This active sense of the eye is inscribed linguistically in the Italian term for an Evil-Eyed person, namely *jettatore*, lit., "one who casts" (*jettare*, "to throw, cast") an Evil Eye. This active eye theory, we shall see, underlines all that is said of the eye in the ancient sources, including the biblical writings. Still in our time, despite the view of an intromission theory of vision that prevails in the scientific community, in folk culture the eyes are imagined as active when we speak of "devouring a beloved with our eyes," or "looking daggers" at an enemy. Many of us are convinced that we can feel the ocular rays of someone staring at us. The capacity of the eye and a piercing glance to strike fear or arouse shame is learned from early childhood in cultures across the globe.[70]

The Eye as Conveyer of Dispositions and Emotions Arising in the Heart

The eye, centuries of observation has shown, also gives signals of internal dispositions and emotions. The muscles of the iris work unconsciously, supplying clues to internal states. The wide open eye of love or of fear, the narrow eye of hatred or of greedy calculation or of suspicion are telltale signals

---

Debray 1992 (gaze); Synnott 1992; Illich 1994.

68. On the the extramission theory and the history of theories of vision see D. O'Brien 1970; Ronchi 1970; Hoorn 1972; Hahm 1978; Burkert 1977; Lindberg 1976; Classen 1993; Jay 1986, 1993; Beare 1996:14–23; Rakoczy 1996:19–37; Winer and Cottrell 1996; Winer et al, 1996, 2002, 2003; D. Park 1998:34–41; Rudolf 2011. See also below, Vols. 2 and 3, on theories of vision in antiquity.

69. Bacon 1890:56.

70. Coss 1992; Gross 1999; Ayers 2004.

of stirrings in the heart. Physicians for centuries have examined the eye for the information it supplies about internal health. The eye, common wisdom has had it, is the "window to the soul." The ancients, having no science of psychology and little interest in personal introspection, relied on external factors as indicators of internal states. They regarded the eye as a key revealer of thoughts and emotions. The eye, they held, was linked to the heart, which in turn was considered the locus of feeling and thinking. God alone, the Israelites believed, could look into the human heart. But the eye gave indications of the dispositions of the heart and through the eye these feelings and their energy were projected onto other human beings. The eye was both a "window on the soul" and a channel and conveyer of energy prompted by attitudes and feelings, both positive and negative, arising in the heart.

The Evil Eye as Conveyer of Envy and Other Malignant Dispositions and Emotions

One of the most malicious of the human dispositions is envy: resentment and displeasure felt from observing "the superiority of another person in happiness, success, reputation or the possession of anything desirable," with the wish that the person be deprived of that asset.[71] From antiquity onward envy has been closely associated with casting an Evil Eye.[72] Envy involves perception, emotion, and action on the part of both the envier and the envied.[73] Envy is directly linked with the eye and the act of looking and observing. "Envy begins in the eye of the beholder, an eye that exaggerates, misrepresents, and selectively chooses things to hate."[74] This connection of eye, looking, and envy is inscribed linguistically in the Latin for "envy," the noun *invidia* and the verb *invidere*. To envy is to "look" (*videre*) "upon" (*in*-[2d meaning]) with an (evil) eye. The older English expression "to overlook" (with an Evil Eye), retained this implication. The action is equivalent to "looking askance at" or "looking obliquely at" with malevolent feeling. An envious Evil Eye is aroused by the sight of another's good looks, youth, health, success in business or on the battlefield, many children, fine animals, good milk production, an abundant harvest, prosperity, fame, wealth, and

---

71. *Oxford English Dictionary* (2nd ed. 1989), *s.v.*

72. See Jahn 1855; Walcot 1978:77–90; Schoeck 1970, 1992; Foster 1972; Maloney 1976 passim; Elliott 1988; McCartney 1992:31–32; Stein 1992:243–44; Rakoczy 1996; Gerschman 2011b.

73. Berke 1988:44.

74. Ibid., 36.

honor. This sight produces displeasure and pain, along with the malevolent wish that this asset be destroyed.

Envy is different from jealousy, although the two terms often are used as synonyms in modern discourse. Envy, in terms of its social dynamics, is displeasure at the possessions of others; jealousy is fear of losing to others that which one possesses. Envy is aggressive; jealousy is protective. The Evil Eye is rarely linked with jealousy, but regularly with envy. Schadenfreude, by the way, is the flipside of envy. Envy grieves over another's happiness; schadenfreude is happiness over another's grief. Envy is fueled by the "perception of limited good," that is, the notion that all goods and resources of life are in limited and scarce supply so that the gain of any person or group is thought to occur only at the loss of another person or group.[75] The malevolent feeling, in turn, prompts actions of extreme aggression toward others and can even lead to self-injury. Evil-Eyed and envious persons can harm *themselves* as well as others. Persistent envy can even lead to blindness. "It is likely that certain cases of hysterical blindness are the result of an envy so intense that the person refuses to see anything at all rather than risk seeing any goodness in anyone or anything."[76] Ancient depictions of envious persons, as we shall see, portray them as strangling themselves and through their envy bringing on their own destruction.[77]

An incantation against the Evil Eye still in circulation in Romania illustrates the age-old link of the Evil Eye and envy and declares in violent terms:

> May he burst, the envious one.
> Evil eye he cast.
> May he explode.
> If a virgin spellbinds him,
> May her braids fall off.
> If his wife spellbinds him,

75. On the concept of limited good and envy see the classic studies of Foster 1965, 1972; also Gregory 1975; Seymour-Smith 1986:168–69; Malina 2001:81–107, 108–33; table 3 (131–32) presents an instructive comparison of envy (and the Evil Eye) in "ancient Mediterranean experience" over against contemporary "U. S. experience."

76. Berke 1988:37

77. On the association of envy and the Evil Eye in antiquity see below, chap. 2 and Vols. 2–4; in modern time, see, inter alios, Davidson 1923; Blackman 1927:218 (Egypt); Hocart 1938 (Egypt); Klein 1957, 1975; Wolf 19555 (Latin America); Foster 1965, 1972; Blum and Blum 1970 (Greece); Schoeck 1970, Stein 1974; Evans 1975; Maloney 1976 passim; Stephenson 1979; Ghosh 1983; Siebers 1983; de la Mora 1987; Adamson 1997 (on Melville); Berke 1988:35–77; Dundes 1992 passim; Pocock 1992 (India); Nagarajan 1993 (India); Ibrahim 1994 (Sudan);Gravel 1995; Migliore 1997 (Canada); Nicholson 1999; Aquaro 2004 (Greek Orthodox Christianity); van de Van 2010; Gerschmann 2011a, 2011b.

> May her milk dry up,
> May her breast wither,
> May her child die of hunger.
> If a youth spellbinds him,
> May he burst completely.[78]

The form and content of the incantation are remarkably similar to ancient Near Eastern anti-Evil Eye incantations millennia earlier, as we shall see in chap. 2.

The Evil Eye is alluded to in the Qur'an in a morning prayer for safety from a neighbor's envy [conveyed through an Evil Eye]:

> In the name of God, most compassionate and merciful.
> Say: I seek protection through the lord of daybreak.
> From the evil of what he has created,
> From the evil of twilight,
> From the evil of women who blow on knots,
> From the evil of the envious when he envies.
> (sura 113 *Al-Falaq* ["Daybreak"])[79]

In Islam, as well as among Jews and Christians, the Evil Eye and envy are inextricably related.

Miserliness, a begrudging spirit, and lack of generosity are further dispositions associated with an Evil Eye, especially in the biblical writings.[80]

The Evil Eye as Cause of Harm, Loss, Damage, Illness, or Death

According to the extramission theory of vision, the particles or rays emitted by the eye can wreck harm just as can the rays of the sun. A glaring, staring eye, a penetrating gaze, can burn, wither, reduce to ashes, zap, hurt, injure, damage, or destroy any object struck by the ocular emanations. An Evil Eye was feared as a major cause of illness and death.[81] In considering this under-

---

78. Andreesco-Miereanu 1987; 1989:116–21, esp. 119. The field research on what incantations mothers know and use is of "recent years" (119), i.e. the latter half of the twentieth century.

79. On the Evil Eye in Islam see Volume 4, chap. 2.

80. See Vols. 2–4.

81. Anthropologist George Murdock found in his world survey of theories of illness (1980b) that the Evil Eye was held to be a cause of illness in fifty-four of 139 societies primitive, historical and contemporary (Murdock 1980b:21–22 and Table 2, 22–26). In nine societies it was seen as a predominant cause of illness; in eighteen others, an important secondary cause; and in twenty-seven societies, a minor cause; see also 40, 49 and Table 3. Of 26 Circum-Mediterranean societies, 23 consider the Evil Eye a cause

standing of the Evil Eye, medical anthropology has shown how essential it is to study "the closely interwoven natural-environment, human-biological, and socio-cultural threads forming the behavioral and conceptual network of human responses to the experience of illness."[82] Accordingly, a harmful Evil Eye has been referred to as a "baleful eye," an "oblique eye," an "evil look" or "evil glance" (e.g., *böser Blick*, focusing on the ocular action. *Stare, glare, scowl, frown, glower, penetrating gaze, withering glance, dirty look, looking daggers, grimace, looking askance, overlook, leer, knitting of eyebrows*—all these ocular actions can signal hostility, anger, disapproval, aggression and the like and are emblematic of casting an Evil Eye. Looking obliquely or askance is typically associated with casting an Evil Eye. To *leer* has been defined as "to cast a sidelong glance" (*Webster's New Collegiate Dictionary*). "Stink eye" is a Hawaiian pidgin expression for a disapproving glance, a mean or dirty look. It does not seem to be a version of an Evil Eye with its damaging power, but is similar in terms of its being a hostile and aggressive ocular glance. Tobin Siebers concurs with A. M. Hocart (1938), that "further inquiry into the evil eye must begin with staring."[83] When my aggressive, hostile staring at another person, he notes,

> coincides with an accident or decline in his health, I may face a different kind of accusation [beyond the accusation of un-wanted staring], I may be blamed for harming him. He will say that I possess the evil eye . . . Every race of man shares the idea that the human eye penetrates or pierces, and this belief affirms the fundamental premise of the evil-eye superstition [*sic*] that the eye injures or alters reality. The psychological adjustment necessary to leap from this notion of the belief in the evil eye is relatively small. In fact, it may be easier to understanding the transition from penetrating stare to evil eye than to explain why human beings describe the eye as "piercing."[84]

This widespread notion that people can sense their being watched or stared at or spied on has supported this belief from past to present. Behavior

---

of illness; the next large representation is five of twenty-three Sub-Saharan Africa societies (Table 3, 50–51; see also 58). See also the survey of Roberts 1976, which was based on the data of Murdock and White 1969:328–69 ("only 36 percent of the cultures of the world sample possessed the evil eye belief"[1969:330]). This is the sample used by Roberts 1976:227 and Table 1 (230–33): of the 186 cultures in six major world regions; 67 manifested belief in the Evil Eye (Roberts 1976:229).

82. Pilch 2000:21, citing Unschuld 1988:179.

83. Siebers 1983:29. On the act and psychology of staring and its constituting a weapon of the Evil Eye see Siebers 1983:29–33.

84. Siebers 1983:30, 33.

in primates as well as humans adds additional support—dominant agents using a forceful gaze to command subordination while the submissive party averts the eye or agents manifesting aggression and anger through the hostile stare. At the experiential level, this conduct lends credence to this notion of ocular aggression and the power of an Evil Eye.[85] On the U.S. pop cultural level, this gives us comic book characters such as Superman and his x-ray vision or Evil Eye Fleegle, one of the notable characters of Al Capp's "Li'l Abner" comic strip.[86]

The Evil Eye:
Demonic and Human, Voluntary and Involuntary

Many cultures of the ancient Circum-Mediterranean feared an Evil Eye demon that could attack humans and their loved ones from without. This demon is mentioned or depicted frequently in anti-Evil Eye incantations and amulets. Human beings and animals, however, were also thought to possess and cast an Evil Eye—either involuntarily or voluntarily. "Fascination," William Story noted, "was of two kinds, moral and natural. Those in whom the power was moral could exert it only by the exercise of their will; but those in whom it was natural could not help exercising it unconsciously. And these latter were the most terrible."[87] In this latter case, the Evil Eye was thought to be conferred by nature, inherited as a physical quality like blue eyes or bushy eyebrows or physical deformity. The Evil Eyes of dead animals, of those inheriting the power, of fathers adoring their children, of lovers admiring their beloveds, and even of well-intended popes fall into this latter category. In the Middle Ages, Arab historian Ibn Khaldûn (1332–1406) in his introduction to history, *The Muqaddimah*,[88] discussed the Evil Eye and regarded it as a natural quality, innate and not acquired, and independent of the will and intention of its possessor. He thus distinguished the Evil Eye from intentionally malicious sorcery.[89] Numerous ancient sources reflect this view, although the Evil Eye came under moral censure when linked with the disposition of envy and other malevolent dispositions. Where the Evil Eye was thought set in motion by envy, miserliness, greed, or some other

85. On the Evil Eye and ocular aggression see also Gilmore 1981:197–98; 1987a; 1987b; on disinclination to be stared at among humans and animals see Caillois 1960.

86. On the Evil Eye and Dogpatch's Evil Eye Fleegle see Elliott 1988:42–43. On Al Capp and the comic strip "Li'l Abner," see Berger 1978.

87. Story 1877:154–64.

88. Ibn Khaldun 1967:Ch. 6, §27.

89. See Dundes 1992b:259–60.

negative emotion, it was regarded as voluntarily activated and therefore a moral issue. In this case, fascinators were morally warned and condemned and urged to restrain their Evil Eye. The writings of the biblical communities tend to reflect this latter moral position, although self-fascination (an involuntary act) was also deemed possible. Only in the post-biblical period did Christians link the Evil Eye with an external force, namely Satan/the Devil, the chief of demons who worked his malice through Evil-Eyed humans.[90]

The Human Evil Eye as a Phenomenon of Nature, not an Instance of Magic or Vulgar Superstition

The ancient understanding of the Evil Eye possessed by humans and how it worked was based on the presumption of an active eye and entailed an extramission theory of vision. There are only a few ancient discussions of how the Evil Eye was thought to work, such as the accounts of Aristotle, Plutarch, Heliodorus, and Pseudo-Alexander of Aphrodisias, all discussed in Volume 2. From these sources it is clear, as we shall see, that the Evil Eye was regarded as a *phenomenon of nature and not as a vulgar superstition or instance of supernatural magic.*[91] The question of its being a common superstition was raised only to be rejected, as in Plutarch's dinner conversation on the Evil Eye. Here and in other texts a rational explanation was presented based on experience, observation, and the current knowledge of the day. This involved variations of a theory of emanations thought to be emitted by the eye and damaging any object these emanations struck. While contrary to the modern scientific understanding of the eye and vision, this conception of an active eye prevailed in the ancient world and gave Evil Eye belief and practice their plausibility and power.

In this study we shall seek to understand this ancient *emic* perspective on the Evil Eye and the factors that lent it plausibility and power. Then we shall consider it from a modern Western *etic* perspective, with attention to the various biological, psychological, social, and moral factors at play. A distinction between "emic" and "etic" perspectives, as practiced by anthropologists, enables us to avoid imposing on our ancient sources our modern scientific views and moral judgments. "Emic" pertains to the perspectives, descriptions, and explanations provided by members of a particular culture—in our case, the authors and producers of the cultural sources investigated here. "Etic" pertains to the perspectives, descriptions, explanations and criteria used to analyze a culture by persons *outside* this particular

90. On the post-biblical sources through the end of Late Antiquity see Volume Four.
91. On this issue, see below, pp. 62–68.

culture—in our case, modern historians, classicists, social scientists, or theologians intent on understanding and explaining the data according to modern scientific criteria.[92]

The Fascinators

"Fascinators" are agents who fascinate, i.e. who possess, cast, and injure with, an Evil Eye. We recall that the English terms "fascinate," "fascinator," and "fascination" derive from the Latin *fascinare, fascinator,* and *fascinatio* which are transliterations of the Greek *baskainen, baskanos, and baskania*. Originally, "to fascinate" was to injure with an Evil Eye. Its shift in meaning from ancient negative sense to present-day positive sense parallels the changed senses of "bewitching" and "enchanting." In Italian, these fascinators are known as known as *jettatori* (singular: *jettatore,* from *jettare,* "cast"); i.e. *casters* of the Evil Eye.

Possessors of the Evil Eye could come from all walks of life and knew no social bounds. Across the centuries it has been attributed to commoners and rulers alike, from village locals to kings and queens, priests, rabbis and monks, midwives, beggars, smiths, iron-workers, eunuchs, witches, grave diggers, intellectuals, poets, musicians, football players, and modern-day murderers. Social deviants within the group as well as visiting strangers and exotic alien families or tribes were readily accused. Identifying and labeling the fascinators involved constant stereotyping and stigmatizing.

In earliest time, the Evil Eye was attributed to the gods, mythical figures, fabulous creatures, and an Evil-Eye demon that attacked humans and their possessions. We shall be examining these instances in due course. Eventually, humans and animals also were believed to possess and exercise an Evil Eye.[93] Notorious ancient fascinators included Medusa/Gorgo, Medea, Polyphemus the one-eyed cyclops, certain ethnic groups (such as the Telchines, the Thebians, and the Egyptians), and Aesop the fabulist. In Jewish lore, numerous biblical characters were attributed the envious Evil Eye including Cain, Sarah, Og, the giant, Joseph's brothers, King Saul, and Queen Esther.[94] It was said of Eleazar ben Hyrcanus, Simeon ben

92. On "emic" and "etic" as analytical categories see Pike 1954/1967; Harris 1976; Headland et al. 1990; Barnard and Spencer, eds. 2002:180–83.

93. For fascinators throughout history see Story 1877:147–238; Seligmann 1910 1:65–168; 1922:94–111; Elworthy 1958/1895:1–43.

94. *Midrash Megillah* [Ozar Midrashim 60b]; cf. *b. Megillah* 15b; see Ulmer 1994:114–15.

Yohai[95] and Yohanan,[96] rabbis of the second century CE, that the rays of their Evil Eyes reduced the objects of their glances to ashes. "Wherever the Sages cast their eyes in disapproval, death or poverty resulted."[97] The Evil Eye of Rabbi Eliezer could cause the destruction of the world.[98] Rabbi Yohanan bar Nafcha (died 279 CE) reportedly had "very large eyebrows"[99] and with his Evil Eye killed his brother-in-law, Simon ben Laqish,[100] and also endangered his nephew by admiring him.[101] Among the followers of Jesus, the apostle Paul was accused of casting an Evil Eye on his Galatian converts.[102] Fascinators in ancient times and in the Bible will be discussed in due course. Irish legend tells of a mythical giant warrior, Balor, king of the Fomorians, whose single lethal eye could annihilate entire armies.[103] In modern time persons of fame and renown thought to be fascinators included King Louis XIV and emperor Napolean III of France, King Alphonso XIII of Spain, Queen Maria Amelia of Portugal, Kaiser Wilhelm II of Germany, and King Victor Emmanuel of Italy. King Ferdinand of Naples, it was rumored by the Neopolitans, died not of apoplexy but of an Evil Eye cast by a certain Canon Ojori, "one of the most terrible *jettatori* [casters of the Evil Eye] in Naples."[104] Lord Byron the English poet, the Austrian composer Jacques Offenbach, and numerous Italian counts were also suspected. Not even Roman Catholic Popes have escaped suspicion. Pius IX (1792–1878) as well as his successor Leo XIII (1810–1903) were both feared for their Evil Eye. Pius IX ("Pio Nono"), though praised as very kind, was regarded by the populace as "the most respected and feared jettatore in Rome"[105] because of the numerous calamities to persons and places that occurred when he appeared and offered his blessing. "If he had not the *jettatura*, it is very odd," the Romans said, "that everything he blessed made *fiasco*."[106] "There is nothing so fatal as his blessing," said a

---

95. *b. Shabbat* 33b–34a; *b. Bava Metzi'a* 84a.

96. *b. Bava Batra* 75a; *b. Sanhedrin* 100a.

97. *b. Nedarim* 7b.

98. *b. Bava Metzia* 59b.

99. *b. Taanit* 9a.

100. *b. Bava Metzi'a* 84a; *b. Bava Kamma* 11a; *Pesiqta de Rab Kahana.* 137a

101. *b. Taanit* 9a. cf. Seligmann 1910 1:110.

102. See Elliott 1990 and Vol. 3, chap. 2.

103. Seligmann 1910 1:26–27; Krappe 1927; Crenshaw 1996.

104. Elworthy 1958/1895:28.

105. Seligmann 1910 1:116.

106. Elworthy 1958/1895:25.

contemporary Italian.[107] Now, if he hasn't the *jettatura*, said another, "what is it that makes everything turn out at cross purposes with him? For my part, I don't wonder the workmen at the Column in the Piazza di Spagna refused to work the other day in raising it, unless the Pope stayed away."[108] A rosary that he blessed and that was given as a gift, it was rumored, brought on illness and death.[109] Devout but cautious Roman Catholics kneeling to receive his benediction would extend a *mano cornuta* toward him or women would make the protective gesture under their skirts.[110] Pope Leo XIII, successor of Pio Nono, was suspected of being a *jettatore* possessing an Evil Eye, gossip had it, because so many cardinals died during his pontificate.[111] In mid-twentieth century America, a character known as "Evil Eye Fleegle" was featured in one of the most popular comic strips of the day, Al Capp's "Li'l Abner," dweller of Dogpatch, USA. Dreaded denizen of deepest Brooklyn, Evil Eye Fleegle controlled "nature's most stupefyin' equipment—THE UNLIMITLESS POWER OF THE HUMAN EYEBALL!!" He was, "master of th' WHAMMY—th' most powerful force on oith!!" "His—shudder—single whammy is powerful enough to stop a rampaging elephant dead in its tracks!!" "His double whammy kin melt a locomotive in full flight." "His triple whammy . . . kin toin Lake Erie into a mud flat . . . or win the Noo Yawk Mets a pennant." Using only "th' super-unnatural, trans-spatial power o' [his] INTERPLANETARY WHAMMY," he can even stupify the sun and blast it from its orbit. This deadly character was part of the fictional Dogpatch world of Li'l Abner followed avidly by millions of readers.[112] His well-known creator, Al Capp, is considered by many one of the greatest of U.S. satirists.[113] Fleegle's moiderous eye is more than a figment of Capp's fertile imagination; it has a pedigree in the rich European Jewish tradition that was Capp's heritage.

107. Story 1877:197–99, esp. 198; Gifford 1958:17.

108. Gifford 1958:16–17. On Pius IX, see also Seligmann 1910 1:116–18.

109. Elworthy 1958/1895:26.

110. Ibid., 24–26; Trachtenberg 1939:54.

111. Seligmann 1910 1:118; Budge 1978/1930:365). On the various suspected human fascinators from past to present see Seligmann 1910 1:108–19. On other fascinators (animals, fabulous creatures, transcendent beings, and inanimate entities) see Seligmann 1910 1:120–68. See also Elworthy 1958/1895:21–28, recounting thirteen questions posed by Valletta (1777) concerning maneuvering with suspected *jettatori* (1958/1895:22) and listing noted jettatori of Naples and Rome, including the two popes, Pio Nono and Leo XIII.

112. Capp 1953, 1964, 1978.

113. Berger 1970.

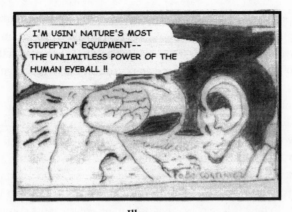

Illus. 1.1

Evil Eye Fleegle and his stupefyin' eye, from Al Capp, *Li'l*
Abner, linedrawing by Dietlinde Elliott

Telltale Features

What are the physical and social features of an Evil-Eyed fascinator? Cultures
vary on this point, but the historical and cross-cultural evidence indicates
that the Evil Eye has regularly been attributed to strangers, enemies, the socially displaced (e.g., widows) and those who are "different" (physically and/
or socially). Especially under suspicion have been persons with ocular irreg-
ularities (e.g., crossed, squinting, blinking, wandering, or deeply-set eyes;
eyes with double pupils or pupils of contrasting colors; twitching eyelids;
bushy eyebrows; joined eyebrows),[114] the blind,[115] the physically disabled or
deformed including dwarfs and hunchbacks,[116] and epileptics such as Pope
Pius IX. A newspaper cartoon by Gary Larson ("The Far Side") smiles at
the notion, still alive today, that something in the eye reveals one to be an
Evil Eye possessor. To a patient undergoing an eye examination the doctor

114. Pitrè (1889) 1884 writing on the Evil Eye in nineteenth-century Italy describes
the anatomical features of a *jettatore* as including "a thin face, dark, sallow; small,
deepset eyes; a hooked nose; a long neck like those who swallow saliva; he's altogether
unpleasant and burdensome, offensive, repugnant (1992:132); see also his description
(1884) of a a Sicilian jettatore as having a "viso magro, al colorito cupo, olivigno, al naso
adunco, especialmente agli occhi biechi e loschi, rossi o blu (cio percosi da una vena),
piccoli, porcigni, ingrottati."

115. Those lacking sight were thought possibly to have been blinded by the gods,
like Oedipus, for having cast an Evil Eye.

116. The disabled and deformed were suspected of enviously Evil Eyeing the
healthy. For an ancient predecessor of the modern Italian "gobbo" (hunchback) see Levi
1941 regarding a mosaic in Antioch, Syria, depicting a hunchback warding off an Evil
Eye and in this study, Volume Two.

exclaims, "Oh, this is wonderful, Mr. Gruenfeld—I've only seen it a couple of times. You have a corneal corruption . . . Evil eye, Mr. Gruenfeld, evil eye!"[117] Widows, widowers, persons living alone, and those with dangerously ambiguous roles also have been suspected. Likewise under suspicion have been persons in competitive relation with the supposed victims of Evil Eye attack or those in the society who customarily are targeted as scapegoats when misfortune strikes.[118] In Evil Eye cultures, looking with an Evil Eye at someone, casting an Evil Eye, is regarded as an act of aggression, with not only personal but also social ramifications and consequences. Evil Eyes can harm and kill. So those suspected of having an Evil-Eye are deemed fair game for ostracizing, punishment, or elimination.

Accusation of Being a Fascinator

Accusation of someone being a fascinator and casting an Evil Eye has been an effective means in Evil Eye and witchcraft societies for discrediting, shaming and ruining the reputation of a rival. In small, face-to-face communities where central authority for adjudicating conflicts is weak or lacking, public accusation of fascination and making it stick can ruin the reputation, credibility and status of the accused in the court of public opinion. One so accused was stigmatized as a social deviant, unreliable, morally questionable, and dangerous to the common good. The purpose and deleterious effect of such accusation was similar to that of charges of practicing magic, sorcery and the occult arts.[119] Such accusations, of which Paul the apostle was a target, as we shall see, were an informal but potent means of social control and negotiation of group identity and boundaries among persons and factions struggling for dominance.[120]

The Fascinated:
Victims of the Evil Eye, Types of Injury, and Dangerous Situations

On the whole, the Evil Eye appears to be regarded as no respecter of persons or classes; it is capable of injuring all sorts and conditions of humankind. Neonates, infants and children prior to their majority, however, are

117. Larson, "The Far Side," *San Francisco Chronicle* 2 April 1992.

118. On the features of suspected fascinators in various cultures see Seligmann 1910 1:66–82.

119. Ricks 1990; Dickie 2001:21–22; Schmidt 2002, among others.

120. See Douglas, 1970b; Elliott 1990; 2005a:159–64; 2011:118–22. On Evil Eye accusation, see Vols. 2 and 3.

regularly considered among its most vulnerable victims. Mortality rates among infants were high in antiquity and account for this fear of the Evil Eye as a threat to infant survival. Today the causes of high infant mortality are traced to malnutrition, chronic illnesses, poor housing conditions, and lack of sanitation and hygiene. Pregnant and birthing mothers likewise are deemed highly vulnerable. Then any and all persons enjoying sound health, youth, beauty, vitality, sudden good fortune, victory in competition and battle, popular acclaim, and favored social status also are prey to the envious Evil Eye. Similarly, no realm of property or life is considered beyond potential damage. Primary concern, however, focuses on those things upon which one's sustenance and survival depend. Thus one's food, family, cattle and crops, means of livelihood, health, and familial reputation are regarded as constantly exposed to Evil Eye attack. The idea that children are chief targets of the Evil Eye continues in today's popular culture.

Types of Injury

The injury and damage from an Evil Eye can range from a passing illness or loss of a single prized possession or defeat in a competition or battle, or curdling of milk or lameness of horses or camels to prolonged sickness, drying up of lactating mother's milk, the withering and dessication of humans, animals, and crops; loss of children or other loved ones; destruction of prized possessions; calamity affecting entire families, tribes or states and personal death.[121] "Among the diseases given by the glance," Story notes, "are ophthalmia and jaundice, say the ancients; and in these cases, the fascinator loses the disease as his victim takes it."[122] In the Scottish Highlands were reports of the sudden illness of humans and animals caused by the Evil Eye and "overlooking," cows having their milk drying up, beer turning sour, pigs dying.[123] In Cairo, a pregnant young bride dies suddenly and an envious Evil Eye was deemed the cause.[124]

---

121. For the Evil Eye as a significant cause of illness see Abbott 1903:139–46; Murgoci 1923; McKenzie 1927:225–62; Seligmann 1927a; Blum and Blum 1965; St Clair 1971:278–302 (autobiographical account); Press 1973; G. M. Foster 1976; Hand 1976; Maloney 1976:14, 138–39, 166, 171, 184, 315–19; Murdock 1980b:21, 27 and passim; Nichter 1981; Migliore 1983, 1990, 1997; Sachs 1983; Parsons 1984; Parsons and Wakeley 1991; Pasquale 1984; Hughes 1985; Rivera and Wanderer 1986; Burleigh et al 1990; Dundes 1992 passim; Bohigian 1997; Pilch 2009a:19 and passim.

122. Story 1988:187.

123. MacLagan 1902:17, 55.

124. Bowen and Early 1993:107.

Dangerous Times, Situations, and Places

Dangerous times and situations when an Evil Eye could strike generally involve instances of life transitions (birth; courtship, marriage and weddings; and dying). They however also include daily occasions of meals and dining, the arrival of visiting strangers or undertaking travel, of displaying and selling one's wares, husbanding animals, enjoying an abundant harvest, building a house, engaging in public and private competitions, victory celebrations, or exposure in large public assemblies, moments of expressing praise or admiration, or receiving requests for alms and aid, and occurrence of sudden and inexplicable illness or misfortune.[125] Places where an Evil Eye could lurk in addition to the table, bedside, shop, barn, and fields include all public spaces and thoroughfares as well as latrines and cemeteries. Hence the careful protection of these spaces with anti-Evil Eye amulets including images of the crescent moon displayed at latrines for warding off the Evil Eye and other inimical forces.

In Arab-Muslim culture, a saying among the Bedouin highlights the deadly effect of the Evil Eye: "The Evil Eye can bring a man to his grave, and a camel to the cooking pot."

Precautions and Protection against the Evil Eye (and Envy)

The belief that the Evil Eye could strike anyone anywhere at any time has called for constant vigilance. Over the centuries, a vast arsenal of apotropaics and amulets have been employed to thwart, repel, and ward off the malignant eye. An "apotropaic," as already noted, is any word, gesture, action or object whose purpose is to fend off and "drive away" evil harmful forces. The term derives from the Greek *apotrepô*, "drive off." An "amulet" is one type of apotropaic; namely, a small object attached to, or worn on, the bodies of living or dead creatures (humans and animals) whose purpose is to safeguard the wearer from evil harmful forces. The power of such apotropaics and amulets appears to have been attributed to the phenomenon of *similia similibus*, "like influences life," "similar entities protect against, or are cured by, similar entities." This principle involves the practical notion of "fighting fire with fire." *Apotropaics* have included spoken and written

---

125. See MacLagan 1902; Elworthy 1958/1895:3–7, 9–11; Foster 1972:172; Maloney 1976 passim; Berke 1988:296 n. 23; Dundes 1992 passim. For antiquity see Pliny, *NH* 7.2.16–18 (withering of crops, death of infants and adults); Philostratus, *Life of Apollonius* 6.12 (loss of life); Plutarch, *Quaestiones Convivales/Table Talk* 5.7; *Mor.* 680C–683B (children, adults "fall[ing] ill and wasting away").

words, prayers, incantations, acts of ridicule, gestures, and precautionary or defensive actions.

Precautions have included the avoidance of complimenting, praising, or admiring the possessions of others;[126] refusal to look into another's eyes; concealment of children and valued items from the prying eyes of others; denial of one's own success and good fortune; restraint of ambition through the practice of moderation; and the sharing of one's goods and possessions to appease an envious Evil Eye.[127] Fear of children being Evil-Eyed led in China to calling them "dogs," "hogs," or "fleas."[128] "In India," Siebers notes, "male children are nicknamed 'dunghill,' 'grasshopper,' or 'beggar,' whereas 'blind,' 'dusty' or 'fly' are reserved for females."[129] Where praise is unavoidable, then the custom is to add expressions such as the ancient Latin *praefiscini dixerim* or the later equivalent Yididish *kein einhoreh,* both assuring that behind the praise "no Evil Eye is intended." The Muslim expression *Mashallah* ("It is as God wills") or the Italian words *Grazie a Dio* ("Thanks be to God") or the further Italian wish, *si mal occhio non ci fosse* ("may the Evil Eye not strike it") all have the similar purpose of assuring that no envy or Evil Eye has prompted the praise. Romanians receive a compliment "by spitting three times and exclaiming *Sä nu-i fie de deochiu*! (Let it not be cause for the giving of the evil eye)."[130]

Gestures and defensive actions have included spitting; the touching of genitals; the display of the *mano fica,* the *mano cornuta,* and the extended middle finger or "high sign" (the *digitus infamis*), the wearing of amulets and display of protective devices in the home, fields, shops, public places and thoroughfares. Amulets carried or worn by humans and animals include necklaces from which are suspended images of a (blue) eye, or a *wedjat/udjat* (Eye of Horus), or replicas of a phallus and testicles (*fascinum)* or of a vulva (cowrie shells), or of a *mano figa*; or a Hand of Fatima (*Hamsa*) or Hand of Miriam (*Hamesh*), or small pouches (*bullae*) containing bits of plants, herbs (especially rue and garlic) or citations of sacred texts on parchment; the wearing of bells, iron earrings, embossed finger rings and bracelets and objects colored red or blue; the tying of red or blue string around the wrists of newborns; the prophylactic use of substances from humans and animals (horn, teeth, hair), of horseshoes and images of lunar crescents, and of stones, gems, metals and medallions on which are inscribed powerful words and potent images; the affixing of phallic images and *fascina* to door

126. See Maloney 1976:102–48; McCartney 1992:9–38.
127. See Berke 1988:48–56; and Volume Two.
128. Siebers 1983:42.
129. Ibid.
130. Ibid., citing Murgoci 1923:358.

lintels and their depiction in threshold mosaics; the painting of eyes on drinking vessels, tombs, and boat prows; and the modern affixing of miniature blue eyes on the bumpers and rearview mirrors of wagons, taxi cabs, and buses, and the wearing of replica blue eyes as pendants and jewelry.[131] Museums throughout the world teem with amuletic materials, much of it against the Evil Eye. Large amounts of this inventory have yet to be catalogued. Ancient instances of these defensive strategies will be discussed throughout the volumes of this study.

Illus 1.2
Mano fica hand gesture (from Seligmann 1910 2:219, fig. 174)

Illus 1.3
Mano cornuta hand gesture (from Seligmann 1910 1:381. fig.70):

Illus 1.4
Digitus infamis/impudicus ("high sign") gesture

Illus 1.5
Bronze winged phallus amulet (from Seligmann 1910 2:257, fig. 189)

131. See Seligmann 1910 2:1–416; Gifford 1958:53–93.

Illus 1.6
Eye of Horus (*wedjat*) on
modern Egyptian postage
stamp

Illus 1.7
Necklace of cowrie shells
symbolizing the vulva, Eye
of Horus pendant (from
Seligmann 1910 1:317, fig.
55)

Illus 1.8
Brazilian mano *figa/higa*
amulet, Brazil (John H.
Elliott collection)

Illus 1.9
Jewish silver Hand
of Miriam amulet
(Hamesh)(from
Seligmann 1910
2:193, fig. 162)

Illus 1.10
Roman *bulla*/pouch worn
as amulet (from Seligmann
1910 2:313, fig. 162)

Illus 1.11
Modern blue anti-Evil Eye beads, St.
Petersburg, Russia (Photo by Alexander
Schmidt, used by permission)

Illus 1.12
Fascinum in threshold
mosaic, Ostia Antica, Italy

Illus 1.13
Pair of eyes on ancient Greek
drinking cup (*kylix*)
(Photo by J. H. Elliott)

Illus 1.14
Pair of eyes on modern
Mediterranean boat prow

Remedies and cures from Evil Eye attack have been thought possible. These are not often mentioned in the ancient sources that we shall be considering. Reports are far more frequent in modern time. Diagnosis and cure can often involve the same ritual. Remedies have consisted of medicaments and healing rituals involving plants and herbs, stones, metals, water and oil, coals and fire, substances from humans and animals (e.g., spittle, blood, urine, bone), the tying of knots, fumigation, prayers, relics, crucifixes, holy objects, votive offerings and more.[132] In some Italian cultures, for example, a ritual (usually performed by an older wise woman) involving water, oil, prayers and incantations is used to detect and cure injury by the Evil Eye. Drops of oil are allowed to fall over water in a basin and attention is given to whether the oil beads or spreads.[133]

The similarity of the protective measures from one culture to another and their long survival down through modern time is truly remarkable. Many of today's customs, gestures, and even jewelry designs trace their roots back to antiquity's Evil Eye belief and practice.

The Good Eye

A "good eye" has been associated with deity and divine supervision, protection, and blessing. The Masons' concept of a benevolent divine eye has even found its way on to the

132. See Seligmann 1910 1:270–399; Maloney 1976:passim; Dundes 1992a:passim.

133. For the ritual and various interpretations see Appel 1976:17–21; Maloney 1976:10; DiStasi 1981:46–48; Buonanno 1984:46–49; for a similar curative in Greece see Dionosopoulos-Mass 1976:45–47; for curatives in India, Maloney 1976:110–13.

U.S. dollar bill. We will have little to say about this concept since as a human quality it appears only rarely in tandem with references to an Evil Eye. Matthew 6:22–23/Luke 11:34 and rabbinic parallels represent exceptions that will be discussed in connection with these texts.[134]

THE ORIGIN AND DISTRIBUTION OF EVIL EYE BELIEF AND PRACTICE

Evil Eye belief and practice has flourished for at least for 5000 years. Cuneiform texts of Sumerian incantations from Mesopotamia dated to the third millennium BCE are the earliest historical written attestation.[135] From Mesopotamia and the ancient Near East the belief appears to have spread across the Fertile Crescent and Palestine to Egypt and North Africa and Ethiopia, to Greece and Rome, and then beyond the Mediterranean basin eastward to India and European Russia and westward to Spain, Portugal, Britain, Ireland and Scotland via Celtic migration, and finally to all four directions of the compass. "Within this central area [European, Mediterranean, and Near East] throughout time the cultures were undoubtedly linked by diffusion and cultural transmission."[136] It appears "contiguously from Scotland at one extreme of its main area of distribution to Sri Lanka at the other" and from Northern Europe to North and East Africa.[137] Anthropologist Clarence Maloney, summarizing the important tabulations and analysis of John Roberts on Evil Eye belief in cross-cultural world perspective,[138] states that "It must have been spread in large measure by the expansion of Indo-European and Semitic-speaking peoples . . . and the early dairy and herding traditions of those peoples may account for the statistical association of the belief with those features."[139] The conclusions of the economic study of Boris Gershman (2011a) on "the economic origins of Evil Eye belief" are consistent with this research of Roberts and Garrison and Arensberg (1976), among others, which points to ancient Mesopotamia and the Circum-Mediterranean

134. On the good eye see Seligmann 1910 1:244–51; Deonna 1965:147–53; Rakoczy 1996:227–45.

135. DiStasi 1981:111–16 suggests that a prototype of the phenomenon is traceable to the Paleolithic period.

136. Roberts 1976:234.

137. Maloney 1976:x–xiv.

138. Ibid., v–xvi, summarizing Roberts 1976:223–78. See also the data of Murdock 1980a.

139. Maloney 1976:xiv; as applied to the biblical communities, see Elliott 1992:55.

region and their agro-pastoral societies as the likely point of origin. Gershman has found a

> robust positive association between the incidence of the belief
> in small-scale pre-industrial societies and various measures of
> wealth stratification . . . [The] belief is more likely to be present
> in agro-pastoral societies which technologically sustain higher
> levels of inequality and where material wealth plays a major role
> in the subsistence economy. Historically, rising wealth inequal-
> ity, a natural by-product of early economic development, might
> have increased the risk of envy-induced destructive behavior
> leading to the emergence of the evil eye belief.[140]

These witchcraft societies of the Circum-Mediterranean also view witches, the Evil Eye, and envy as potent causes of illness and envy—a view "surprisingly rare elsewhere in the world."[141] According to anthropologist David Gilmore, belief in the Evil Eye is "probably one of the few true Mediterranean universals. It is also one of the oldest continuous religious constructs in the Mediterranean area."[142] From the "old world" the belief made its way to North, Central and South America via the ethnic traditions brought by colonists from the "old countries."[143] The spread of Islam took it to Indonesia as well.

The Evil Eye was once thought to be a universal belief. More systematic historical and anthropological investigation of the phenomenon, however, now indicates a dissemination more restricted in scope. A cross-cultural survey of 186 societies has identified sixty-seven cultures, thirty-six percent of the total world sample, as evidencing belief in the Evil Eye. One hundred nineteen cultures, on the other hand, manifest no presence of Evil Eye belief.[144] Distribution of the belief globally over time is thus extensive but not universal. It is, nevertheless, found in all of the six major regions of the world: sub-Saharan Africa (28 cultures), Circum-Mediterranean (28

---

140. Gershman 2011a:1.

141. Murdock 1980b:21; cf. pp. 49, 57, 58, with comparative statistical evidence.

142. Gilmore 1982:198 and 178–79 on the Evil Eye.

143. Roberts 1976:234; Hand 1976/1980; see Maloney 1976:xii–xiii for a map of the belief's global distribution.

144. Roberts 1976:229 and 230–33. This percentage concurs with the earlier survey of Murdock and White (1969:329–69) that found that "only 36 percent of the cultures of the world sample possessed the evil eye belief" (Murdock and White 1969:330). The belief is not found among native Americans in North, Central, and South America except where European colonization left its impact nor in Sub-Saharan Africa except where Islam has been influential, nor in Oceania. For over half the peoples of the earth Evil Eye belief is not attested.

cultures), East Eurasia (34 cultures), insular-Pacific (31 cultures), North America (33 cultures), Central and South America (32 cultures). In the ancient Near East and Circum-Mediterranean region, however, it appears to have been ubiquitous. It has been found in Jewish, Christian, Islamic, Hindu, and Buddhist traditions and, more generally, the cultures of most pre-literate societies. It is mentioned repeatedly in the Hebrew and Greek Bibles of the Old and New Testaments, though this is generally not apparent in modern translations, which render the original terms not literally but according to presumed sense. Evil Eye belief and practice is still prominent today in Italy and Spain, Greece and Turkey, the Arabic countries, India and Sri Lanka, as well as in ethnic pockets of immigrant communities populating the cities of the "new world."

Beside its distribution in space, we can trace its spread over time from the cuneiform tablets of third millennium Sumer to yesterday's newspaper. The *Hamburger Abendblatt* reports an incidence of children chasing a women thought to have an Evil Eye.[145] Patients in hospitals are still attributing strange illnesses to Evil Eye attacks.[146] Jewish grandmas are still muttering *genahoreh/kain ein horeh* (Yiddish: "no Evil Eye"); women are still wearing Hand of Fatimah and Hand of Miriam pendants. Babies are still equipped in hospitals and nurseries with red or blue apotropaic bracelets; church festivals are still distributing anti-Evil Eye amulets. Evil Eye accusations still abound in novels, films, and television series. The belief and its accompanying practices represents an important cross-cultural phenomenon with extraordinary staying power. A 2009 survey conducted by the Pew Forum on Religion and Public Life and reported in the *Chicago Sun-Times* in 2009[147] reports that about sixteen percent of Americans believe in the "evil eye"— that certain people can cast curses or spells with their eye.[148]

It is a phobia prevalent in societies living at subsistence levels and marked by intense struggle over limited resources, in emigrated ethnic groups maintaining traditions of the "old country," and among individuals in highly competitive situations and afflicted with strong emotional feelings

145. Johner 1977:3.

146. For folk medical aspects and a physician's perspective on the Evil Eye see Hand 1992; Dossey 1997.

147. Gorski 2009.

148. On the evidence of pre-modern societies see the studies of Jahn 1855; Story 1877; Elworthy 1895/1955; Seligmann 1910; Budge 1978/1930:354–65; Gravel 1995; Rakoczy 1996 etc. For reports on the Evil Eye in modernity see, amid the mountain of research, the essays in Maloney 1976 and Dundes 1992; MacLagan 1902; Gifford 1958; Campbell 1964:324–38; St. Clair 1971; Hand 1976/1980; Hauschild 1979; Herzfeld 1981; Maple 1983:893–94; Buonano 1984; Gilmore 1987; Dossey 1997; and the studies listed below (studies by various disciplines).

bordering on paranoia. Its presence continues to be an expression of the fear and dread of noxious evil that accompanies and overshadows the human condition and the suspicion of enemies intent on harm and injury through their glaring eyes and gaze. Down through the centuries and across the globe belief in the existence of the Evil Eye and fear of its deadly power has continued to arouse dread, shape behavior, and affect social relations.

A belief so ancient in history and so widely disseminated cannot but have developed variations over time and across the globe. The belief has proved flexible and malleable in its less central features as it spread from culture to culture and generation to generation. Specific cultural expressions of the belief across the centuries and the continents, conditioned by varying ecological, economic, social, and political factors, likewise advise against superficial generalizations concerning its meanings and social functions. Within these limits, however, and despite all its variations, it is possible to say something about this belief in general and several of its characteristic and persistent features. There is a constancy in several of its basic features that is quite remarkable. A comparison of ethnographic reports from diverse areas of the globe, as well as the essays in Maloney (1976) and Dundes (1992), all confirm this impression of similarity and stability of several features of Evil Eye belief and practice over the centuries and across the globe.

THE MATRIX AND CONDITIONS
OF EVIL EYE BELIEF AND PRACTICE

To understand the salient features of Evil Eye belief and practice and the distribution of the Evil Eye belief across the centuries and around the globe, it is essential to consider the ecological, economic, social, and cultural conditions prevailing in the societies initially holding this belief. These are factors of the physical and social matrix which sustain the belief and lend it plausibility and power. These conditions have been studied and summarized by anthropologists and others.[149] We will take them into account in our study of the belief in the antiquity and the biblical communities. Despite variation in certain details from earliest Sumerian conditions to those of Late Roman antiquity, from the first appearance of combined agriculture and animal husbandry to the advanced agricultural society of Roman late antiquity, the

149. See the summaries by Maloney 1976:v–xvi; Roberts 1976:223–78; Spooner 1976; Garrison and Arensberg 1976; Bowie 2006:200–236. See also Murdock 1980b; and Hauschild 1979b, discussing the Evil Eye as a cause of illness. On cultural aspects of ancient Evil Eye societies see also Elliott 1991:150–51; Rakoczy 1996 passim; Malina 2001.

circumstances supporting Evil Eye belief and practice in antiquity (ecological, economic, social, cultural) have tended to remain constant. Our summary of these conditions here will pertain to circumstances supporting the belief also in ancient Mesopotamian, Egyptian, Greek, Roman, biblical and post-biblical cultures as well.[150]

Ethnographic and anthropological studies of Evil Eye cultures have noted that the belief has flourished under specific ecological, economic, social and cultural conditions.[151] The societies we shall be studying –from Sumer to late Roman antiquity—range from early agrarian societies with mixed economies of herding and agriculture (Sumer) to later advanced agrarian societies (Rome and late antiquity).[152] They tend to be marked by a mixed economy of intensive agriculture and pastoralism, technological specialization, writing and records, a monied economy, cultural complexity, patrilineal descent, patrilocal residence, political autonomy, concentration of executive power, belief in high gods, and child socialization stressing the importance of obedience, sexual restraint, physical aggression, pain, low trust in others, industry and responsibility.[153] These are "agonistic societies" marked by intense aggression, competition, and struggle for survival under often tenuous ecological conditions.[154] Ocular aggression is one expression of this agonism. Staring, glaring, and shooting menacing looks at perceived rivals, critics, enemies, and outsiders is one form of competitive face-off. These societies are fraught with internal tensions (between, e.g., nomads and settlers, herders and farmers). Social stratification distinguishes two classes (the few "haves" [2–3%] and the vast majority of "have nots" [97–98%]) with mediating mechanisms of patronage and clientism. This social disparity is conducive to the development of envy conveyed, according to

150. The conditions nurturing the belief in the *modern era* require a separate analysis.

151. For the following see especially Roberts 1976:235–62 and thirty-eight tables of factors. See also Garrison and Arensberg 1976, esp. 294–97 and the brief summary of Elliott 1991:150–51. The economist Boris Gershman (2011a; 2011b) who arrives at similar conclusions treats Evil Eye belief as a product of envy avoidance. He analyses the economic and social factors prompting envy and envy-avoidance.

152. For extensive descriptions of these societal types see, e.g., Lenski and Lenski 1987; Sjoberg 1960.

153. Roberts (1976:262) summarizes: "The variables, then, that will be important in further work [i.e. research on the Evil Eye] are: social status, property, focused authority, industry, responsibilty, obedience, sex, physical aggression, trust, and pain . . . The investigation of these patterns should lead to a theory of envy, and from that to a theory of the belief in the evil eye" (262).

154. For ancient Greece see also the historical-sociological study of Gouldner 1969; for the Circum-Mediterranean in general see Gilmore 1982:189; 1987b; and for Andalusian Spain, see Gilmore 1987a.

common opinion, by an Evil Eye directed against rivals.[155] This competition extends to families, and in polygynous cultures like those of the Hebrews, rivalries among wives where then Evil-Eyed envy often appears, as the Bible recounts.[156] In these societies the belief prevails that all the goods and resources of life are in scarce and limited supply so that one group's gain occurs at another's loss, thereby further fueling conflict, resentment, and Evil-Eyed envy. Evil Eye societies are also collectivist in nature, promoting orientation and loyalty to the group rather than to the welfare of individuals, with strong group influence or control over group values, expectations, norms, and sanctions.

Vision is valued as a primary mode of verification, and there is recognition of the power of the eye and the intense stare to cause discomfort, signal aggressive feelings, or convey intense amorous desire. As "witchcraft societies," they reckon with the existence of both witches and the Evil Eye possessors whose power can injure or destroy.[157] "The person who casts the evil eye is often presumed to be hostile, envious, and not conforming to cultural codes, i.e. not obedient or responsible."[158] Honor and shame, pivotal values in these societies, are symbolized by the male and female genitals, respectively—the same symbols deemed effective in thwarting the Evil Eye.

Poor sanitation and unhealthy living conditions in these societies resulting in high morbidity and morality rates, especially high infant mortality, support the notion that infants and nursing mothers were especially vulnerable to the Evil Eye. A rudimentary knowledge of disease causation allows the attribution of illness and death to demons and a neighbor's hostile Evil Eye rather than to microbes and viruses. The cause of illness and misfortune is thus attributed to personal agency (human, demonic, divine) rather than to impersonal forces. Evil Eye cultures also hold that

155. The presence of evil eye belief [and envy] is associated with social and political inequality according to Roberts 1976:261.

156. See Vol. 3. Murdock (1980b:61) indicates that the Evil Eye was feared where polygyny was practiced.

157. Anthropologist Phillips Stevens (1996:238) classifies the Evil Eye as "a specific institutionalized form of witchcraft belief." Witchcraft societies recognize "a mystical power that develops in certain persons and enables them to work harm directly, without magic and without invoking spiritual assistance." The Evil Eye, like witchcraft, can work independently of the bearer's knowledge and without his/her intention, It is energized by strong negative emotions like anger, hatred, and especially envy. The Evil Eye, however, "does not involve the manipulation of visual or verbal symbols, nor is the power learned or artificially acquired. The evil eye power is innate within the individual, so it is best explained in the context . . . of witchcraft." On witchcraft societies of the Circum-Mediterranean and Ancient Near East as the matrix of Evil Eye belief see below, 70, 73 and n. 266; see also Vols. 2 and 3.

158. Roberts 1976:261.

the reputation, well-being, and honor of family and friends is under constant challenge. This is in line with a sense of being under constant attack from hostile forces (human, demonic, and divine), which fuels a feeling of vulnerability, dread, and a need for effective means of protection. In these "high context cultures" it is assumed that "everybody knows" who needs to know and what is needed to know, so that detailed information generally is limited and compressed. This is in contrast to modern individualist "low context cultures" that require minute and extensive information on everything from architectural blueprints to repair manuals and operating instructions. High context "everyone knows" knowledge includes the phenomenon of the Evil Eye, how it works, who are the possessors, the victims, and how it can be warded off. As a result, while the Evil Eye is mentioned frequently in the ancient sources, descriptive detail of how it works and whom it hurts is rarely provided. The extended comments of Plutarch and Heliodorus are unusual and, for modern researchers, happy exceptions. The Bible too makes repeated mention of the Evil Eye, but aside from Sir 14:3–10 the references are minimal in length and detail. This constellation of ecological, economic, social, and cultural conditions provided the seed bed and matrix of Evil Eye belief and practice and the setting in which the Evil Eye belief assumed plausibility and power.

RESEARCH ON THE EVIL EYE FROM PAST TO PRESENT

Sources of Evidence of Evil Eye Belief and Practice

Evidence of Evil Eye belief and practice abounds from 3000 BCE on. In the ancient world, on which this study focuses, it comes from a wide spectrum of sources ranging from Mesopotamian incantations to Byzantine art and amulets. A vast company of ancient authors, as we shall see, mention or allude to the Evil Eye and its malignant glance in their writings, from Homer and Hesiod in the eighth century BCE to Greek, Latin, Jewish, and Christian writers down through Late Antiquity (sixth century CE). Beside direct mention of the Evil Eye in literary works, sacred texts, personal letters, papyri and inscriptions, philosophical and historical treatises, incantations and prayers, sermons, theological commentaries, and liturgical formulations, there is the plethora of indirect traces of the belief in the form of thousands upon thousands of anti-Evil Eye amulets uncovered in archaeological digs and excavated sites. These include images of the Eye of Horus, of Evil Eyes attacked, and anti-Evil Eye designs on door plaques and tombs, carvings on stone, mosaics, statuary, art (frescos, funery art etc.), architecture and jewelry—all designed to neutralize and ward off the malicious eye. Among the ancient written texts are the sacred literature of the Hebrew and Christian Bibles as well as the parabiblical writings, Jewish Mishnah, Talmud and rabbinic texts, and the writings of the Christian church fathers. Evil Eye belief in Islam is attested since the statement of Muhammad, "The influence of an Evil Eye is a fact . . ."[159] The prayer at daybreak for protection from evil including "from the evil of an envier when he envies" (*Qur'an*, sura 113), also has been linked with the belief because of the traditional association of the Evil Eye and envy. From the Middle Ages, Renaissance, and Reformation eras to the modern period, the Evil Eye is mentioned in poetical, philosophical and theological works.[160] Specific treatises on the subject begin appearing in the West in the 1400s.[161] In modern time, research by archaeologists, historians, and classicists has been joined by travelers' accounts of relevant experiences in Evil Eye cultures, medical practitioners' interviews with patients, ethnographic reports and studies, as well as references to the Evil Eye in current literature, art, music, the cinema, television, sports, daily newspapers, comic strips and cartoons, and virtually all domains of modern life.

Popular and Scholarly Study on the Evil Eye

Evil Eye belief and practice has been a focus of both popular and scholarly attention. Research ranges from more popular general studies on the subject[162] to investigations from varying academic perspectives (history, classics, anthropology, ethnology, sociology, psychology, ophthalmology, medicine, folklore studies), to study of particular cultures, and geographic areas.[163] Research on the Evil Eye in these various cultures, sub-cultures, and geographical regions is extensive.[164]

159. *Sahih Muslim,* Book 26, number 5427.

160. Story 1877:183–205.

161. See below, pp. 48–49.

162. See Story 1877:147–238; Elworthy 1895/1958; Seligmann 1910, 1922, 1927; Park 1912; Gifford 1958; Lykiardopoulos 1981; Berke 1988:35–56, and numerous encyclopedia articles listed in the bibliography.

163. Overviews and assessment of research on the subject include the brief comments of Alan Dundes (1992:260–65, from the Renaissance to the present); and Pierre Gravel (1995:23–31); and the more detailed historical review and assessment of the scholarly discussion by Thomas Hauschild (1979:10–236); on these works see below.

164. For the Circum-Mediterranean region: Grossi 1886; Coote Lake 1933; Moss and Cappannari 1976; Gillmore 1982:197–98.

For Italy: Marugi 1815; Nobile 1815; Arditi 1825 (Naples); A. De Jorio 1832/2000

(Naples); W. Story 1877:147–238; Salomone-Marino 1882; Pitrè 1884, 1889 (reprinted in Dundes 1992:130–42), 1913; Grossi, 1886; Rolfe and Ingleby 1888:106–26; Trede 1909; Stocchetti 1941; Pazzani 1948; Satriani 1951; Moretti 1955; De Martino 1959; Brögger 1968; Berry 1968; Giancristofaro 1970; Coppola 1971; Gallini 1973; Appel 1975, 1976; 1977; Bruzza 1975; Foulks et al. 1977; Migliore 1977; Lopasic 1978; Hauschild 1979; Izzi 1980; Bronzini 1981; DiStasi 1981; Di Tota 1982a, 1982b; Galt 1982; Gatto 1982; Pavesi 1995; Pelligrino 1996; Centini 2002; Benvenuto and Pozzoli 2008 (Naples); De Ceglia 2011 (Naples). For further literature see Dundes 1992:131–32, 313.

For Sardinia: Valla 1894; Wagner 1913; Moretti 1955; Gallini, 1973; Lopsaic 1978.

For Corsica: Bertrand-Rousseau 1976, 1978.

For Malta: Zammit-Maemple 1968.

For Spain: Salillas 1905; Wagner 1913; Villena 1917; Vasconcellos 1925 (and Portugal); Gonzalez Palencia 1932; Ball 1967; Diego Cuscoy 1969; Pitt-Rivers 1971:198, 204; Cátedra Tomás 1976; Irimia and Fernandez de Rota 1976; Díaz Ojeda and Sevilla. 1980; Díaz Ojeda 1982; Fariña 1982: Erkoreka 1984, 1995, 2002, 2005; Espinosa 1985:75–76 (Spain and American Southwest); Gilmore 1987:154–170 (Andalusia); Sanfo 1987; Sanz Hermida 2001.

For Greece (modern): Dodwell 1819 2:30–37; Lawson 1910:8–15; L. Arnaud 1911, 1912; Schmidt 1913; Hardie 1923; Gubbins 1946; Georges 1962; J. K. Campbell 1964; R. Blum and E. Blum 1965, 1970; Knecht 1968; Dionisopoulos-Mass 1976:42–62; M. Herzfeld 1981, 1986; Dundes 1992:107–8; Storace 1997; Veikou 1998; Kottis 1999; Koyen 2002; Papanikolas 2002; Apostilides 2008:52–58, Chryssanthropoulos 2008 (the Greeks of Australia).

For North Africa: Doutté 1909:317–27; Oyler 1919; Brugnatelli 1987; Touhami 2007; 2010.

For Morocco: Westermarck 1926 1:414–78; Stillman 1970.

For Tunisia: J. M. Teitelbaum 1976:63–75; Schefold 1982:134–40;

For Egypt:Lane 1895/1973; Gardiner 1916; Blackman 1927:71, 218; Griffiths 1938; Hocart 1938; Sainte Fare Garnot 1960; Fodor 1971; Spooner 1976:76–84; Ghosh 1983; Dundes 1992:313; Inhorn 1994:205. For ancient Egypt, see Chapter Two below.

For Ethiopia, Abyssinia: Worrell 1909, 1910; Staude 1934, 1954; Reminick 1974, 1975; Vecchiato 1994; Matsuzono 1993; Finneran 2003.

For the Middle East: Spooner 1976:76–84.

For Lebanon: Harfouche 1965.

For Indo-European and Semitic: Dundes 1992:257–312.

For Palestine: Einszler 1889; Canaan 1914:28–32; Jaussen 1924.

For Israel and Jews: Brav 1908 in Dundes 1992:44–54; Lilienthal 1924; Löwinger 1926; Shrut 1960; Noy 1971; Kirschenblatt-Gimblett and Lenowitz 1973; *Encyclopedic Dictionary of Judaica* 1974:181; Palgi 1978:132–39; Ashkenazi 1984; Levy and Levy Zumwalt 1987, 2002; Issroff 1991; Dundes 1992:44–45; Zumwalt 1996, Schmid 2012.

For Turkey: Garnett 1890, 1891; Johnson 1924–25; Kuriks 1930; Gülerman 1933; Küçükerman 1988.

For Arabs, Islam and Muslim countries: Meltzl de Lomnitz 1884; Garnett 1891; De Vaux 1910:457–61; Seligmann 1910 1:16–17, 340–41; 2:341–43, 361–62; Westermarck 1926:414–78; Herber 1927; Djordjevic 1934, 1938; Koebert 1948; Grandqvist 1950:76–81; Marçais 1960; Kriss and Kriss-Heinrich 1962; Spooner 1976:76–84; Teilelbaum 1976; Sheikh-Dilthey 1990; Ibrahim 1991; 1994 (Sudan); Donaldson 1992; Kanafani 1993:128–35; Patai 1983:29, 145, 154; Abu-Rabia 2005; Kahl 2006 (Muslim and Christian commonalities); Camp 2009; Bille 2010.

For Persia/Iran: DeCunha 1886–1889:149–53; Frachtenberg 1918:419–24

Despite the innumerable references or allusions to the Evil Eye in the ancient world, treatises on, or sustained discussions of, the subject are rare in antiquity.[165] Plutarch's "Symposium" or "Table Talk" on the Evil Eye (c. 100 CE) is the sole extended discussion of the phenomenon in ancient secular literature.[166] Briefer comments are offered by Alexander of Aphrodisias, a peripatetic philosopher at Athens (c. 200 CE),[167] and Heliodorus in his romance novel, *Aethiopica* (c. 250 CE). The Evil Eye is mentioned frequently

---

(Zoroastrian); Lindquist 1936; Donaldson 1938:13–23; Barth 1956; Spooner 1976:76–84.

For India: DeCunha 1886–1889; Joshi 1886–1889; Sastrian 1899; Thurston 1912:109–120; Euthoven 1924; Modi 1924:123–28; Cooke 1926; Woodburne 1935; Rosner 1958; Ripka 1965; Crooke 1896/1968 2:1–84; 1913; Rosner 1958; Gonda 1969; Crooke and Enthoven 1972:276–307; Pocock 1973; Maloney 1976:102–148; Mutu Chidambaram 1980; Nichter 1981; Rajamokan 1987; Pocock 1991, 1992; Nagarajan 1993:200–201.

For Saudi Arabia: Sheikj-Dilthey 1990.

For Asia: Rypka 1965 (Hyderabad).

For Ceylon/Sri Lanka and Buddhist countries: Gombrich 1978.

For the Philippines: Flores-Meiser 1976:149–62.

For Oceania: Parsons 1984.

For Scotland: Napier 1879; Mackenzie 1895; J. G. Campbell 1900; A. Carmichael 1900; Maclagan 1902; T. Davidson 1949, 1950, 1992:143–49; and bibliography in Dundes 1992:143–44.

For Ireland (and Celts): Mackenzie 1895; Henderson 1911; Gregory 1920:127–52; Crenshaw 1996; Pauli 1975; Synder 2001.

For Guernsy: Dewar 1970.

For Germany: Knortz 1899; Wolters 1909; Wewerka 1965.

For Rumania: Hermann 1888; Murgoci 1923.

For Slovenia: Djordjevic 1938.

For Albania: Elsie 2001; Pederson-Bidoshi 2006.

For Northern Europe: Feilberg 1901; Hemmer 1912/1913; Eisen 1927 (Estonia); Å. Campbell 1933; Landtman 1939 (Finland); R. Corso 1959 (Poland); Vuorela 1967 (Finland).

For North America (USA and Canada): Gamache 1946, 1969; Gifford 1960, 1971; West 1974; Hand 1976; Hartman and McIntosh 1978. Sicilian Canadians: S. Migliore 1997; European Americans: L. C. Jones 1951; Italian-Americans: Swiderski 1976; Foulks et al. 1977; Hartman and McIntosh 1978; DiStasio 1981; Migliore 1983, 1990, 1997 (Sicilian Canadian); Buonanno 1984; Malpezzi and Clements 1992; Greek-Americans: Georges 1962; Slovak-Americans: Stein 1974; Syrian- and Lebanese-Americans: Naff 1965; Ukranian Canadians: Hanchu Hanchuk 1999:42–45.

For Latin America: Hornell 1924 (Trinidad);.Wolf 1955; Vega 1968 (Guatemala); Simeon 1973 (Guatemala); Cosminsky 1976; M. Kearney 1976, 1981 (Mexico); Burleigh et al. 1990; Sault 1990 (Mexico); Rebhun 1995 (Brazil); Burleigh et al. 1990.

165. See Walcot 1978:77–90 on ancient Greek sources and now Rakoczy 1996; see also Story 1877:147–238 on sources from antiquity to the nineteenth century.

166. Plutarch, *Quaestiones Convivales* (*Convivial Questions/ Symposium/Table Talk*) Book 5, Question 7, 1–6 (*Moralia* 680C–683B). For discussion of this text see Vol. 2.

167. Alexander of Aphrodiasas, *Prob. Phys.* 2.53.

in the Bible, regularly in condemnatory terms, as will be discussed in Volume 3. In ancient Jewish and Christian circles of the post-Biblical period, mention is made often of the Evil Eye (numerous rabbis, Basil, Jerome, John Chrysostom, Augustine, among others). The only sustained discussion of the topic is Basil of Caesarea's homily on envy.[168] This Cappadocian theologian, consistent with other church fathers, links the Evil Eye with envy and traces both to the Devil's malignancy.

In the Middle Ages and beyond, many luminaries, including Albert Magnus, Roger Bacon, Thomas Aquinas, Dante Alighieri, Martin Luther, and William Shakespeare referred to the Evil Eye.[169] Engelbert, Benedictine abbot of Admont (c. 1250–1331), published his *Tractatus de fascinatione* c. 1331.[170] From the 1400s onward, treatises on the subject began to appear: de Villena (1411, 1422);[171] Diego Alvarez Chanca (1499);[172] Ficino (1576);[173] Frascatorius (1555);[174] Vairus (3 vols., 1583, 1589);[175] Alsarius (1595);[176] Del Rio (1599);[177] Gutierrez (1653);[178] Frommann (1675);[179] Valletta

168. Basil of Caesarea. "Homily 11, Concerning Envy." *Peri phthonou PG* 31, cols. 371–86; for discussion of this text see Volume Four, Chapter Two.

169. See Story 1877:183–205; and the list of Seligmann 1910 2:472 n. 1.

170. See Fowler 1970.

171. Enrique de Aragon, Marqués de Villena [1384–1434], *Tratado de aojamiento o fascinología* (1411, 1422, 1425). For new editions, see F. Almagro and José Fernández Carpintero, 1977; Anna Maria Gallina, 1978. In her edition of Villena's tractate, Anna Maria Gallina discusses the Evil Eye in Spain and Medieval, Renaisance, and later works treating the phenomenon (1978:29–54).

172. Alvarez Chanca 1499/2001.

173. Marcilio Ficino, *Opera Omnia*, 1576.

174. Hieronymus Fracastorius, *De Sympathia et Antipathia Rerum*, 1555.

175. Leonardus Vairus [1540–1603], *De fascino. libri tres*, 1583 (Paris), 1589 (Venice). Vairus was Italian bishop of Pozzuoli, Italy.

176. Vincentius Alsarius [c. 1576–1631], *De invidia et fascino veterum libellus*, Lucae, 1595. Summarized in J. G. Graevius, *Thesaurus Antiquitatum Romanarum*. Leiden: Franciscus Halma and Petrus van der Aa, 1694–1699, vol. 12:885–99.

177. Martin Antonio Del Rio, S. J. [1551–1608] (Salamanca, Spain), *Disqusitionum magicarum, libri sex in tres tomos partiti*, 1599–1600/1603. For an ET see P. G. Maxwell-Stuart 2000, who, however, translates *fascinatio* as "spell" or "enchantment."

178. Johannes Lazarus Gutierrez, *Opusculum de fascino*, 1653.

179. Johannes Christian Frommann, *Tractatus de fascinatione novus et singularis*, 1675. A total of 1067 pages in 4° plus two page epilogue, 43 page index and 3 pages of errata. A physician, his intent was to contribute to the Church's eradication of fertility rituals and the like.

(1787/1819);[180] Marugi (1815);[181] Arditi (1825);[182] de Jorio (1832);[183] Davies (1856); and Grossi (1886).[184]

Modern critical scholarship on the Evil Eye in antiquity begins in 1855 with Otto Jahn's pioneering essay, "Über den Aberglauben des bösen Blickes bei den Alten" ["On the Superstition of the Evil Eye in Antiquity"]. In this essay of eighty-three pages and five plates, Jahn (1813–1869), an influential classicist,[185] first delineated key features of the belief[186] and then discussed and illustrated the various means employed in Greco-Roman antiquity for warding off the Evil Eye.[187] The study was primarily descriptive in nature, with little analysis of the complex of beliefs and social dynamics typical of this concept.[188] Succeeding works enlarged the focus of attention but followed this descriptive pattern. In 1877 William W. Story added to his earlier writing *Roba di Roma* four additional chapters devoted to the Evil Eye (147–238), which, like Jahn, were descriptive, rather than theoretical, in

180. Nicola Valletta [1750–1814], *Cicalata sul fascino volgarmente detto jettatura,* 1777. The latest of many subsequent editions is *Cicalata sul fascino volgarmente detto jettatura* edited by Umberto Attardi, with a hypothesis by Renato de Falco, Naples: Colonnese, 1988. Valletta wrote about "fascination popularly called jettatura" in Naples. He was a Neopolitan poet and professor of law. He took the Evil Eye most seriously and was considered himself a *gran jettatore* (Jahn 1855:31). He tells of his personal experiences of the Evil Eye and its lethal effect, offering no theory of explanation but passing on traditional folklore. On Valletta and *Cicalatta* see Elworthy 1958/1895:17–22; Croce 1945; De Martino 1963:170–71 and Hauschild 1979:53–57. A critical response to Valletta was published by A. Schioppa in 1830.

181. Giovanni Leonardo Marugi, *Capricci sulla jettatura,* 1815 (poems on *jettatura*).

182. Michele Arditi, *Il fascino e l'amuleto contro del fascino. Illustrazione di un antico basso-rilievo rinvenuto in un forno della città di Pompei* ["The Evil eye and the amulet against the Evil Eye. Discussion of an ancient bas-relief discovered in a bakery in the city of Pompeii"], 1825, concerning a *fascinum* [phallus and testicles] in bas-relief on the wall of a bakery, accompanied by the inscription "HIC HABITAT FELICITAS" ("Here happiness dwells").

183. De Jorio's 1832 publication, *La mimica degli antichi investigata nel gestire napolitano* [Gestural expression of the ancients in the light of Neapolitan gesturing] contains much information on Neopolitan anti–Evil Eye gestures, several of which, he maintained, originated in Greco-Roman antiquity. In 2000 this important word was translated into English: *Gestures in Naples and Gesture in Classical Antiquity.* See the review of J. Acocella 2000.

184. Grossi (1886) includes terms for Evil Eye in various ancient and modern languages.

185. On Jahn and his significance in the world of scholarship see Müller 1990; 1991; Calder at al. 1991.

186. Jahn 1855:28–30.

187. Ibid., 40–110 and five plates.

188. Schlesier 1991 presents an unconvincing challenge to Jahn's early dating of the evidence of the Evil Eye.

nature. Jules Tuchmann (1830–1901), a French ex-musician and self-taught research librarian, published an extensive series of articles (more than ninety segments) on "la fascination" in the French folklore journal, *Mélusine*, vols. 2–11 (1884–1912). His research in the Bibliothèque Nationale resulted in a massive collection of data from numerous sources in many languages; but it was never collected and published in one encompassing study. A parody on Tuchmann's sad story by folklorist Arnold van Gennep appears in Alan Dundes's anthology (1992) as "The Research Topic: Or, Folklore Without End."[189] Tuchmann had "spent his entire life amassing material on the Evil Eye, which by the age of 54 had involved his mastering 843 languages and dialects, and who died at his library seat [in Paris] leaving eighteen million notes of no use to anyone."[190]

One oft-cited volume is Frederick Thomas Elworthy's, *The Evil Eye: An Account of this Ancient and Widespread Superstition* (1896 and numerous subsequent reissues).[191] Broad in scope and rich in illustrative detail, it is one of the few scholarly monographs on the Evil Eye in the English language. In 1902, the physician Robert Craig Maclagen published a descriptive account of Evil Eye belief and practice in Celtic tradition and the Scottish highlands.[192]

Another physician, Hamburg ophthalmologist Siegfried Seligmann, in 1910 published a massive two-volume work, *Der böse Blick und Verwandtes* [The Evil Eye and Related Subjects]. This collection of data was supplemented by two further publications by Seligmann describing popular conceptions of the eye's particular power (1922)[193] and a history of amulets, including means for healing and protection, especially in relation to the Evil Eye (1927).[194] The 1910 double volume offers a panoramic survey of Evil Eye belief and practice from past to present and across cultures and has never been translated. This *omnium gatherum* is almost a thousand pages in length and richly illustrated; its index of primary and secondary literature contains over 2,100 entries. A "table of languages" lists terms for Evil Eye in thirty-nine languages.[195] Volume 1 presents a categorized survey

189. Dundes 1992:3–8. On Tuchmann and his research see Gaidoz 1912.

190. Bowie 2006:216–17.

191. The 1958 edition of the volume is cited in this study. William Graham Sumner, in his classic study *Folkways* (1906/1960), describes both the concepts of uncleanness and the Evil Eye (1960:428–38) as "products of demonism" (1960:428; see also 433–38 on the Evil Eye).

192. Maclagen 1902. On Scotland and the Evil Eye see also above, n. 164.

193. Seligmann 1922.

194. Seligmann 1927.

195. Seligmann 1910 1:48–63.

of documented features of the Evil Eye and healing rituals. Volume 2 lists and categorizes means of protection, with the conclusion reviewing previously offered "hypotheses and explanations." Seligmann's own explanation concentrates on the nature of the eye, the gaze, and the power of verbal suggestion.[196] Like Elworthy, his contemporary, Seligmann collected and categorized relevant material, but cited sources isolated from context and offered no comprehensive theoretical model for analyzing this rich bounty of data. His verdict was that the Evil Eye is "an ancient folk concept, born of ignorance and superstition, but mixed with a small kernel of truth."[197] His combined works remain, however, the fullest collection and descriptive treatment of the subject through the early twentieth century and are cited frequently in the present study.

This linking of the Evil Eye with superstition crops up also in Sigmund Freud's famous essay *Das Unheimliche* ("The Uncanny," 1919). Freud wrote of the Evil Eye as "one of the most uncanny (*unheimlichsten*) and most widespread forms of superstition (*Aberglaube*)," without, however, subjecting it to more extensive analysis.[198] The 1958 publication of American ophthalmologist, Edward S. Gifford, combines a description of Evil Eye belief and practice[199] with an account of the folklore of the eye and vision.[200] He concludes that "the fear of the evil eye may represent aggressive impulses turned upon the self because of a guilty need for self-punishment associated with forbidden sexual strivings."[201] Other works identified by Alan Dundes (1992:261) as "landmark studies" include Edvard Westermarck on Evil Eye belief in Morocco (1926);[202] Karl Meisen's two essays in the *Rheinisches Jahrbuch für Volkskunde* on the Evil Eye in antiquity and early Christianity (1950) and in the Middles Ages and modernity (1952); and the study of classicist Waldemar Deonna on symbolism of the eye across the globe published posthumously in 1965.[203]

---

196. Ibid., 2:417–75.

197. "ein uralter Völkergedanke, hervorgegangen aus Unwissenheit und Aberglaube, aber gemischt mit einem kleinen Körnchen Wahrheit" (Seligmann 1910 1:9).

198. Freud, "Das Unheimliche," *Gesammelte Werke*, edited by Anna Freud et al., vol. 12:227–278, esp, 252–53: "Eine der unheimlichsten und verbreitetsten Formen des Aberglaubens ist die Angst vor dem 'bösen Blick.'" ET "The Uncanny," 1955:217–52.

199. Gifford 1958:3–104: the act of fascination, fascinators, the fascinated, protection, and the Evil Eye today.

200. Ibid., 105–93.

201. Ibid., 104.

202. Westermarck 1926 1:414–78.

203. On the eye, eye symbolism, and the gaze across cultures see Mundt 1870; Ferenczi 1913, 1956; Reitler 1913; Seligmann 1922; Rolleston 1942; Hart 1949; Frey 1953;

The collection of fourteen anthropological essays on the Evil Eye assembled by anthropologist Clarence Maloney and published in 1976 marks another major milestone of research on the Evil Eye. Evidence of Evil Eye belief and practice in regions around the globe is subjected to critical social-scientific analysis and theoretical interpretation. Maloney's introduction[204] calls for considering "the core of the complex in cultural evolutionary terms" and "the essential meaning of it in behavioral terms."[205] He distinguishes "potential theoretical approaches"[206] and "potential historical approaches."[207] Thomas Hauschild's ethnological study, *Der Böse Blick* (1978; 2nd ed. 1982), joins theoretical analysis with fieldwork research on Evil Eye belief and practice in Southern Italy, with a focus on both the bio-psychological and the sociological aspects of the belief and associated practices. The anthology edited by folklorist Alan Dundes, *The Evil Eye* (1981; 2nd ed. 1992) contains fourteen descriptive and six interpretive essays. The last is Dundes's own interpretative proposal that underlying and undergirding Evil Eye belief and practice is an age-old distinction between wet versus dry and the forces and symbols of life versus those of death.[208] Pierre Gravel's wide-ranging anthropological study, *The Malevolent Eye* (1995), examines cross-cultural evidence of the eye as linked with male and female genitals as a potent symbol of fertility, manna, and rituals of production and reproduction.[209]

In comparison to these more broad-ranging and cross-cultural studies, Jahn had focused attention on Evil Eye belief in the ancient classical world, the context of significance for our investigation. This pioneering work, regularly cited in subsequent studies, was never translated into English. Jahn's interest in the topic had been piqued by the publication of a report concerning the "Woburn Marble," a striking marble bas-relief of a large

---

Gifford 1957, 1958; Déonna 1965; Gonda 1969; Meerloo 1971; Hess 1975; Koenig 1975; Argyle and Cook, 1976; Jaeger 1979; Hirschberg 1982; Potts 1982; Cavendish-Deutsch 1983 4:885–94; Siebers 1983; Meslin 1987; Seawright 1988; G. Simon 1988; Huxley 1990; Classen 1993; Jay 1993; Bohigian 1997, 1998; Fredrick 2002; Keeley 2002; R. Mack 2002; Shapiro 2003. For a medieval treatise on the eye and its moral implications see Peter of Limoges, *Tractatus moralis de oculo*, c. 1274/75–1289; ET: *The Moral Treatise on the Eye* (2012).

204. Maloney 1976:vii–xvi.

205. Ibid., vii.

206. Ibid., vii–x.

207. Ibid., x–xvi.

208. The second edition (1992:313–19) updates the 1981 bibliography (298–312).

209. Koerper and Desautels 1999 follow Gravel in seeing linkages of the eye, Evil Eye, vulva, fertility, and sex-based symbolism.

eye attacked by an array of encircling enemies dating from the late second century CE and found at Woburn Abbey, England.[210]

He proceeded to collect and compare literary and iconographic evidence of Evil Eye belief and practice that related to the details of the marble bas-relief. He concluded that such an analysis of the evidence can demonstrate common features of Evil Eye belief and practice and aspects of the belief's historical development.[211]

The study of another German classicist, Thomas Rakoczy, picks up where Jahn left off. Rakoczy's 1996 investigation of the Evil Eye in Greek literature, *Böser Blick, Macht des Auges und Neid der Götter* (Evil Eye/Glance: Power of the Eye and Envy of the Gods) is the

Illus 1.15
Woburn Marble, relief of Evil Eye attacked (from Elworthy 1958/1895:137, fig. 34)

most complete analysis of the Greek evidence to date. It is both historically and thematically organized, with meticulous discussions of the relevant Greek texts, which are expanded in number and cited extensively. In tracing the belief historically down through the Christian patristic period, Rakoczy shows both consistencies in Evil Eye belief and practice over time as well as how, when, and where the belief is articulated and modified in ancient Greek and Roman cultures. His careful text analysis is accompanied by significant social-scientific insights. His data and conclusions support conclusions I reached in my earlier publications on Evil Eye belief and practice in the ancient world and the Bible. In these volumes I will be referring extensively to his work, which is available only in German but certainly deserves a wider audience. Rakoczy makes the important point that belief in an Evil Eye was not viewed in antiquity as a vulgar superstition, but was thought to rest on accurate observation and scientific knowledge of the time. The plausibility of the belief was founded on the premise that the eye was an active rather than a passive organ, a theory that prevailed in Western science until the 1700s. Our study of the ancient evidence takes both points into consideration. While Jahn, Seligmann, and Rakoczy provide valuable comparative

210. On this important bas-relief see Vol. 2. For illustrations of the relief see Jahn 1855 Pl. 3, no. 1 (discussion: 30–32, 96–100); Seligmann 1910 2:115, fig. 123 (discussion: 152–56); Lafaye 1926:987, fig. 2887; Elworthy 1958/1895:137, fig. 24 (discussion: 138–41)

211. Jahn 1855:110.

material from the ancient world, none examines the biblical evidence, thus leaving a void that the present study aims to overcome.

Explanatory Theories

Much of what has been written about the Evil Eye is reportorial in nature, with little if any attempt at theoretical explanation—as in the early studies of Jahn, Story, Elworthy, and Seligmann.[212] Moving beyond description to explanation of the data, more recent analysis has examined the belief from a variety of theoretical perspectives: ethnological, anthropological, folklorist, sociological, and psychological, among others. Ancient theories representing the folk level of knowledge and rationalization focused on ocular emissions (extramission theory of vision) linked with envy and other malevolent dispositions, along with homeopathic notions (sympathy/antipathy) of contact and contagion. Modern theories, distinguishing extramission and intromissionary theories of vision, have considered a diversity of factors at differing levels of analysis: worldview systems; ecological conditions; history of the belief's diffusion; semiotics; factors of culture and folklore; folk healthcare systems; binary oppositions; concepts of manna and fertility and of evil and illness; social structures and processes of interaction; social deviancy and boundary maintenance; individual and social control mechanisms; ocular aggression and hostile staring; coping strategies; and psychologies of paranoia, eye and gaze, rivalry, envy, and malevolent emotions.[213]

212. Seligmann concludes with a chapter on "Hypotheses and Explanations" (1910 2:417–75), but it is more descriptive than analytical in nature.

213. For theories, overviews and assessments see Seligmann 1910 2:417–475; McDaniel 1918; Freud 1919; H. C. Evans 1925; Greenacre 1925–1926; Vasconcellos 1925; McKenzie 1927:225–62; Gordon 1937; Stocchetti 1941; Gamache 1946, 1969; Grandqvist 1950:76–81; Roheim 1952; Tourney and Plazak 1954; Gifford 1957, 1958; Caillois 1960 ("Medusa complex"); Haimowitz and Haimowitz 1966; Vereecken 1968; Arieli 1970; Schoeck 1970 (envy and Evil Eye); Meerloo 1971; Press 1973; W. N. Evans 1975; Argyle and Cook, 1976; Dionisopoulos-Mass 1976; Garrison and Arensberg 1976; Kearney 1976, 1984:86, 197–202 (paranoia theory); Machovec 1976; Maloney 1976:v–xvi, 102–48; Roberts 1976; Spooner 1976:279–285; Appel 1977; Foulks et al. 1977; Bertrand-Rousseau 1978; Brown and Levinson 1978 (vantage point of "politeness theory"); Hauschild 1979:108–171, 237–334; Stephenson 1979; Díaz Ojeda and Sevilla 1980; Murdock 1980b:20–27 (Evil Eye as form of witchcraft); Bronzini 1981; DiStasi 1981; Herzfeld 1981, 1984, 1986; Nichter 1981; Achté and Schakir 1982; Díaz Ojeda 1982; diTota 1982; Galt 1982; Domash 1983; Ghosh 1983; Migliore 1983, 1990, 1997; Simizu 1983; Siebers 1983:27–56; Buonanno 1984; Carroll 1984; Erkoreka 1984, 1995, 2002, 2005; Hughes 1985; Rheubottom 1985; Perdiguero Gil 1986; Rivera 1986; Berke 1988:35–56; Djéribi 1988; J. Mack 1988; Sault 1990; Ibrahim 1991, 1994; Parsons and Wakeley 1991; Zinvovieff 1991 (gossip as the verbal equivalent of the Evil Eye); Coss 1992; Dundes 1992:262–266; Stein 1992; Adalsteinsson 1993; De Forest 1993:129–48;

Tobin Siebers, *The Mirror of Medusa* (1983), insists on the phenomenon and psychology of staring as the starting point of an explanation of Evil Eye belief and practice.[214] He indicates features of the fascinator (*jettatore*) that often mark him/her as a stranger, outsider, but actually an insider whose membership in the group is put to question.[215] Evil Eye accusation "relates intimately to [in-group] rivalry."[216] "The evil eye is also a means of maintaining a distance between them [competing groups] in order to prevent an act of physical violence."[217] In regard to compliments, praise and dispraise, and accompanying expressions of "no Evil eye intended," Evil Eye belief "provides a [cognitive] frame within which the disruptive and ambivalent nature of praise [and dispraise] is rendered more stable."[218] The Evil Eye has been pegged a "communicable disease" with deleterious social impact. It is an ambiguous "contagion" that spreads throughout the community and transforms victims of the Eye into victimizers of others.[219] Evil Eye belief "forestalls . . . a complete pattern of social violence" (misfortune followed by diagnosis, search [for fascinator], accusation, and murder of the fascinator).[220]

> When misfortune occurs, the evil-eye belief offers a systematic procedure for making searches, accusation and cures. When the fascinator is identified, the ritualistic procedure often does not allow punishment because accusations themselves acts as cures. If the accusation does not effect the cure, it is probable that a ritual sublimates violent retribution into symbolic gestures or

M. Jay 1993; Vecchiato 1994; Gravel 1995:23–31; Pavesi 1995:43–51; Haimowitz and Haimowitz 1996; Stevens 1996 (Evil Eye belief as an instance of "magical thinking," witchcraft, and conceptualization of power); Dossey 1997:60, 115–24, 1998; Caisson 1998; D. Park 1998; Veikou 1998; Gross 1999; Hedayot and Pirzadeh 2001; Sanz Hermida 2001; Durand and Barlow 2002:33–72, esp. 65 (fear of Evil Eye as instance of psychopathology); Keeley 2002; R. Mack 2002; Ayers 2004; Abu-Rabia 2005; Bowie 2006:200–236; Devish 2007; Apostolides 2008; Apostolides and Dreyer 2008; Bille 2010; Mesner 2010; Ross 2010; Stein and Allcorn 2010; van de Ven et al. 2010; Gershman 2011b.

Concerning the earlier theory of Mesmer (1814), Hauschild (1979:58–62) has observed that Mesmer was the last recognized scientist of Germany who still believed in the power of the Evil Eye and attempted to explain this power as an instance of mesmerizing.

214. Siebers 1983:27–56.

215. Ibid., 35–40.

216. Ibid., 41, following Teitelbaum 1976.

217. Siebers, 1983:41.

218. Ibid., 42, following Douglas 1966:64.

219. Siebers, 1983:44–45.

220. Ibid., 46.

imitative executions. Retaliatory impulses are immediately
caught in the web of sanctioned ritualistic procedure, structure
to channel desires by imposing less violent solutions.[221]

Evil Eye belief allows for unintentionality as witchcraft accusations
do not. Moreover, it is not the individual but the community that "decides
whether the crime was intentional, and the verdict will usually depend on
the intensity of the crisis at hand."[222] "The degree of crisis generates the
evidence that defines the accused as either a witch or a fascinator."[223] Witchcraft accusations are responses to serious social crises (as, for example, the
Salem witch trials) prompting a search of volitional agents of malice who
are then subjected to punishment, expulsion, or execution. "In the evil-eye
event, the degree of violence has not risen to uncontrollable heights . . . The
belief operates at the level of prevention, creating representations such as
amulets, gestures, and rituals for the purpose of hindering violent contact
between individuals . . . The community neither projects malicious intent
nor seeks to murder the victim [i.e. the fascinator]."[224] Maintaining con-
straint on envy, deviant behavior, and the escalation of violence, the belief
promotes an isolation of the fascinator as object of psychological violence,
and serves to "maintain the existing social order."[225]

Sam Migliore's study, *Mal'uocchiu: Ambiguity, Evil Eye, and the Language of Distress* (1997), reviews eight theories focusing on various interrelated phenomena.[226] Combining elements of these theories, he views Evil
Eye belief as a means "to explain, express, and cope with the personal experiences of suffering."[227] It is a form of argument and a mechanism for voicing
grievances publicly. It can serve as "a commentary on the moral character
of 'self' and 'other,' a means of impression management; a comment on social distance; and a technique that can be used in an attempt to control the
behaviour of others."[228] "It provides people with a means by which they can
take action when confronted by misfortune (consult a traditional healer,
avail self of therapeutic ritual; self-protection)."[229] The Evil Eye complex

221. Ibid., 48.
222. Ibid., 50.
223. Ibid., 55.
224. Ibid., 56.
225. Ibid., 56.
226. Migliore, 1997:13–16.
227. Ibid., 55, 72.
228. Ibid., 97.
229. Ibid., 52–53.

possesses a constellation of stable features and at the same time a flexibility that allows it to be taken in a variety of directions.

While a number of researchers favor a merger of approaches and composite theories to account for all the data,[230] there is at present no single encompassing explanatory model that has gained scholarly acceptance.[231] Maloney lists seven features of the belief that reappear across cultures.[232] The essays that follow indicate a wide range of its functions in social interaction and offer a variety of theories. Folklorist Alan Dundes, *The Evil Eye*, points out important folk ideas crucial to the Evil Eye belief complex. "The evil eye belief complex," he argues, depends upon four "interrelated folk ideas in Indo-European and Semitic worldview:" (1) life depends upon liquid and blood (symbols of life, so that wet and dry, life and death, are logical oppositional pairs); (2) goods and resources are in limited supply so that one person's gain comes at another's loss; 3) life entails an equilibrium model modulating envy between the haves and the have-nots; 4) in symbolic terms, a pair of eyes may be equivalent to pairs of breasts or testicles; a single eye, equivalent to a phallus, vulva or anus; spittle and spitting equivalent to semen and ejaculation; mother's milk or male semen can be symbolized by an eye, and threats to one's supply of such precious fluids can be manifested by the eye or eyes of others.[233] Along symbolic lines, moreover, Evil Eye texts and iconography suggest an assumed homology between the human face and the human genitals: two eyes aside a nose on the male face matched by two testicles aside a phallus, with nose and phallus having a similar shape; female mouth and vagina (facial and genital orifices; *vagina dentata*); eyebrows and pubic hair; spittle/saliva and semen—both liquids of life.

Our approach in this study will be to expand the list of salient features of the belief as well as the list of folk ideas accompanying and supporting this belief in antiquity so as to understand its meaning and function in the Bible and its cultural context. Any adequate approach to the issue has to consider a total web of interrelated factors: the environmental, human biological, psychological, socio-cultural (including religious), and moral threads that inform and shape Evil Eye belief and practice.

230. Spooner 1976:282 notes that several theories are complimentary rather than conflicting. Stein (1992), Hauschild (1979), Dundes (1992) and several essays in the Maloney volume (1976) are among those studies employing multi–disciplinary approaches.

231. Spooner (1976:281–84) delineates the limitations of even current composite theories.

232. Maloney 1976:vii–viii.

233. Dundes 1992b:266–77.

This book presents in English material from the German studies of Otto Jahn (1855), Siegfried Seligmann (1910), Thomas Hauschild (1979) and Thomas Rakoczy (1996), as well as from important French studies (Perdrizet, Deonna, and others), none of which has been translated into English. It also reorganizes and updates with numerous new studies these earlier works and those of Story (1877), Elworthy (1895), and Gifford (1958) on the Evil Eye, and Budge (1930) on Evil Eye related amulets. It draws deeply from the anthropological and ethnographic studies in the anthologies edited by anthropologist Clarence Maloney (1976) and folklorist Alan Dundes (1992) and from additional research of the social sciences. It goes beyond any of these works in its sustained attention to the Evil Eye in the Bible and its cultural matrix.

All of these studies make only passing reference to biblical texts on the Evil Eye. None devotes so much as a chapter to the biblical material, though many mention one of more of the biblical passages. The tendency of exegetical research of the Bible, on the other hand, has been to take little, if any, note of biblical references to the Evil Eye or to read these texts in isolation of their historical and cultural contexts.

Biblical Studies on the Evil Eye

Despite repeated mention of the Evil Eye in the Jewish and Christian Scriptures, despite its ubiquity in the environment of the biblical communities, and despite the continuation of Evil Eye belief and practice in Israel and Christianity down to the modern era, no critical monograph on the Evil Eye in the Bible has ever been written.[234] Exegetical studies of biblical passages mentioning the Evil Eye prior to the mid-1980s have been few in number and attend more to literary and theological matters than to the cultural significance of the Evil Eye.[235] Observations in the biblical commentaries are sporadic, brief, and made in passing. Modern Bible translations tend to replace rather than translate the original terms for Evil Eye, providing an assumed sense of the expression rather than a literal rendition. As a consequence, the general reader of the Bible is left uninformed of its presence in the Bible and of its existence as a phenomenon of ancient cultural history. Readers also are left in the dark about the implications of this concept and

234. The recent volume of Robert A. Aquaro (2004) is quite limited in scope and substance. Focusing more on envy than on the Evil Eye, it does not qualify as an adequate and comprehensive analysis of the Evil Eye in the Bible and the Christian tradition. See also Aquaro 2001.

235. For earlier New Testament studies see Vol. 3, chap. 2.

its accompanying customs for the meaning of the texts in which it occurs, and the nature of the social relations and dynamics and cultural values to which it points. The present study aims at closing this surprising gap in exegesis and at situating these biblical texts in their cultural contexts. Our study will display the frequency with which reference to the Evil Eye is made in the Bible and the parabiblical literature, and the values and behavior which Evil Eye belief expresses and encourages. We shall examine in detail all the biblical texts referring explicitly to the Evil Eye as well as those containing possible allusions.

Underlying Evil Eye belief and practice is an understanding of the eye as an active rather than receptive organ and a so-called "extramission theory of vision" according to which the eye projects ocular rays or particles of energy. These ocular notions were prevalent in the ancient world and basic to the plausibility of a harmful Evil Eye. We will discuss them below in extensive detail. Siegfried Seligmann[236] pointed this out over a century ago, but this crucial observation had virtually no effect on what exegetes wrote concerning biblical Evil Eye texts. The tide only began to change in recent decades when Betz (1979),[237] Allison (1987, 1997), Elliott (1988),[238] and Rakoczy (1996) all pointed to the extramission theory of vision underlying the notion of the Evil Eye in the ancient world and lending the belief plausibility. As a result, exegetes are now building on this research, as will be discussed in Volume 3. Commenting on the cultural world of the Bible and the need for understanding biblical texts in their proper cultural contexts, for example, biblical exegetes Philip F. Esler[239] and Richard L. Rohrbaugh[240] both open their volumes with illustrations concerning the Evil Eye. David A. Fiensy's study on *Jesus the Galilean* (2007) also begins with Jesus's comment on the Evil Eye as something typical of his teaching and culture.[241] Bruce J. Malina has added an illuminating essay on envy and the Evil Eye to his expanded edition of *The New Testament World: Insights from Cultural Anthropology* (2001).[242] And John J. Pilch, in his in-depth analysis of illness and healing in the New Testament (2000a), explains that the ancient and biblical view that a major cause of illness is the Evil Eye is best understood as

236. Seligmann, 1910 2:454–62.

237. See also Betz 1992; 1995:437–53.

238. See also Elliott 1990; 1991; 1992; 1993:67–69; 1994; 2004; 2005a; 2005b; 2007a; 2007b; 2008; 2011; 2013; 2014; 2015.

239. Esler 1994:19–21.

240. Rohrbaugh 2007:3–4.

241. Fiesny 2007:11–22; see also Fiensy 1999.

242. Malina 2001:108–33.

a "folk-conceptualized disorder." "Since all illness is culturally constructed, a more accurate term [for the sickness resulting from the evil eye] would be *folk-conceptualized disorder*" or "*culture-bound*" syndrome. "No medical anthropologist identifies such human problems as misconceptions or superstitions."[243] Additional relevant studies are now also at hand.[244]

METHOD, AIMS, AND PROCEDURE OF THIS STUDY

Evil Eye Belief and Practice in Their Ancient Context

This study presents for the first time a comprehensive analysis of all explicit references to the Evil Eye in the Bible in fresh English translation, along with other texts where the phenomenon is likely implied. Since the meaning of these texts is determined by their literary and social contexts, the study is contextual in nature. Merging the perspectives of exegesis and the social sciences, it examines these texts in their physical, historical, economic, social, and geo-cultural contexts. It investigates these texts and their contents to relation to the surrounding cultures where the Evil Eye was such a prevalent and prominent aspect of everyday life. This includes the earliest extant references to the Evil Eye, which are found in Mesopotamian texts (Sumerian, Akkadian, Assyrian, as well as Ugaritic), then its appearances in Egyptian sources, and thereafter references in the abundant Greek and Roman data.

In the light of evidence from these sources and their contexts, we will then examine all explicit references to the Evil Eye in Israel's Bible (Hebrew and Greek "Old Testaments"), the parabiblical writings, and the New Testament. This will include the Deuteronomic warnings against Evil-Eyeing and withholding aid to needy neighbors and starving kin; an anxious King Saul enviously Evil-Eyeing an adored David; sages condemning the Evil Eye as the worst of sins; King Solomon as a potent figure for thwarting the Evil Eye; Jesus comparing the good eye of generosity to the Evil Eye of stinginess and illiberality and censuring the Evil Eye of envy; and Paul engaging with his opponents at Galatia in mutual Evil Eye accusations. Our ultimate aim is to arrive at a culturally informed understanding of the Evil Eye phenomenon in antiquity and at a culturally-informed understanding of the pertinent biblical Evil Eye texts and what they meant. In the process, we shall describe

243. Pilch 2000a:19.

244. On New Testament texts see Neyrey 1988; 1990; Pilch 1996; 2000a:19, 80, 85–86, 126, 133, 134, 152; 2000b; 2000c:51–52; 2002; 2004; 2012:176–81; Pilch and Malina 1998:59–63; Esler 1998; Nanos 2002:181–82, 184–91, 251–52, 278–80 and passim. On Old Testament texts and the recent studies of Wazana 2007; and Kotzé 2006; 2007; 2008; see the critical discussion in Vol. 3, chap. 1.

for an English-speaking audience the milestone studies of the Evil Eye in antiquity—the research of Jahn, Elworthy, Seligmann, Rakoczy, and other key contributions, including works not translated into English. Our discussion also updates relevant primary source material (and studies thereof) that have appeared since Jahn and Seligmann. We hope with this accumulated evidence to refute the theological doubters and naysayers who recognize no mention of the Evil Eye in the Bible on the misguided assumption that this was an ignorant "superstition" that could hardly be entertained by inspired biblical authors and would surely not be enshrined in the pages of Sacred Scripture.

We shall examine Evil Eye belief and practice in the Bible *contextually*, that is, as a phenomenon whose features, meaning, and importance are established within a total historical, ecological, economic, social, and cultural context.[245] It is this matrix and constellation of interrelated factors that determine the features, meaning, functions, plausibility, and power of this widespread belief. This matrix provides information on the linguistic terminology for "Evil Eye," the ecological conditions and salient features of ancient Evil Eye belief and practice, as well as the social scripts, cultural values, psychological states, and typical behaviors entailed in Evil Eye belief and practice across ancient societies. We will be considering the three basic components of the ancient cultures presenting Evil Eye belief and practice: the physical environment, the social environment, and the ideational environment, with the first two as the context for the third, which exists not in material reality but only in the human mind.[246] In relating biblical statements on the Evil Eye to those of the surrounding cultures, we are interested in both comparisons and contrasts—where biblical and extra-biblical features coincide or diverge. The examination of these similarities and differences will help put the biblical texts and their emphases in high relief.

Treating Evil Eye Belief as Folklore Rather Than Magic

With Evil Eye belief and practice we are in the domain of folklore and folk cultural beliefs. This comprises "traditional knowledge, customs, oral and artistic traditions among any community (or sector of the community) united

245. Gravel seeks "to place the Evil Eye back in the cultural context in which it originated" (1995:3). He links the Evil Eye with symbols of fertility and sexuality: "virtually all amulets, all gestures, all imprecations that protect against the Evil Eye are sexual in character" (1995:6). However this thesis is to be assessed, his insistence on contextualizing the study of the Evil Eye is methodologically right on target.

246. Murdock 1980b:53–54.

by some common factor, such as a common occupation, co-residence, or a common language or ethnic identity . . . The essence of folklore is its spontaneous or organic nature: that is to say, it is a result of the experiences and interpretations of experience of persons engaged in social interaction."[247]

In this volume we abandon the custom of earlier studies that have approached and portrayed the Evil Eye belief as an instance of "ancient superstition" or "magic" (e.g., Jahn, Elworthy, Brav, Seligmann among numerous others). These categories have been exposed as ill-defined, value-ladened, and prejudicial. They represent modern, Western views on, and attitudes toward, ancient, non-Western thought and behavior. Most often the label "magic" has a pejorative taint in modern discourse, generally with the implication of "primitive," "unenlightened," and non-scientific (or "pre-scientific") thinking. The earlier widespread employment of these concepts in conceptualizing magic, however, has come under intense criticism in recent scholarship. There is no current consensus on the definition and substance of magic, or miracle, or even religion, while there is wide agreement concerning their subjectivity of use and flexibility of meaning dependent on context: "my religion is your superstition; my miracle and medicine is your magic."[248] Writing on ancient Egypt, Geraldine Pinch, an Orientalist at Cambridge University, observes that "[d]ivisions between religion, magic and medicine which seem obvious to us would not necessarily have been meaningful to ancient Egyptians."[249] Pliny's *Natural History,* rabbinic traditions, and the Christian biblical and postbiblical literature similarly show that no clear and consistent distinction was made between medicinal/scientific techniques, magical techniques, and religious rituals. The category and definition of "magic" are thus highly problematic.

The designation "magic" in ancient and modern texts reveals little if anything about the actual nature and behavior of the thing so identified. The term functions more as a pejorative label for something alien or disapproved than as a neutral descriptor. Employed by rival persons or groups competing for hegemony and control, labels and accusations of magic were enlisted as verbal weapons in contests between rivals for dominance. The term was employed in the differentiation of "our" approved behavior

247. Seymour-Smith 1986:120, s.v. "folklore"; see also Dundes 1965.

248. See D. E. Aune's instructive 2007 survey of recent research on "magic" in antiquity; on magic see also D. E. Aune 1980, 1986. For a survey of theories concerning magic see also Cunningham 1999.

249. Pinch 1994:123. Although Pinch titles her volume *Magic in Ancient Egypt* she has readily and frankly acknowledged the limited value of this "magic" classification (ibid., 9–17). We will cite her work below in our discussion of Egypt and the Evil Eye. This keen observation applies to the ancient world generally.

and rituals from the illegal, fraudulent, immoral, or anti social acts of our enemies. Its aim and effect was to vilify rather than clarify. As a cultural construct, the concept of magic, moreover, varies from culture to culture and period to period. No definition of magic is universal.

One representative definition covering most of the features generally attributed to magic is that of J. A. Scurlock, writing on magic in the Ancient Near East in the *Anchor Bible Dictionary*:

> In its broadest sense, 'magic' is a form of communication involving the supernatural world in which an attempt is made to affect the course of present and/or future events by means of ritual actions (especially ones which involve the symbolic imitation of what the practitioner wants to happen), and/or by means of formulaic recitations which describe the desired outcome and/ or invoke gods, demons, or the spirits believed to be resident in natural substances.[250]

This definition may capture some aspects of the repelling power of amulets and apotropaic strategies. But it does not accord with thinking concerning the eye itself, which is regarded as a *natural*, not supernatural, phenomenon. The eye is a natural organ, whose potent glance requires neither the intermediary function of priests or medicine men nor the intervention of supernatural forces. Over the centuries, the shifting understandings of nature (upon which knowledge rests) has affected shifts in what is considered magic and superstition. This shift, along with the accompanying moving boundaries between rational and irrational, natural and supernatural, it has been noted,[251] have made the concepts of "magic" and "superstition" useless for analyzing the phenomenon of the Evil Eye.[252] Famed anthropologist

250. Scurlock 1992 4:464–68, esp. 464.

251. Rakoczy 1996:211–12.

252. For a recent and provocative discussion of "magic as a mode of discourse" shaped always by specific contexts and employed to designate, denigrate and marginalize "the Other," see Stratton 2007, esp. 1–38. In contrast to notions of a "magical worldview" as "degenerate religion" (maintained, e.g., by Barb 1963 and others), Stratton still finds merit in use of the term "magic" by regarding magic as a constellation of ideas, practices, and institutions and as involving a discourse of efficacy that is continuous with (public) religion and rooted in a common universe of symbols. Discussing "Beliefs and Iconography: Prophylactic Symbols and Amulets" (Ch. 2), she considers the Evil Eye and apotropaics (grafitti, floor mosaics, and literary evidence) including the apotropaic eye, phallus, horn, Medusa-head, various animals and birds, as well as potent apotropaic gestures like spitting, urinating, and even defecating. For a historical overview of research on magic since the 1920s, see Bremmer, "The Birth of the Term 'Magic'" (1999), who stresses the plurality of meanings over time and across groups. He concurs with Fowler (1995) on the problematic meaning and use of "magic." For

Edmund Leach wrapped up a lifetime's reflection on magic with the verdict, "As for magic . . . I can only say that, after a lifetime's career as a professional anthropologist, I have almost reached the conclusion that the word has no meaning whatsoever."[253] Clarence Maloney, in his introduction to the collection of anthropological essays on the Evil Eye that he edited, states emphatically that "clearly, we are not dealing with a 'superstition' that can be dismissed with jokes, but with a belief important enough to diffuse over half the world."[254]

The labels of "magic" and "superstition" provide little heuristic aid for understanding Evil Eye belief and practice.[255] Both terms have been used in antiquity, as in the present, to stigmatize and dismiss beliefs and practices of individuals and groups deemed to be "different from us" and "inferior to us" cognitively, culturally, and morally. When speaking of the Evil Eye, the ancients rarely if ever did so in connection with what they called magic. When describing magic and sorcery, on the other hand, they never cite the Evil Eye as an instance.[256] When Plutarch raises the question of its being a form of superstition, he answers it in the negative and submits a rational explanation of how it functions. Pliny the Elder, we shall see, spoke repeatedly of the Evil Eye and of magic, but not in the same breath. He makes no mention of the Evil Eye in his extended discussion of magic and remedies for illnesses prescribed by the Persian Magi (*Natural History*, book 30), whom he is intent on exposing as quacks.[257] Currently, anthropologists recognize that traditional, pre-industrial societies as well as modern ones, think and act in accord with reason and the scientific knowledge available. Despite distinctly different worldviews and assumptions about how the events of

useful discussions, see also Winkelmann 1982; Penner 1989; Jeffers 1996; Glucklich 1997; Schäfer and Kippenberg 1997; van Binsbergen and Wiggermann 1999; Collins 2000; Downing 2003; Klutz 2003:1–9. On Hellenistic magic specifically and the issue of definition, see also Golden 1976; Segal 1987, 1995; Dickie 2001; Bailliot 2010. On magic as a modern Western concept that distorts historical life, and on the uncritical use of the term "magic," see, most recently, Horsley 2014:37–100.

253. Leach 1982:133.

254. Maloney 1976:xv–xvi.

255. Martin (1997) offers an excellent critical discussion of the emic and etic issues involved in the interpretation of terms such as "superstition" and "magic." The need for attention to native plausibility structures and constructions of reality is especially stressed. See also Martin 2004.

256. Recent research on the Evil Eye or on magic in antiquity appears skeptical toward relating of the Evil Eye to magic. Matthew Dickie's 2001 compendium on ancient magic, for example, refers only occasionally and in passing to the Evil Eye. Marco Frenschkowski's substantive review of magic in the ancient world (2010) contains not a single thematic mention of the Evil Eye, referring to it only thrice in passing.

257. Pliny, *NH* 30.1.

everyday life are to be explained, traditional societies, like modern Western societies, build theories from traditional axioms describing experience and observation. Then they test hypotheses derived from these theories. They proceed, in short, as do scientifically-minded people today.[258] Classifying the cognitive processes of such peoples as "magical thinking" flies in the face of this evidence and from the outset warps and distorts our investigation of these peoples and their Evil Eye beliefs and practices. In fact, even though they had concepts of magic and witchcraft, they did not discuss the Evil Eye as something magical but as an actual phenomenon whose operation can be explained on rational grounds. On the other hand, some scholars, like Siebers, continue to view the Evil Eye as an instance of magic and superstition. Siebers argues that that the Evil Eye and narcissism illustrate "the structuring principles of superstition" in human behavior from past to present and that the imitative logic of superstition is best illustrated in the Medusa myth.[259] The basis of this argument, however, is erroneous, at least with respect to antiquity. It is not the case that "the evil-eye belief thrives by attributing a *supernatural* difference to accused individuals."[260] The Evil Eye was held to be a natural, not supernatural, phenomenon and explainable on logical physical grounds. Recently Antón Alvar Nuño, in a 2008 article on the Evil Eye in the classical world, has cogently argued that current research on magic and superstition shows that neither of the fluid concepts is useful for understanding the Evil Eye. "El mal de ojo no es una actividad mágica" ("the Evil Eye is no magical activity"). Its chief features were not consistent with those of magic; it was not proscribed as magical or superstitious in the ancient world; but in fact was included under the umbrella of Roman state religion (see the god *Fascinus* and related cult).[261]

Our study shows that the ancients thought of the Evil Eye rather as a phenomenon of nature and attempted to understand and explain it on rational grounds (according to the existent state of knowledge). Thomas Rackokzy makes this crucial point in his excellent 1996 study on the Evil Eye in Greek antiquity. We shall allow the ancient sources to speak for themselves without prejudging them as indications of magical thinking and ignorant superstition. We shall treat the Evil Eye—as the ancients regarded both the Evil Eye and witches and witchcraft—as power-charged phenomena of nature not to be dismissed but to be taken seriously. Evil Eye

258. See Marwick 1982:460–68 on "Witchcraft and the Epistomology of Science."

259. Siebers 1983:22.

260. Against Siebers 1983:xii, emphasis added.

261. Alvar Nuño 2006–2008:104–12; see also Alvar Nuño 2009–2010, 2012a, 2012b.

possessors were not necessarily regarded as witches, nor witches as necessarily possessors of an Evil Eye, as far as we can tell from the sources. But
both witches and fascinators were regarded as similarly endowed by nature
with special power that had to be reckoned with. Witches like Medea could
employ an Evil Eye, but an Evil Eye was by no means the exclusive possession of witches or magicians. An Evil Eye could be wielded by any living
entity, human or divine, demon or animal. The biblical authors appear not
to have attributed an Evil Eye to God or demons or animals, but only to
humans, and they condemned it as a malicious human vice. Only in post-
biblical time did the Christian church fathers associate the Evil Eye with
the devil and denounce Evil Eye possessors as tools of Satan, the demon
par excellence. Beginning in the fourth century CE, Christian authorities
associated the magical arts with paganism, idolatry, and heresy. Magicians
and magic were condemned and criminalized,[262] but not the Evil Eye. Evil
Eye belief and practice was deplored as satanic in origin but was spared
criminalization and flourished unchecked.

In this study we shall respect this ancient perspective on the Evil Eye.
We shall attempt to understand Evil Eye belief and practice as presented and
explained by the ancient authors themselves on their own terms. This focus
on an "emic" perspective (the view of the ancient informants) by no means
rules out employing modern social-scientific theory and taxonomies for
our understanding the phenomenon today (an "etic" perspective).[263] But we
shall attempt to stay as close as possible to the terminology and mentalities
of our ancient informants. So in this study we shall treat the Evil Eye as it
seems to have been regarded in the ancient world; namely as a phenomenon
of nature open to rational explanation.[264]

We might add in this regard that modern study of the gaze or stare
behavior of humans and animals—starring and being starred at—may
show how the ancients could find the notion of an active eye so natural
and plausible. Over the centuries and across cultures, the eyes themselves
have remained potent conveyers of a variety of emotions and "a provocative source of social stimulation, and this may account for the intense fascination with the eyes [and ocular features and symbols] by many cultural
groups."[265] Numerous scientific experiments have shown the sensitivity and
unease of animals and humans at being the object of another's intense stare

262. See Frenschkowski 2009.

263. On the terminology and distinction of emic and etic, see Harris 1976; Headland et al. 1990.

264. This is the position also of Thomas Rakoczy in his 1996 study of the Evil Eye
in antiquity, *Der böse Blick*.

265. Coss 1992:182. See also Caillois 1960.

or gaze.[266] Among humans, this experience prompts feelings of anxiety or fear of hostile intent on the part of the starer, as noted by psychologist Richard G. Coss.[267] Belief in an Evil Eye, Coss proposes, is rooted in and bolstered by this negative experience, which is universal in the world of humans and primates. In the world of football, boxing, and other contact sports, the scowl is an omnipresent means of defiance and intimidation. In Andalusian Spain and other Mediterranean societies, ocular aggression is directly linked with the Evil Eye.[268] Thus one significant contribution to the persistence of the Evil Eye belief over the centuries and into modern time, Coss suggests, is the physiological reality of eye contact and aversion, ocular aggression and the biopsychological nervous arousal in virtually all species of the animal world.[269]

Colin Andrew Ross takes this observation a step further and argues, against the current prevailing intromission theory of vision, that there are data indicating an "electrophysiological basis of Evil Eye belief." Western science's rejection of evil eye beliefs, he proposes, "may be based on an erroneous rejection of a widespread component of human consciousness, the sense of being stared at, which may in turn be based on a real electrophysiological signal."[270] Ross represents an interesting yet clearly minority view in this discussion. In our study, in any case, we shall see the paramount role attributed to the eye in ancient Circum-Mediterranean societies as primary source of information and as active agent of ocular intimidation and aggression—basic building blocks to the belief and practices concerning an Evil Eye.

The reasoning apparently behind the design, production, and use of anti-Evil Eye amulets in antiquity seems consistent with what has been labeled a "magical" idea of causation. The armchair ethnologist Sir James

---

266. Radin 1997:27–30, 155–56. Laboratory studies have been conducted over eight decades of persons staring and being stared at by others over a distance, with the stared-at person unaware of when the starer was staring at him or her (studies listed by Radin 1997:313 nn. 25 and 34). "These studies resulted in an overall effect of 63 percent where chance expectation is 50 percent. This is remarkably robust for a phenomenon that—according to conventional scientific modes—is not supposed to exist. The combined studies result in odds against chance of 3.8 million to 1." (155; see also 156, fig. 9.2). See also biologist Sheldrake 2003 on experiments regarding the sense of being starred at.

267. Coss, 1992 (1974). On the psychological aspect and the link of staring and the Evil Eye see also Siebers 1983:29–35.

268. Gilmore 1982:197–98; 1987.

269. Coss 1992; see, similarly, Meerloo 1971.

270. Ross 2010. For a critical response see Mesner 2010.

Frazer (1854–1941), author of the famed and influential *The Golden Bough*,[271] dubbed it the "law of similarity," according to which "like influences like" (*similia similibus*).[272] This "law," however, is also an acknowledged and respected principle of medicine and illustrates the difficulty in determining where medicine ends and so-called "magic" begins. Our discussion below of amulets and instances of representations of eyes deployed to repel an Evil Eye will take up this issue of "like influences like."[273] The problematic labels of "magic" and "superstition," however, will be avoided in this study of Evil Eye belief as prejudicial, misleading, and useless as analytical and explanatory concepts.

The Evil Eye and Witchcraft Societies

We will, however, be speaking of witchcraft since Evil Eye belief and practice has been shown to be characteristic of what anthropologists call "witchcraft societies."[274] Witchcraft is not a synonym for, or subset of, superstition or magic, contrary to earlier scholarship. Witches, as defined by anthropologists and ethnographers, are persons of a culture who are thought to be replete with power to affect the lives and fortunes of others, both positively and negatively. Witchcraft societies are those that reckon with the existence and capabilities of such powerful persons. This includes the biblical communities.[275] Evil Eye belief is a feature of such witchcraft societies,[276] just as it is prominent in societies presuming the existence of supernatural spirits (both benevolent and malevolent, angels and demons) that influence and affect human life and fortune. Belief in powerful witches and threatening demons/spirits is typical of the ancient societies that we shall be examining in this study, including the biblical communities, and illustrative of the prevailing mental and emotional climate that was home to the dreaded Evil Eye. These witchcraft societies, it must be noted, operate with systems

271. Frazer, *The Golden Bough*, originally 2 vols., 1890. 3rd enlarged edition of 12 vols., 1906–1915.

272. Frazer, *Golden Bough*, 3rd ed., Vol. 1: Part 1, *The Magic Art and the Evolution of Kings in 2 vols.*, vol. 1, Ch. 3, Sympathetic Magic, 52–219, esp. 52. The other basic principle of causation, according to Frazer, is that of "contact/contagion."

273. See Vol. 2.

274. See Douglas 1970b:xxvi–xxvii; Spooner 1970; 1976:76–84, 279–85; Reminick 1976:96–100; Garrison and Arensberg 1976:319–24; Murdock 1980b:49, Table 3, 50–51, 57–63. On witchcraft societies of the Circum-Mediterranean and ancient Near East as the matrix of Evil Eye belief, see Vol. 3, chap. 2.

275. See Neyrey 1990:181–217.

276. See Murdock 1980b; Roberts 1976.

of thought that are bound by rules of reasoning and criteria of truth and falsehood. So belief in witches, spirits, demons, and the Evil Eye cannot be judged as an instance of benighted superstitious thought. Texts like that of Plutarch reveal how the belief made sense to intelligent, critically thinking persons. In witchcraft societies, Evil Eye accusations have the same purpose as accusations of practicing witchcraft—to delegitimize, discredit, and demote those accused. The implication of the accusation is that the eye of the fascinator(s) and its oblique glance have a pernicious effect upon victims and a divisive effect upon communities.

Evil Eye Belief and Practice in Context— Emic and Etic Perspectives

By contextualizing the subject of our study and viewing it as a cultural construct related to other ancient cultural constructs produced by ancient societies in their specific geographical, historical, socioeconomic, and cultural (including religious) settings, we aim at avoiding a culturally biased, ethnocentric, and judgmental treatment of our subject. The meaning and plausibility of the Evil Eye in the ancient world are determined and constrained by the historical, social, and cultural contexts of thought, worldview, language and behavior that prevail in given societies. This is as true of Evil Eye belief and practice as it is of all other ancient concepts and customs. This matrix-shaped meaning includes ecological and environmental factors, social structures and dynamics, along with the prevailing state of scientific knowledge, worldviews, values, norms of conduct, modes of personal socialization, and the experiences of everyday living.

The chapter and volumes that follow will explore and update what is known about the Evil Eye in the cultures of the ancient Near East and Circum-Mediterranean. What did the ancients believe about the Evil Eye? How was this belief expressed in their language, literature, art, architecture, adornment, and manner of speaking and acting? What concepts were associated with and supportive of this belief? In what environmental, economic, social and cultural conditions and circumstances did it flourish? What danger was it thought to pose? How did it strike? What persons or forces wielded an Evil Eye? Who was vulnerable to its power? Where and when could it strike? Why did it arouse fear and dread? With what dispositions and emotions was it connected? What moral values did it represent and reinforce? How did it affect social relations and personal behavior? How did persons and groups attempt to protect themselves from an Evil Eye and from being suspected of wielding an Evil Eye? For the biblical communities, what role did the Evil Eye assume in their everyday life and behavior? How was it related to thought about God and fidelity to the divine will? What did the sages, Jesus and the apostle Paul have to say on the subject? Answers to all these questions require a contextualized approach to the issue.

Such an approach will include our adopting from anthropology the useful distinction between "emic" and "etic" realms of discourse. As indicated above (see pp. 26–27), "emic"[277] denotes discourse reflecting the viewpoint, conceptual categories, and explanations provided by members *belonging to* a particular culture—in our case, the authors and producers of the ancient cultural sources investigated in this study. "Etic"[278] denotes discourse, categorization, explanations and criteria used to analyze a culture by persons *outside* this particular culture—in our case, modern historians, social scientists, or theologians intent on understanding and explaining the data according to modern scientific criteria. "Emic" identifies "folk rationalizations and explanations" of everyday experience based on knowledge prevailing among certain populations at a given time and place. For investigators of the Bible and biblical cultures, the Bible provides "emic" accounts and explanations. We modern day readers and investigators, on the other hand, bring to the Bible, and the entire body of evidence from the ancient world, our modern etic perspectives, theories, conceptual categories and bodies of knowledge. Observing this distinction between emic and etic perspectives aids our avoiding an ethnocentric and anachronistic imposition of modern Western views and values on ancient Near Eastern and Circum-Mediterranean cultural systems, beliefs, and practices. Accordingly, we shall attempt to understand these ancient sources on their own terms, logic, and rationality, without prejudging them as expressions of "primitive" modes of thought, "ignorant superstition," or irrational "magical" notions.

Finally, as to the comparative method employed in this study, we might ponder the reluctance of two researchers to envision the Evil Eye as a fixed concept. Mediterranean anthropologist Michael Herzfeld has proposed that the term "Evil Eye" should not be used in cross-cultural comparisons, according to M. W. Dickie, "on the ground that the term is frequently employed to refer to beliefs that have little in common with each other, although he [Herzfeld] does think that it has a proper application."[279] Dickie, a classicist,

277. "Emic" is derived from the linguistic category "phonemic" (sounds meaningful to native speakers).

278. "Etic" is derived from the linguistic category "phonetic" (the study and systematization of speech sounds)

279. Dickie 1995:12, referring to Herzfeld 1984:448–50, and 1986:108 n. 3. For similar cautions and appeal for a semiotic focus on the symbol system as a whole, see Herzfeld 1981.

has written extensively on the Evil Eye[280] and envy,[281] and is sympathetic to this suggestion. He claims that,

> In the case of classical antiquity and of the late Roman world, the term evil eye as such is hardly used at all and then only under the influence of certain scriptural passages of uncertain import. The terms used most often are, by Greek speakers, *phthonos* and *baskania*, and by Latin speakers, *invidia* and, *fascinatio* or *fascinus*. What men [*sic*] feared under these headings was not a single object with a secure and fixed identity but a complex of objects with shifting identities, and identities that coalesce. Very often what they feared will have been inchoate and will have lacked any real identity. The more or less constant factor in this constellation of fears was the fear of envy: men were afraid lest their good fortune would draw envy on their heads. They might fear it would come from their fellow men, demons, the gods, fortune, the fates, and a malign supernatural power they called simply *phthonos* or *invidia*.[282]

Fear may have lacked a clear focus and explanations for misfortunes were "fluid" and included "a combination of forces, for example, envious demons working though envious human beings," or the effect of *phthonos* or *invidia*.[283] Our study will put these claims of Herzfeld and Dickie to the test. We will attempt to see whether reference to the Evil Eye as a stable and threatening ocular phenomenon with a cluster of salient features is more extensive than Dickie allows, and whether there is more consistency in what ancients thought and said about the Evil Eye than Dickie and Herzfeld seem prepared to allow.

Aims of the Study

One broad aim of this study is to provide a sorely needed update on the deluge of research on the Evil Eye since the classic works of Jahn, Elworthy, and Seligmann at the turn of the twentieth century. Seligmann's two-volume work of 1910 is unsurpassed for its documentation and wealth of material. The bibliography in this present volume listing works on the Evil

280. Dickie 1987; 1990; 1991; 1993a; 1995; 2000.

281. Dickie 1983; 1987; 1992; 1993b.

282. Dickie 1995:12, citing Gregory of Nyssa, *Oratio funebris in Meletium*, PG 46, col. 856, and John Chrysostom, *Commentarius in epistulam 1 ad Corinthios*, PG 61, col. 106.

283. Ibid., 12–13.

Eye is the largest of its kind since Seligmann. English summaries of foreign language studies are included, along with abundant graphic representations and illustrations.

Our more specific aim is to present the *first monograph* treating all the Evil Eye texts of the Bible within the context of Evil Eye belief and practice across the world of the Circum-Mediterranean and ancient Near East, from Sumeria (3000 BCE) to Roman Late Antiquity (600 CE). The analysis treats the biblical texts in relation to their specific geographical, historical, economic, social, and cultural (including religious) contexts. These contexts include Mesopotamian, Egyptian, Greek, and Roman thinking and practice concerning the Evil Eye, along with post-biblical developments In Israel and early Christianity. The diffusion of Evil Eye belief and practice in antiquity is a dramatic instance of cross-cultural sharing and influence. The volumes of our study constitute foci of attention, not cases of isolated development. They examine particular cultures in roughly sequential historical periods. This does not presume, or intend to suggest, however, that these cultural communities existed independent of one another. To the contrary, we must envision a lively and extensive synergism and cultural commingling. This, as we shall see, is especially the case with regard to belief and practice concerning the Evil Eye.

Issues of Translation:
Striving for Consistency in Translation

Our subject requires that we engage in detailed linguistic analysis at points in order to identify relevant texts and their meanings, and also to assess conventional translations. Our study aims at consistency in the translation of relevant key terms so that the reader is apprized of all explicit mentions of the Evil Eye in the ancient sources. The translations in this volume are my own unless otherwise indicated. In several instances I have modified existing translations. Although there is repeated mention of the Evil Eye in the Bible—-as the venerable King James Version shows—modern translations of the Bible fail to make this clear. These translations are regularly inconsistent in their rendition of terms for "Evil Eye" in the original languages. Virtually all modern Bible versions, as we shall see, translate the Hebrew and Greek terms for "Evil Eye" not literally but according to some assumed sense, favoring such words and expressions as "envy," "bewitchment," "spell," "malice," "begrudge," "be hostile toward," among others. As a consequence, today's Bible reader is left unaware of the frequent reference to the Evil Eye in the original texts and gains no insight into the connection between current customs revolving around this belief and its significance in the biblical writings.

Conventional translations of Evil Eye texts in secular writings are characterized by a similar variation in the modern terms selected. Here too the translations leave the reader unaware of the frequency of reference to the Evil Eye in the original texts. Here too the reader is left ignorant of the regularity of its association with particular salient features and components of the Evil Eye belief complex. I shall remedy this situation by rendering all Evil Eye terminology of original texts consistently with "Evil Eye," "harm with an Evil Eye" or, its equivalent, "fascination," "fascinate," "fascinator," and the like. This will be done with both biblical and non-biblical texts. This entails no presumption of a fixed singular meaning to these terms. A range of meanings is allowed, with context being determinative. It is possible, if not likely, that in some instances the original term "Evil Eye" connoted "malice," or "malignity," or "bear ill will," or "(be)grudge" or "envy" or "be miserly toward," or "slander" and the like.[284] My aim, however, is to expose the frequency of reference to this phenomenon and the varied contexts in which it appears in both the biblical and extra-biblical sources. For this purpose consistency of terminology is essential.

Plan of the Study

Since this belief and its associated practice can be accurately understood only in relation to specific historical, social, and cultural contexts, we begin with the earliest references to the Evil Eye in antiquity—the evidence from ancient Mesopotamia and Egypt (chap. 2 below). In the case of Mesopotamia, our chief sources will be incantations directed against the Evil Eye. Here will begin our assembling of features regularly associated with the Evil Eye and details of protective practice. Egyptian sources will entail art and occasional literary references to the Evil Eye. The largest body of evidence, however, will consist of the plethora of anti Evil Eye amulets, various forms of the *udzat* or "Eye of Horus" that once circulated in abundance in Egypt and then made their way throughout the Mediterranean world and the Fertile Crescent.

Volume 2 treats the evidence of Evil Eye belief and practice in Greek and Roman cultures down through Late Antiquity (c. 600 CE). This comprises our largest body of evidence and the broadest diversity of sources (literature, papyri letters, inscriptions and epigrapha, art, sculpture, mosaic

284. See, for example, the standard *Greek–English Lexicon* of Liddel–Scott–Jones 9th ed. 1940, sub *baskainô*.

designs, plaques, and an arsenal of anti-Evil Eye amulets). Here we will list and discuss key elements of the Evil Eye belief complex along with further salient features of Evil Eye belief including strategies for warding off the Evil Eye and envy. Volumes 1 and 2 set the stage for a contextual reading and interpretation of Evil Eye belief and practice in the Bible and the biblical communities (Vols. 3 and 4).

Volume 3, chap. 1 identifies and discusses all the references to the Evil Eye (explicit and implicit) occurring in the Hebrew and Greek Old Testaments and the related parabiblical texts (e.g., *Testaments of the Twelve Patriarchs*, *Testament of Solomon*, the Dead Sea Scrolls, and the writings of Philo and Josephus). In this chapter we will see the frequency of references to the Evil Eye, its several nuances, the similarity of its features to those of the surrounding cultures, and some notable distinctive biblical features. Possible allusions will also be considered.

Volume 3, chap. 2 identifies and discusses all references to the Evil Eye in the New Testament; namely, in the sayings of Jesus (Matt 6:22–23/Luke 11:33–36; Matt 20:15; and Mark 7:22) and the apostle Paul's letter to the Galatians. Possible implicit references will also be considered. We will see a consistency between these references to the Evil Eye and preceding biblical tradition. Similarities with and differences from pagan thought and practice also will become apparent.

Volume 4, chap. 1 tracks evidence of Evil Eye belief and practice in postbiblical Israel through Late Antiquity (second to seventh centuries CE). Dread of the Evil Eye and the condemning of envy continue unabated. The literary as well as material evidence expands in these centuries and includes the literature of the Mishnah, Talmud, and Jewish lore, and the abundant remains of anti-Evil Eye protectives found in excavated houses, vestibule mosaics, synagogues, grave sites and elsewhere.

Volume 4, chap. 2, parallel to chap. 1, surveys the literary, epistolary, and material evidence of Evil Eye belief and practice in postbiblical Christianity through the Roman and Byzantine periods (second to seventh centuries CE). This comprises references in the writings of the Apostolic Fathers, the apocryphal *Acts of the Apostles* (Thomas, John), and numerous writings of the Church Fathers. As in chap. 1 of Volume 4, a broad range of material and iconographic evidence also is included.

Volume 4, chap. 3 concludes our study and summarizes what we have learned about the Evil Eye in the Bible and its ancient cultural context. We close with some final reflections on the roles that Evil Eye belief and practice played in the ancient world and on the roles they have continued to play in everyday thinking, feeling, and conduct.

Many readers today who have encountered belief in the Evil Eye consider this as nonsense and dismiss it as a relic of ancient superstition. Numerous others, on the other hand, regard the Evil Eye today as it was regarded generally in antiquity, as something physically real, dangerous, and destructive, but also as a force that can be averted in various ways. Whether one "believes in" the Evil Eye or not, the traces of this belief across the pages of history calls for examination and explanation. A venerable axiom of sociology holds that beliefs, whether true or false, are always real in their consequences. Those who believe in and dread the Evil Eye think, plan, and act in particular ways. They have developed what to them are rational explanations based on experience. They have devised a range of behavioral strategies for dealing with the Evil Eye, which they take to be a constant threat. These modes of behavior have led to habits and customs of action that have endured from antiquity to the present. In this study we prescind from the question of whether the Evil Eye is real or not, and rather examine the contours and traces of this belief and its impact on human and social behavior in the ancient world and the biblical communities.

"The evil eye," declares classicist Thomas Rakoczy, "is with certainty the most widespread concept of folk belief, both geographically and historically, and today a majority of modern languages still have at their disposal countess terms for the evil eye and its effect."[285] The late Alan Dundes, a preeminent folklorist who compiled an anthology of twenty-one essays on Evil Eye belief and practice across the globe (1st ed. 1981; 2nd ed. 1992), insisted, quite rightly, that "the evil eye is not some old-fashioned superstitious belief" (1992:viii). Nor is it solely of interest to antiquarians. "The evil eye continues to be a powerful factor affecting the behavior of countless millions of people throughout the Indo-European and Semitic world. Certainly in India, in the Arab world, and among Circum-Mediterranean peoples—and their descendants in North and South America—one will find without difficulty innumerable illustrations of the remarkably pervasive and persistent influence of the evil-eye belief complex."[286]

Our study concentrates on an early phase of this long and colorful history—the Evil Eye in the Bible and its ancient cultural context. It will be the first book-length exegetical analysis of the Evil Eye in the Bible and related literature. It will be comparative as well as cross-disciplinary in method, involving a merging of history, linguistics, literary and social-scientific criticism, and exegetical analysis and synthesis. Beside illuminating biblical texts and biblical culture, and along the way correcting inadequate modern

285. Rakocsy 1996:39.
286. Dundes 1992:viii–ix.

translations, it will inform readers of the origin and meaning of numerous practices once rooted in Evil Eye belief that are still in vogue today—such as avoiding praise, tipping at meals, tying blue and red threads to the wrists of newborns, not admitting one's good fortune publicly, spitting three times, using prophylactic hand gestures including the "high sign," or uttering certain protective expressions such as "ptui-ptui-ptui" or "toi-toi-toi"; "Mashallah," "keineinhore," "Gratia a Dio," or "thanks be to God." In this way readers are assisted in understanding the behavior of persons for whom the Evil Eye remains a daily reality. In the process, similarities across cultures will become apparent as well as the striking persistence and pervasiveness of Evil Eye belief and practice from antiquity to the present, from Sumeria to San Francisco, from ancient incantations to yesterday's internet blog.

2

MESOPOTAMIA AND EGYPT

THE EVIL EYE IN MESOPOTAMIA AND RELATED CULTURES

Introduction

To prepare for a reading of the biblical texts on the Evil Eye—our chief concern—it is necessary to consider these texts in relation to the cultures and currents of thought and practice in which the biblical communities were at home. In this way we can read them within their appropriate historical, social, and geo-cultural contexts and frames of reference. The purpose of this chapter is to review the earliest written and material evidence of this belief—the cultures of Mesopotamia and Egypt.

Evil Eye belief and practice is one of the oldest and most widely-spread instances of ancient popular culture. It has been found throughout the areas of the ancient Circum-Mediterranean[1] and ancient Near East, the cultural matrix of the biblical writings.[2] Thomas Rakoczy, reflecting the general view, identifies the Evil Eye as the most widely spread concept of popular

---

1. The "Circum-Mediterranean" territory embracing the lands and cultures surrounding, and reliant on, the Mediterranean Sea, is a geographical and cultural area displaying a sufficiently high degree of ecological, social and cultural similarity to lead anthropologists to regard and study it as a distinctive geographical and cultural region.

2. On this world in general, see, for example, the recent volumes of Sasson 1995; Kuhrt 1997; and Woodward 2004. On Sumeria see Kramer 1963.

belief, both geographically and historically.[3] Evidence ranges from 5,000 year old Sumerian incantations to abundant literary references and ubiquitous amulets and apotropaics of late Roman antiquity (sixth cent. CE). The first recorded instances of Evil Eye belief and practice come from one of the world's most ancient civilizations, Sumer, located in Mesopotamia, the land "between the two rivers," the Tigris and the Euphrates, modern day Iraq. According to E. A. Wallis Budge, former Curator of Antiquities at the British Museum, "The oldest mentions of the Evil Eye are found in the texts which the Sumerians, Babylonians and Assyrians wrote in cuneiform upon clay tablets; the Sumerian texts date from the third millennium before Christ, and they form the base of the later Babylonian and Assyrian magical literature."[4] Sumerian incantations were chanted formulations used to ward off and defend against various harmful powers including the Evil Eye. This is where our investigation begins.

Geographically, Evil Eye belief and practice is thought to have spread from Mesopotamia southward through the Fertile Crescent to Egypt and then throughout the lands of the Circum-Mediterranean of Greek and Roman times. Putting the Evil Eye belief into world perspective, anthropologist J. M. Roberts concludes his ethnographical survey: "The geographical distribution of the cultures possessing the evil eye belief supports the statement that the belief became culturally elaborated in the Near East (broadly defined)."[5] Anthropologist Clarence Maloney concurs: "the belief originated in the Near East with the evolution of complex peasant-urban cultures and spread in all directions. It is statistically associated today with such features as plow agriculture and dairying, as well as pre-modern urbanization."[6] T. Schrire has noted that amulets, whose "primary object is to protect the wearer against the effects of evil and the Evil Eye," have been found dating from pre-historic times. "The Egyptians and Sumerians had a very strong belief in the Evil Eye and commonly wore amulets for protection. From Egypt the belief spread centrifugally to other parts of the Old World.[7] We begin our journey, therefore, with an examination of the Evil Eye in Mesopotamia. Thereafter, we shall consider traces of this belief in Egypt of the earlier Pharonic and then later Ptolemiac periods.

3. Rakoczy 1996:39.
4. Budge 1978/1930:358.
5. Roberts 1976:261, see 234–60.
6. Maloney 1976:xi, following the data analysis of Roberts.
7. Schrire 1982:6.

Sumerian and Akkadian Texts

The earliest historical mention of the Evil Eye comes from the ancient Near East and the Mesopotamian civilization of Sumer.[8] Sumerian incantations dating from the third millennium BCE refer to the Evil Eye and these are followed by incantations in bilingual Sumerian-Akkadian texts, then Akkadian, Ugaritic, Phoenician, and Aramaic texts.[9] Bounded by the Tigris and Euphrates rivers and extending from Baghdad southward to the Persian Gulf, Sumer was one of the world's earliest and most influential civilizations (c. 3000–1700 BCE). It was a network of small competing city-states, which survived on an agricultural base and achieved brilliant advances of technological and scientific sophistication (irrigation systems, mathematics, pharmacology, astronomy), communication (system of writing), law, and education. Sumerians are credited with the invention of writing (in cuneiform script, wedge-like impressions made into moist clay tablets) around 3200 BCE. Sumerian civilization was penetrated by the Akkadians (c. 2350–2100), Semites from the north and west of Sumer, who exerted increasing influence over Sumer from King Sargon of Agade (c. 2340–2230 BCE) onward. They established a transitional Semitic rule (2300–2100 BCE) until the revival of Sumerian power c. 2100–1720 BCE. With Akkadian ascendance, the Akkadian language became the lingua franca of this region (c. 2100–600 BCE). Bilingual incantations were employed that were formulated in both Sumerian and Akkadian and written in cuneiform script. Akkadian and Sumerian linguistic and literary traditions then merged to form a Sumero-Akkadian language (also written in cuneiform).[10] From the Old

8. Budge 1978/1930:358.

9. Evil Eye belief and practice in Sumerian, Akkadian, Babylonian, Assyrian and Ugaritic cultures have been discussed by numerous authors including Lenormant 1878:40–42; Fossey 1902:50; Seligmann 1910 1:12, citing one Akkadian incantation; Jastrow 1905 1:285; Langdon 1913:11–12; Ebeling 1938, 1949; Contenau 1947:259–63; Virolleaud 1960; van Dijk 1967:262; Farber 1981:52, 60–68; Farber 1984:70; Krebernik 1984:55, 59–63; Cunningham 1997 (who classifies these as religious rather than "magical" texts); Thomsen 1987, 1992; Seawright 1988; del Olmo Lete 1992a; 1992b:255–59; 1999:379–84; 2010; Veldhuis 1992; Hunter 1993; Cavigneaux 1996; Cavigneaux and Al-Rawi 1993, 1994, 1995a, 1995b; Wasserman 1995; Ford 1998, 2000; Hamp 2000:15–19; Pardee 2002; Geller 2003, 2004, 2007; B. R. Foster 2005; Barjamovic and Trolle Larsen 2008; Mouton 2009 (also Hittite sources on "evil eyes" in plural, 426–32); Kotzé 2013. On the Evil eye in Zoroastrian literature see Frachtenberg 1918:419–24.

10. "Akkadian was an inflected language, conveying part of its meaning by tone and pitch. The Akkadians conquered a literate people [the Sumerians] whose pictograms generally represented physical objects rather than sounds. But they were more interested in developing phonetic writing. The fusion of the Akkadian language and Sumerian literacy resulted in a simplified cuneiform script, which helped transform pictograms into a syllabic script. The existence of fewer characters was a boon to the diffusion of

Babylonian period (1850–1530) onward if not before, Akkadian began to supplant Sumerian and became the main language spoken in Mesopotamia until about 500 BCE when it was supplanted in the Persian period by Aramaic, an alphabetic script borrowed from the Canaanites. The advantage Aramaic had over other Middle Eastern languages enabled it to become the main international language of trade and diplomacy.

Evidence of Evil Eye belief and practice is found in all these periods. In addition to Sumerian, Akkadian, and bilingual Sumero-Akkadian incantations, texts in Ugaritic or from Phoenicia, as well as in Aramaic,[11] and then in Syriac, Coptic, and Mandaic in the Common Era display remarkable similarity in how the Evil Eye was described, how it was thought to function, and how it could be avoided or overcome.

The Sumerians and Akkadians were polytheists whose cosmology, E. A. Wallis Budge, the renowned Egyptologist has noted (1978/1930:82), especially at the level of popular religion, included a lively belief in potencies visible and invisible, powers terrestrial and celestial, and potentially harmful forces including daimons and witches as agents of both good and evil—a set of beliefs typical of peoples throughout the ancient world.[12] These were cultures, their clay tablets inform us, who searched for information about the present and future regarding personal and familial health and fortune, the welfare of the king, outcomes of battles, quality of the harvest, weather conditions, and similar practical concerns. This information was sought from such sources as astrology, dreams (oneiromancy), study of the entrails of sacrificed sheep (extispicy) or of animal livers (heptoscopy), or attention to freak births (teratoscopy) or pebbles (psephomancy) or oil offered to the deities (lecanomancy).[13] To shape the course of events in their daily lives, they consulted witches and wizards and employed, among other things, curses and blessings, incantations and prayers, sure of their intended effect. Anthropologists classify and study societies with such beliefs as "witchcraft societies," with "witchcraft" used strictly as a descriptive term with no

literacy. Akkadian's advantage over other Middle Eastern languages was so great that in the mid-second millennium, even after papyrus was replacing the clay tablet, it became the main international language of diplomacy and trade" (Mann 1986:152).

11. Contenau, Conservateur of Oriental antiquities and Islamic art at the Louvre, Paris, observes: "La croyance à ce qu'on nomme de 'mauvais oeil,' universellement répandue, est attestée chez les Babyloniens" (Contenau 1947:260; see pp. 259–63 on the Evil Eye; p. 261, fig. 24 for a fresco of the Evil Eye in Dura-Europos). The first millennium evidence for Akkadian Evil Eye incantations was two Assur tablets now in the Vorderasiatisches Museum in Berlin and edited by Ebeling, discussed later by Thomsen and Ford.

12. See also Oppenheim 1977:171–227.

13. See Hallo 2005.

negative implication.[14] All the cultures we shall be examining in this study, including the biblical and post-biblical communities, fall into this category. It is in such societies that Evil Eye belief and practice have been found to flourish.[15]

"The Sumerians," Budge noted, "invented and developed a system of writing, and the inscriptions which they wrote on tablets of clay and stone suggest that they lived anxious lives and were in perpetual fear of the attacks of hosts of hostile and evil spirits which lost no opportunity of attempting to do them harm. To protect themselves against these they employed charms and spells and incantations, and in order to destroy the operations of the Evil Eye they wore amulets of various kinds, both inscribed and uninscribed."[16] Incantations, in particular, were often employed for preventing or curing illness and warding off evil. These were chants[17] uttering powerful words designed to ward off hostile spirits, illness, and other forms of malignity. In the Greek world, the famous philosopher and medical expert Pythagoras (582–500 BCE) also used singing as a means of healing: "He had prepared songs for bodily illnesses, by the singing of which he cured the sick" (Porphyry, *Life of Pythagoras* 33). Spells and incantations were so-called "performative acts" in which the speaking and chanting was intended to set in motion the action described by the words. The words of such incantations were also inscribed on clay tablets in cuneiform script. These included many that were employed to ward off the dangerous Evil Eye and keep it at bay. These clay tablets inform us that their writers were persons searching also for informa-

14. Anthropologist Mary Douglas (1970b: xxvi–xxvii) has indicated six salient features of witchcraft societies, which also tend to foster belief in the Evil Eye: (1) clearly drawn external social boundaries; (2) confused internal social relations; (3) close and continual interaction within a society; (4) poorly developed tension-relieving techniques; (5) weak central authority for adjudicating quarrels and strife; and (6) disorderly but intense conflict. On witchcraft and the Evil Eye, see also Devish 2005, esp. 389–90, 402–3; Bowie 2006:200–236. On the image of the witch and witchcraft in standard Babylonian literature, see Abusch 1989, 2002, 2008; Abusch and van der Toorn 1999; Abusch and Schwemer 2011; Farber 1995; Cryer and Thomsen 2001:56–90.

15. Douglas 1970b:xxvi–xxvii; Spooner 1976a, 1976b; Reminick 1976:96–100; Garrison and Arensberg 1976:319–24; Murdock 1980:49, Table 3, pp. 50–51, 57–63. On witchcraft societies as the matrix of Evil Eye belief, see also Vol. 3, chap. 2.

16. Budge 1978/1930: 82; for illustrations of Babylonian and Assyrian amulets, see Budge 1978/1930:82–126, 283–90. Plate XI (page 89) shows a cylinder-seal dated, with a representation of a row of horned animals with an eye above them (British Museum, no. 1073900). Dated prior to 2500 BCE, this seal shows the great antiquity of the eye in general as "symbol of divine protection" (Budge 1978/1930: 91). On Assyrian-Babylonian amulets, see also Thompson 1903–1904, 1910.

17. "Incantation" and "chant" derive from the Latin *cantare*, "to sing"; "charm" derives from *carmen*, "song." On incantations in general, see Bourghouts 1978; Ludwig 1989; Scurlock 2002.

tion about personal health and fortune in the present and future, the health of the king, outcomes of battles, the quality of the harvest, weather conditions, and similar practical concerns. To shape the course of events in their daily lives and afford themselves protection from evil forces, including the Evil Eye, they employed, among other things, curses and blessings, incantations and prayers, sure of their intended effect.

This belief in, and dread of, an eye that causes injury and disaster is consistent with Sumerian production of "eye idols" and the apparent worship of a goddess of childbirth and protector of the newborn. An excavation (1937–1938) at the ancient Mesopotamian site at Tell Brak, Syria, in the Khabur valley (fourth millennium BCE) found remains of an "Eye Temple" in which were thousands of "eye idols" (thin-bodied figures surmounted by pairs of eyes).[18] The best supported theory associates these eye idols with the worship of the goddess Ninhursag, Sumerian goddess of childbirth.[19] These eye idols and the worship of the protecting goddess of childbirth were likely linked to Evil Eye belief, since newborns, infants and birthing mothers have been deemed especially vulnerable to the Evil Eye in all Evil Eye cultures.[20] Traces of these eye symbols from c. 3000 BCE have subsequently been found in numerous regions of the ancient Circum-Mediterranean and beyond. Prophylactic eyes also have been found in profusion in the tombs of the kings of Ur.

In the Assyrian and later periods, stones were engraved with protective eyes and used as votives.[21] O. G. S. Crawford (1957) examined ancient engravings of circles on stone and interpreted these as eyes attesting to an ancient fertility cult associated with an "eye goddess" or "face-goddess." This cult, he suggests, originated in the Fertile Crescent during the third millennium BCE and then spread, over time, to Anatolia, Thessaly, Italy, Sicily and Malta, Iberia, Brittany, Ireland, Britain, Africa, the Canary Islands, and southern Ethiopia. He makes brief mention of belief in the Evil Eye as a development and modern survival of this cult.[22] Left unexplained, however,

18. See Mallowan 1947:198–210, 1965.

19. See Mallowan 1947, 1965; Potts 1982:2, fig. 1; Brandon 1983:888 for illustrations of these eye idols (1983:888–889). An eye idol statuette is in the National Museum, Aleppo, Syria. For illustrations of the Tell Brak idols (British Museum) see *ISBE* 2 (1982):249 (British Museum) and Di Stasio 1981:95, who also presents an illustration of eyes on a Sumerian seal-impression of the third millennium BCE (Oriental Institute, the University of Chicago).

20. On the perceived dangers surrounding childbirth, babies, and mothers, see Scurlock 1991.

21. See Contenau 1947:242–45; Deonna 1965:98–99 and notes 3–4; and Mallowan 1965.

22. See especially Crawford 1957:139–42; see also Mallowan 1965.

is how fertility was associated with the eye or why the eye should symbolize a fertility goddess.[23] Likewise unclear is whether the circles unquestionably depict eyes and if so, how they are connected with Evil Eye belief and practice in particular. A counter proposal holds that the circles represent not eyes but breasts, symbols of fertility. Pierre Gravel pursues these questions in his 1994 analysis of the connection of eye and fertility to the Evil Eye belief.[24]

Evil Eye Texts

Incantations mentioning the Evil Eye provide the chief source of explicit evidence of Evil Eye belief and practice in ancient Mesopotamia. Graham Cunningham (1997) lists 448 Mesopotamian incantations dating from 2500–1500 BCE. There are sixteen from about 2500 BCE. Most are from the Old Babylonian period (1830–1530 BCE), with 236 in Sumerian and 92 in Akkadian coming mostly from Nippur. Akkadian textbooks of the *Šurpu* and *Maqlū* contained incantations and prayers employed by knowledgeable priests for the relief of persons suffering illness from known and unknown causes. Both Sumerian and Akkadian incantations were directed against dangerous things such as snakes, scorpions, dogs, flies, the evil *udug*, the *galla* ("demon"), illnesses of various kinds (affecting the eye, bile, heart, lung), against the child-killing demoness Lamashtu, witchcraft, and evil demons causing illness.[25] They also concern matters relating to the health of the king, pregnancy and birth, protection of mother and newborn, and the relief of agricultural problems.[26] Among the causes of illness mentioned are flies, worms, witches, warlocks, other demons, hostile humans, and the Evil Eye.[27]

Later Babylonian healing incantations from this region (1830–1530 BCE) generally invoked the assistance of the great gods, named the spirit or demon to be controlled, and then with an exorcism formula ordered the demon to leave the afflicted person. Earlier Sumerian and Sumero-Akkadian incantations mentioning the Evil Eye did not yet follow this threefold

23. On an eye divinity, see also Van Buren 1955.

24. On eye symbolism in Mesopotamia (and Israel), including the Evil Eye, see Seawright 1988; see also Potts 1982.

25. On demons and spirits, see Tamborino 1909; Thompson 1903–1904; Gordon 1957; Colpe 1976; Abusch 1989. On the baby-snatching and child-killing demoness, see also Scurlock 1991; van der Toorn 1999.

26. Cunningham 1997:162–65.

27. Ibid., 177. On the Evil eye causing illness, see Black et al. 1992:63, 67.

pattern but did explicitly name the Evil Eye. In the bilingual Sumero-Akkadian texts mentioning the Evil Eye, Sumerian *igi-ḫul* ("Evil Eye," *igi* = "eye," *ḫul* ="evil") was rendered in Akkadian as *īni limuttum* or *īnu lemuttu* ("Evil Eye").[28] The Ugaritic equivalent of Akkadian *īni* or *īnu* ("eye") is *'nn* ("eye"). "Eye" without the attribute in these languages could also imply "Evil Eye," as also in Hebrew (*'ayin*), Mandaic (*aina*), and Arabic (*'ayn*).[29]

Explicit mention of the Evil Eye appears "as early as the pre-Sargonic period" (2500–2350 BCE) according to Cunningham,[30] who cites as an example a line from the *Instructions of Suruppak (ED)* vii 4':[31] "With your eyes (*igi*), do not do evil x." However, "no incantations directed against it are attested until the Old Babylonian period."[32] He lists four Sumerian texts from this period (1830–c. 1530 BCE): Nos. 149 (BL 3; Thomsen 1992, no.5), 184 (TCL 16, 89; Thomson 1991, No. 4 = AO 8895 [Ebeling 1949:206–208]), 289 (YOS 11 70 i 1'-14'; Thomsen 1991, No. 1), 290 (290a =YOS 11 70 i 15'-23'; 290b = YOS 11 71; Thomsen 1992, nos. 2B, 2A); 291 (YOS 11 70 i 24'-ii 7'; Thomsen 1992, no. 3). Sumerian texts 289, 290A, 290B, 291 are in YOS 11 (Old Babylonian era, 1830–c. 1530). There is, in addition,[33] an Akkadian text from Susa from the Sargonic period (2350–2150 BCE) describing a ritual against the Evil Eye (MDP 14, 90).[34] "This ritual involves transferring the Evil Eye's damaging effect to a sheep as a neutral carrier; the sheep and its evil are then destroyed. Further instances of such transfer are provided in Old Babylonian incantations, with one Sumerian incantation, for example, referring to the transfer of the Evil Eye's effect to animal hair, and another to the transfer of illness to a goat."[35]

Seven Mesopotamian incantations mentioning the Evil Eye are listed by Marie-Louise Thomsen (1992:20–22): *five Sumerian incantations* (YOS 11,70 I 1'-14'; YOS 11,70 I 15'-23'= YOS 11,71; YOS 11, 70 I 24'-II 6'; TCL

---

28. Budge 1978/1930:358; Ford 1998:205 and passim.

29. Ford 1998:205. For the Sumerian, Geller (2004:52) prefers the rendition "evil face" to Evil Eye," but the frequent references to "looking" make "Evil Eye" more apt.

30. Cunningham 1997:59, 177.

31. Following Civil 1984:282.

32. Cunningham 1997:59.

33. See ibid., 59.

34. Translated by Foster 1993:55 (I.3); 3rd ed., 2005:65 (I.4b).

35. Cunningham 1997:172. On a Sumerian text mentioning healing of the effect of an Evil Eye with a mixture of oil and water, see Ebeling 1949:209 (Langdon, BL 3); for the use of incense for the same purpose see Thomsen 1992:29; compare the later Greek ritual given in Heliodorus, *Aeth.* 4.5.3–4. On analogous healing procedures in modern time, see, for Greece, Arnaud 1912:511–14; Schmidt 1913:603–5; Hardie 1923; Campbell 1964:339; Blum and Blum 1970:145–47; for Italy: Brögger 1968:15–17.

16, 89);[36] BL 3, 3–9, partly a duplicate of TCL 16, 89;[37] *a bilingual Sumerian-Akkadian incantation* 17, pl. 33 = STT 179 = BM 54626.[38] And an *Akkadian incantation* (VAT 10018 = CT 17;[39] but see also VAT 13683).[40] To this list Thomsen adds five further passing references to the Evil Eye in other incantations and rituals, which include references to its destroying a child[41] and its mention together with an evil face, evil mouth, evil tongue, evil lips, and evil spittle.[42] To Thomsen's list can now be added the important Ugaritic incantation against the Evil Eye, KTU[2] 1.96, presented and discussed extensively by J. N. Ford.[43] These various texts display noticeable similarities in motifs and themes. Ford comments extensively on these similarities as well as on their commonalities with texts in other languages and periods. Our consideration of these texts will follow a rough chronological sequence, interrupted occasionally by texts of later periods illustrating similar wording or motifs.

One Sumerian anti-Evil Eye incantation (c. 1830–1530 BCE) reads:

1. The eye is a single ox, the eye is a (single) sheep,
2. the eye is numerous men, the mouth is numerous men,
3. the Eye is Evil, the most evil thing.
4. Asarluhi saw this,
5. he went to his father Enki in the temple
6. (and) he spoke (thus) to him:
7. "My father, the eye is a single ox, the eye is a single sheep!"
8. A second time he spoke:
9. "What I shall do I do not know, what can cure him?"
10–11. Enki answered his son Asarluhi:
12. "My son, what do you not know? What can I add?
13. "My son, what do you not know? What can I add?
14. What I know, you also know.
15. Go my son, black wool and white wool
16. bind around his head."
17. The Evil Eye of the evil-doing man
18. may it be slaughtered like an ox!

---

36. Ebeling 1949:206–7.
37. Ibid., 208–9.
38. See Pinches 1901:200.
39. Ebeling 1949:203–5; Geller 2004.
40. Ebeling 1949:209–11.
41. Thomsen 1992:21, no. 9
42. Ibid., 21–22, nos. 10–12.
43. Ford, "KTU[2] 1.96," 1998: 201–78.

It is an incantation against the evil eye.

(YOS 11,71 = YOS 11,70 I:15'–23')[44]

Here the Evil Eye is declared to be "the most evil thing" (line 3) and is compared with an ox and a sheep targeted for slaughter (lines 1, 7, 18).[45] It is also depicted, like a mouth, as an attribute of a man (line 17) or numerous men (line 2). Eye and mouth are juxtaposed (line 2). It has been noted that Akkadian texts connect an Evil Eye and an evil mouth.[46] Later Latin writers similarly relate Evil Eye (*malus oculus/fascinatio*) and evil tongue (*mala lingua*).[47] The wisdom Enki passes on to his son, Asarluhi (lines 4–14), involves a remedy for curing a victim made ill by the Evil Eye—binding his head with black and white wool (lines 15–16). The incantation concludes with the statement that it is an evil-doing man that possesses (and casts) an Evil Eye, and it ends with the wish that this Evil Eye be slaughtered like an ox (line 18).

One of the earliest Akkadian Evil Eye texts on record dates from the Archaic Sargonic period (2300–1850 BCE). Though less descriptive of the Evil Eye itself, it details a ritual for expelling the noxious Evil Eye from the dwelling of a man afflicted by the Evil Eye:

> One black virgin ewe: In (each of) the corners of the house he will lift it up(?). He will drive out the Evil Eye and the [ ] . . . In the garden he will slaughter it and flay its hide. He proceeds to fill it with pieces of . . .-plant. As he fills it, he should watch. The evil man [ ] his skin. Let [him] ca[rry (it) to the river], (and) seven (pieces of) date palm, seven (pieces of) oak, and seven (pieces of . . .) let him submerge. (MDP 14, 90: 1–8)[48]

A parallel to these anti-Evil Eye texts with rituals is an anti-Evil Eye purgative ritual involving a libation of beer, prayer, a threefold repetition, and an incense burner. The ritual is to insure that "the Evil Eye shall not

44. Transliteration and translation by Thomsen 1992:30.

45. On the other hand, the mention of ox and sheep in other incantations as *victims* of the Evil Eye (TCL 16, 89:5 [Thomsen 1992:23; Ford 1998:258]; VAT 10018:9 [cf. Ebeling 1949:204; Thomsen 1992:24; Ford 1998:258]; IM 90648:5 [Cavigneaux and Al-Rawi 1994:85; Ford 1998:258]; and a Mandaic text [Drower 1937:594, lines 8–12]) might suggest that here too ox and sheep and numerous men are the stated victims of the Eye.

46. See Lenormant 1878:40; Thomsen 1992: 21.

47. See Catullus 7.12 (*mala fascinare lingua*); Virgil, *Eclogues* 7.28. It is possible that this connection of speaking and looking is implied as well in the standard Greek word family for Evil Eye, namely *baskainô* and paronyms; see Vol. 2.

48. Translation by B. R. Foster 2005:65 [1993:55]; see also Thomsen 1992:22 n. 12.

(approach) the man" (BAM 374 obverse, 3–8).[49] In another ritual (CT 17, 33:11–14) Enki cures the person afflicted by the Evil Eye by wiping his body with bread. To keep the Evil Eye at bay, the seed of the allumzu plant and juniper oil were prescribed (BAM 1, 60).[50] The thought that the Evil Eye is the worst of evils reappears centuries later in the Greek Bible (Sir 31:13).

From the Old Babylonian Period also comes a Sumerian "Lamentation over Sumer and Urim" (c. 1925 BCE) tracing the fall of the cities to the potent Evil Eye of Enlil, the chief Sumerian deity. Lord of the Storm, and "the shepherd of the black-headed people," Enlil, in an act of destruction of the loyal households, "put the Evil Eye on the sons of the loyal men, on the first-born," and "sent down Gutium from the mountains."[51] The attribution of an Evil Eye to the gods recurs in early Greek texts,[52] but finds no parallel in the biblical writings.

Further incantations from the Old Babylonian/Classical Period (1830–1530 BCE) reveal additional aspects of the belief. An Akkadian incantation from this period describes the threat of the Evil Eye to infants and mothers in childbirth and the damage it causes when breaking into a home:

> It [the Evil Eye, *īnum*] has broken in, it is [looking] everywhere!
> It is an enmeshing net, a closing bird snare.
> It went by the babies' doorways and caused havoc among the babies,
> It went by the door of mothers in childbirth and strangled their babies
> Then it went into the jar room and smashed the seal,
> It demolished the secluded stove,
> It turned the locked (?) house into a shambles.
> It even struck the chapel, the god of the house has gone out of it.
> Slap it in the face! Make it turn around!
> Fill its eyes with salt! Fill its mouth with ashes!
> May the god of the house return! (BM 122691)[53]

The Evil Eye is spoken of here as an independent entity (with face, eyes, and mouth) invading homes, threatening pregnant women, strangling babies, and demolishing the contents of the house and its shrine (whose god was

49. Text cited in Thomsen 1992:27. For further remedies, see also YOS 11,70 II 3–7 15–25 = YOS 11, 71 (Thomsen 1992:31) and texts listed in Thomsen 1992:21–22, nos. 8–12.

50. See Thomsen 1992:27.

51. Kramer 1969.

52. See Vol. 2,

53. Translation by Foster 2005:176, II.22b. See also Farber 1981, esp. 62; transliteration and translation in Ford 1998:205–6.

absent). The vulnerability of babies and pregnant mothers to the Evil Eye is a particularly recurrent theme in the incantations and Evil Eye texts across the centuries.[54] Karel van der Toorn identifies the "god of the house" with the dead ancestors who are driven from the house by the constant crying of babies, or by the demoness Lamashtu and her Evil Eye, or both. The function of lullabies was to still this crying, repel the Evil Eye, and thereby protect the family.[55] An incantation of E-NU-RU[56] addresses the demoness Lamashtu and speaks of the demoness "casting eyes on the body of a man . . . on the hand of a man, on the foot of a man."[57] A ritual concerning Lamashtu mentions blue and red cords that bind her,[58] the same colors used in later practice to ward off the Evil Eye.[59]

Nathan Wasserman suggests that the mention of "eye" (igi) in an Old Babylonian incantation from Sippar, S 2/532 (= IM 90648), implies more specifically the Evil Eye of the demoness Lamashtu.[60] Ford also allows that the reference to the Evil Eye in BM 122691 may pertain to the demoness Lamashtu.[61] The conclusion of BM 122691 calls for a counter-attack with a slap of the face, salt in the eyes, and ashes in the mouth, along with the desire that it turn back on its possessor and that the god of the household come back to protect the home. Salt and ashes would dry up the Evil Eye and cause it to wither, precisely the same damage it was thought to cause its living victims. This would be consistent with the wish that it "turn around" and harm itself, a motif that reappears in the Greek and Latin apotropaic inscriptions "back to you" (kai sy and et tibi respectively).[62]

A bilingual Sumerian-Akkadian incantation from this same Old Babylonian Period (1830–1530 BCE) mentions the blurred eyes of Evil Eye possessors caused by a demon, the Eye's roaming about, the domestic havoc caused, the Evil Eye as cause of illness and harm, and the remedy for curing it:

54. See Ford 199:209–10 n. 22, referring to Mandaic and Arab traditions centuries later; for Mesopotamian incantations, see Farber 1981; 1984; and 1989.

55. Van der Toorn 1998. The entire volume in which his essay is contained (Abusch and van der Toorn 1998) is rich in relevant information. On Lamashtu and newborns in general see Wiggermann 2000.

56. Langdon 1919:13.

57. Text in Contenau 1947:184–85, citing Langdon 1919:13.

58. Contenau 1947:181.

59. See Vol. 2.

60. Wasserman 1995.

61. Ford 1998:210 n. 22.

62. Ford, 1998:248–51, lists numerous texts with this "return" theme. On kai sy and et tibi as Evil Eye motifs, see Vol. 2.

1b. [Blurred (eyes)] (*dalhu, dalhati*) which bind, (they are) an *alû*-demon which envelops a man;

2b. Blurred (eyes) which bind,

3b. They are (eyes) which ensnare (the inhabitants of) the land,

4b. They are (eyes) which cause people illness.

5b. The roaming Evil Eye

6b. It looked into the outer corner (of the house) and desolated the outer corner,

7b. It looked into the inner corner (of the house) and desolated the inner corner,

8b. It looked into the living quarters of (the inhabitants of) the land,

10. It looked upon the roaming man, so that he incessantly bent his neck (in submission) like a cut (and) broken tree.

11. Enki saw this man,

12. placed bread on his (the patient's) head

13. approached bread to his body

14. prayed for him the prayer of life.

25. The Eye (*igi*, Sumerian; *īni*, Akkadian) which looked at you to cause suffering

26. The Eye (*igi*, *īni*) which looked at you to cause evil.[63]
   (CT 17, 33=STT 179 = BM 54626)

Mention of defective eyes as a telltale feature of the Evil Eye occurs in other sources as well.[64] Ford cites several texts in different languages and from different periods of time.[65] These blurred Evil Eyes are traced to a demon that envelops humans (line 1); they bind, ensnare, and cause illness (lines 2–4). On the prowl, the roaming Evil Eye destroys with a look both residences and the human inhabitants (lines 5–10, 25–26). To heal one injured by the Evil Eye, bread was applied to the body and prayer was offered.

A Sumerian incantation from the Old Babylonian Period (1830–1530 BCE) gives a more extensive list of *targets and damages*:

1. The eye (is) a dragon, the eye of the man (is) a dragon,

2. the eye of the evil man (*igi lu-níg-ḫul-d[ím]-ma*) (is) a dragon.

3. It (sc. the Evil Eye) approached heaven—it did not rain.

63. Pinches 1901:200. Transliteration of the Sumerian and Akkadian versions of the text and translation of the Akkadian in Ford 1998:203–4 (lines 1–4, 5–8, 10; cf. 1998:261; translation of the Akkadian lines 11–14 in Thomsen 1992:26–27; translation of lines 25–26 in Ford 1998:220. Cf. also Cavigneaux and Al-Rawi 1993:195–205.

64. For example, TCL 16, 89; BAM 514 III.

65. Ford 1998:261–68.

4. It approached earth—herbs did not grow,

5. It approached the ox—its yoke opened,

6. It approached the cattle pen—its cheese was destroyed,

7. . . . .

8. it approached the young man—(his) belt was torn (?),

9. it approached the young woman—she dropped her garment,

10. it approached the nurse with child—her hold became loose,

11. It approached the vegetables—lettuce and cress became bad.

12. It approached the garden—the fruits became bad.

13. The eye of the mountain came out of the mountain,

14. the wild ram lets its shining horns come out.

15. May the Evil Eye (like?) the sick eye be cut off,

16. may it be split open like a leather bag

17. may it go to pieces (like) the potter's *pursītu*-pot on the market place.

18. While standing, while standing,

19. while standing at the mouth (entrance?) of the street,

20. it opposes the young man who has no personal god.

21. Let the eye turn into a wind,

22. Asar in Abzu

23. may he not undo it![66]

(TCL 16, 89)

According to this incantation, the range of the Evil Eye extends from earth to heaven (lines 3–4). It ruins crops (line 4), and an ox yoke (line 5), milk/cheese (line 6), a young man's belt (line 8), and causes a young woman's shame (from losing her garment); it endangers an infant in a nurse's care (line 10), ruin vegetables and fruits of the garden (lines 11, 12). It iself, however, is vulnerable to the power of the curse and attack. It can be overcome (lines 15–17). It is equated with or compared to a sick eye (15), with the wish that it be cut off (15), split open (16) and smashed to piece (17), and turned into a wind (21). It attacks a young man who has no personal god (20).

Erich Ebeling's translation of lines 21–23[67] makes good sense and is consistent both with lines 15–17 and similar attacks on, or containment of, the Evil Eye in other texts and amulets:

21. wie das Auge eines Hundes möge es (zer) schlagen werden,

66. Transliteration and translation in Thomsen 1992:31–32 (= Cunningham 1997, Text 184); cf. also Ford 1998:243, 258, 260.

67. Ebeling 1949:207.

22. Asari lasse es die Torleibung (?!)
23 nicht überschreiten!

21. May it be battered like the eye of a dog.
22. May Asari keep it from
23. crossing the threshold!

In this rendition, the wish is that the Evil Eye be shattered like the eye of a dog (21) and that Asari keep it from crossing the door threshold or inner part of the door entrance.[68] This is consistent with the use of apotropaic items in the third and second millennia to protect temples, palaces, and private houses.[69] This practice continued and spread in later time, with much evidence from Roman antiquity.[70] A Middle Eastern example from the seventh century BCE is a Phoenician plaque once attached to the entrance to a house and reading:

> Flee, O "Eyer" (with the Evil Eye), from (my) house,
>
> From (my) head, O "Consumer of Eyes,"
>
> From the head of the dreamer when he dreams;
>
> Let his eye see perfectly!

This charm is from the scroll of the Enchanter.[71]

Many apotropaics located at doors and thresholds are designs intended to ward off the Evil Eye, similar to the *fascinum* at the door entrances of Pompeii and Ostia Antica.[72] This Phoenician sample is accompanied by a command directing the Evil Eye to "beat it," "scram," not only from the domestic premises but also from the speaker's own head, dreams, and thoughts. This expression also is found in numerous Greek and Roman samples.[73]

Another Sumerian Babylonian incantation strikingly similar to the preceding one also mentions the devastation caused by the Evil Eye: prevention of rain, damage of domestic animals and milk, and injury to young men and women. It also includes a remedy for relieving a man sick from the Evil Eye.

68. Ibid., 208.
69. See the study of Braun-Holzinger 1999.
70. See Vol. 2.
71. From Arslan Tash, Syria; see Cross 1974:489; Beyerlin 1978:249–50.
72. See Vol. 2, on *fascina*.
73. See Vol. 2.

1. The eye *ad-gir,* the eye a man has . . .

2. The eye afflicting man with evil, the *ad-gir.*

3. Unto heaven it approached and the storm sent no rain; unto earth it approached and the fresh verdure sprang not forth.

4. Unto the oxen it approached, and their herdsman was undone.

5. Unto the stalls it approached, and milk was no longer plentiful.

6. Unto the sheepfolds it approached, and its production . . .

7. Unto homes (of men) it approached, and vigor of men it restrained.

8. Unto the maiden it approached, and seized away her robes.

9. Unto the strong man . . . severed

10. Marduk beheld it.

11. What I know, thou also knowest.

12. Seven vases of meal-water behind the . . .

13. Seven vases of meal-water behind the grinding stones.

14. With oil mix.

15. Upon his face apply.

16. As thou sayest the curse,

17. (Thy) neck toward the sick man raise.

18. May the queen who gives life to the dead purge him.

19. . . . .

20. May Gunura her boat . . . .

21. Curse. Incantation of the house of light.[74]

The Evil Eye is envisioned here as an eye possessed by a human and causing evil to other humans (lines 1–2). At the same time, the Evil Eye is depicted as an independent roving entity, akin to a demon, impairing nature (blocking rain from heaven and fresh growth from the earth, line 3) or attacking domestic animals (oxen, sheep, and milk production, probably of goats, lines 4–6), homes and their inhabitants (a male whose sexual vigor is restrained, a maiden who perhaps was violated and shamed, a strong man from whom something was severed, lines 7–9). The god Marduk witnessed it (line 10), and other deities are invoked (lines 18, 20). Line eleven refers either to the speaker recounting the event to others, or to the following remedy of an illness caused by the Evil Eye (lines 12–20). The cure involves

74. Text and translation in Langdon 1913:11–12, Plate no. 3; reprinted as in Langdon 1992:39–40. Ebeling 1949:208–9 presents a transliterated text and a variant translation. Ebeling also noted parallels between lines 1–2, 7, 8, 9 and Louvre Museum AO 8895 = TCL 16, 89 and between lines 18–20 and the bilingual incantation CT 17, 33. For a new copy and edition see also Geller 2003.

meal-water mixed with oil, which is applied to face of the sufferer (lines 12–15) while accompanied with a curse (line 16). The entire text is identified as both an incantation and a curse (line 21).

Erich Ebeling renders lines 1–2 as:

> 1. Auge (in Gestalt einer) böse(n) Schlange, Auges des Menschen
> (in Gestalt einer) böse(n) Schlange
> 2. Auge des Bösegewichtes,
> (in Gestalt einer) böse(n) Schlange.

> 1. Eye (in the form of) an evil serpent, Eye of a man
> (in the form of) an evil serpent
> 2. Eye of an Evil-doer
> (in the form of) an evil serpent.[75]

On this reading, there is an association of Evil Eye and serpent, similar to the identification of the Evil Eye as a dragon in the preceding incantation. Serpents as well as demons are attested as causes of illness in the incantations from the pre-Sargonic period onward. Jewish and Christian amulets of the post-biblical period may reflect an echo of this motif in their depicting cavaliers on horses piercing with their lances both dragons and Evil Eyes.

Ebeling (1949:209) renders lines 17–21 as:

> 17. binde an den Hals des Kranken (sie?) an.
> 18. Nintinugga, reinige (?) das Rohr!
> 19. Damu möge (das böse Auge) mit der Doppelaxt zerschlagen,
> 20. Gusirra möge mit dem Pfahl es beseitigen(?)!
> 21. *é-nu-ru*-Beschwörung

> 17. bind (it?) to the neck of the sick person
> 18. Nintinugga, purify (?) the channel!
> 19. May Damu slaughter (the Evil Eye) with the double ax,
> 20. May Gusirra dispatch it with a stake/lance.
> 21. *é-nu-ru*-Curse.[76]

On this reading, something is bound to the neck of the sick person (for curing the illness caused by the Evil Eye?) (line 17). Lines 19–20 call on deities to attack and slay the Evil Eye with double-ax and a stake or lance. Numerous parallels to these sentiments occur in later Evil Eye amulets of

---

75. Ebeling 1949:208. See also the duplicate in Louvre Museum AO 8895, lines 1–2 = TCL 16, 89: 1–2 (Genouillac 1930, Pl. 159.).

76. Ebeling 1949:209.

the Roman period (first–sixth cents. CE) where amulets are worn around the neck to repel the Evil Eye and where amuletic images abound of an Evil Eye attacked by animals or an Evil Eye (demoness) lanced by a rider (cavalier) on horseback.[77]

A Ugaritic incantation[78] from the site of Ras Shamra on the Syrian coast (c. 1400–1200 BCE) is the focus of an excellent extensive analysis by James Nathan Ford.[79] Ford notes the influence of the Mesopotamian features of the Evil Eye belief and its several salient features, including the "return" motif, on later Evil Eye texts and amulets:

1. The Eye (*'nn*), it roamed and darted;

2. It saw its "brother"—*how* lovely (he was)!

2b, 3 its "brother"—*how* very seemly!

3b, 4. Without a knife it devoured his flesh,

4b, 5. without a cup it guzzled his blood;

5b, 6. (It was) the eye (*'n*) of an *evil* man (that) saw him,

6b. the eye (*'n*) of an *evil* woman;

6b, 7. (It was) the eye (*'n*) of a *merchant* (that) saw him,

7b. the eye (*'n*) of a potter,

8. the eye (*'n*) of a gatekeeper.

8b, 9. May the eye (*'n*) of a gatekeeper return to the gatekeeper!

9b, 10. may the eye (*'n*) of the potter return to the potter!

10b, 11. may the eye (*'n*) of the *merchant* return to the *merchant*!

11b, 12. may the eye (*'n*) of the *evil* man return to the *evil* man!

12b, 13. may the eye (*'n*) of the [evil woman] re[turn] to the *evil* woman!

14. [Incantation against the (evil) eye.] (*mnt 'n*)
(KTU² 1.96 [= RS 22.225 = CAT 1.96 = UDB 1.96])[80]

77. See Vol. 4.

78. Ugaritic is a West Semitic language written in alphabetic cuneiform. It is consonantal, with each character reproducing a sound (of a consonant, but not vowels) and also written in cuneiform on clay tablets.

79. Ford 1998; see also Ford 2000 for additions and corrections.

80. Transliteration and translation in Ford 1998:202, with his italicizations. Virolleaud 1960 is the first publication of this text. Del Olmo Lete 1992a was the first to establish that this incantation was about the Evil Eye and not the goddess Anat; he was followed by Ford 1998 and others. See also del Olmo Lete 1992b:255–59 and 1999:379–84 (both summarizing 1992a), and 2010. Del Olmo Lete's latest rendition (2010:52) is closely similar to that of Ford given here, rendering *'nn. hlkt*, line 1, as "restless Eye." Compare the transliteration and divergent translation of CAT 1.96 in Parker 1997:225–28 [trans. by Mark S. Smith], which offers a less plausible translation.

The "Eye" of line one (*'nn*)[81] stands as a synecdoche for the entire Evil-Eyed person, as lines 2–12 make clear. This same *pars pro toto* usage appears in other Mesopotamian incantations and also in later biblical Evil Eye texts as well (Prov 23:6 [HT]; Sir 14:10). The Evil Eye/Evil-Eyed person can strike not only external enemies but also a "brother," a member of one's own social group.[82] This is a theme[83] also found in Greek and Roman sources[84] and numerous biblical Evil Eye texts (Deut 15:7–11; 28:54–57; Sir 14:8; Tob 4:5–19; Matt 6:22–23/Luke 11:34–35; Matt 20:1–15). The "loveliness" of the brother is thought to attract the attention of the Evil Eye (lines 2–3). This notion that beauty and handsomeness arouse an Evil Eye remains for centuries a regular feature of the Evil Eye belief complex.[85] The damage caused by the Evil Eye here is gruesome: the devouring of a neighbor's flesh and blood. Deuteronomy 28:54–57 presents an equally gruesome biblical scenario involving the devouring of placenta by the Evil-Eyed husband and Evil-Eyed wife.[86] The motif appears millennia later in an eighteenth-century Ethiopian incantation and prayer concerning the *'ainat*, the demonized Evil Eye: "Depart, *'ainat* . . . God drive you away, accursed one, who devours flesh and drink blood. . . . Go away and never return."[87] The danger to family and friends posed by the Evil Eye, its roaming about and "devouring" action, the types of its possessors, and the wish that the Eye *turn back against its malicious possessor* are all themes and motifs found in other Sumerian, Akkadian, and bilingual incantations as well (e.g., VAT 10018:1–21; CT 17, 33). This incantation, Ford observes, "aims at neutralizing the evil through a process of *reversal*" and thus appropriately ends with an expression in which the term referring to the evil doer (*btt*) is literally reversed, letter by letter,

The excellent study of Ford 1998 is the most comprehensive and instructive analysis of this incantation to date, with del Olmo Lete 2010 offering a generally positive response. On this text see also Pardee 2002:161–66; Wyatt 2002 (and p. 375 for further literature).

81. The Ugaritic for Evil Eye (*'nn*) is the equivalent of Akkadian *īni lemmuttu* and Sumerian *igi ḫul*.

82. This "brother" is not "the other eye of the [ocular] pair" (against Wyatt 2002:375–376) but, as Pardee notes, the target and victim of the one casting the Evil Eye (Pardee 2002:164, n. 13).

83. On the Evil Eye as a hypostasis, see Hamp 2000:15–19.

84. See Vol. 2.

85. For ancient Hebrew, Mandaic, and Arabic parallels, see Ford 1998:222–28; for modern instances see several of the essays in Maloney 1976 and Dundes 1992. See also Vols. 2 and 4.

86. See Vol. 3, chap. 1 on Deut 28:54–57. For the motif in later Aramaic incantations, see Ford 1998:232.

87. The author's translation of text in Ford 1998:233, citing Worrell 1914/1915:95–96 (German).

into the verb 'return' (*ttb*)."[88] "The same technique of sending the evil eye back to its 'master,'" Ford notes, "is used in the Akkadian incantation against the evil eye IM 90648, which, following commands to banish the evil eye, ends with the injunction (line 20): . . . 'May the (Evil) Eye return to [its] master!'"[89] A parallel appears centuries later in an Arabic book of magic, *Kitab Mujarobat*:

> O God, send back the eye of the caster of the evil eye upon him, and upon his closest relations(s), and into his possessions, and his children, and the person(s) dearest to him, and seize his (evil) word(s) from between his lips and his (evil) glance from between his eyelids, and send back, O God, his eye upon him.[90]

Further examples of this technique of exorcism and "return" counter-attack against the initiator of the evil are found in Akkadian, Egyptian texts and Aramaic incantations.[91] Later Greek and Latin equivalents of this command to "return to sender," as it were, occur in the Greek expression *kai sy* ("back to you," lit. "you also") and the Latin exact equivalent, *et tibi*.[92]

On the whole, the description here of features of an Evil Eye are akin to descriptions of demons elsewhere (e.g., roaming, eating of flesh, drinking of blood, causing illness and death).[93] Later Greek Evil Eye lore merges the two and speaks of a *baskanos daimôn*.

An Akkadian text (early first millennium BCE) mentions a roaming witch, who also injures with her Evil Eye:

> 1. The witch who roams the streets, . . .
>
> 8. As for the handsome man, she robbed him of his virility.
>
> 9. As for the beautiful maiden, she took away her attractiveness.
>
> 10. With her evil glare (*ina nekelmêša*), she took her sexual charm;
>
> 11. She looked upon (*ippalisma*) the young man and robbed him of his manliness;
>
> 12. She looked upon (*ippalisma*) the maiden and took away her attractiveness.
>
> (*Maqlū* III:1, 8–12)[94]

88. Ford 1998:251.

89. Ford 1998:248–49.

90. Translation by Ford 1998:249–51; cf. Qur'an, sura 67:3b-4. On this *Book of Magic*, see Romdon 2000.

91. Ford 1998:248–51.

92. On these Greek and Latin expressions, see Vol. 2.

93. See Ford 1998:230–32

94. Thomsen 1992:28; cf. Ford 1998:228–29. The *Maqlū* is an Akkadian incantation

In other incantations, it is the Evil Eye that roams (CT 17, 33; KTU² 1, 96; BM 122691); here it is the witch who "roams," who "looks," and has an "evil glare," stripping handsome young men of their virility and maidens of their attractiveness. Thus she is an Evil-Eyed witch on the prowl. Her victims, like those of the Evil Eye, are attractive persons in the prime of youth and sexual vigor. This link of Evil Eye and witch parallels lines of a Sumerian incantation from the Old Babylonian period: "May the evil *udug*, the evil *galla* [. . .] the evil man, the Evil Eye (*igi-ḫul*), the evil mouth, the evil tongued, the witch (and) the warlock stand aside" (YOS 11, 90).[95]

This link of Evil Eye and evil tongue will reappear in Greek and Latin texts and may be implied in the Greek root *bask-* (cf. *phask-*) which can designate both an Evil Eye and an Evil Tongue. Ford notes the similarity in the description of a witch and of an Evil Eye—both "roam," both are attracted by the beauty of young males and females, and both harm their victims by looking at them.[96] This illustrates the place of the Evil Eye belief in witchcraft societies in general and the close association of Evil Eye and witch in particular.

An Akkadian incantation from the Neo-Assyrian Period (911–609 BCE) provides a yet fuller account of the possessors of the Evil Eye, the damage it causes, and the remedy for destroying it.

1. . . . Eye (*e-nu*), eye (*e-nu*)! It is hostile,

2. It is eye of a woman, it is eye of a m[an],

3. it is [ey]e of an enemy, it is anyone's (?) eye,

4. it is eye of a neighbor, it is eye of a neighbor (woman), eye of a child minder (?), it is the eye!

5. O eye (*e-nu*), in evil purpose, you have called at the door,

6. The threshold shook, the beams quaked.

7. When you enter(ed) a house, O eye (*e-nu-um-ma*), [ ].

8. You smashed the potter's kiln, you scuttled the boatman's boat,

9. You broke the yoke of the mighty ox,

---

text (early first millennium BCE) that details the performance of a lengthy anti-witchcraft, or *kišpū*, ritual.

95. Cited in Cunningham 1997:104 as Text 307. The similar linking of Evil Eye and evil tongue/mouth appears in *Udug Hul*, Tablet 3, Text 1 (CT 16, 31) cited below, p. 101.

96. Ford 1998:228–29.

10. You broke the shin of the striding donkey,

11. You broke the loom of the expert weaver,

12. You deprived the striding horse of its foal (?) and the ox of its food (?)

13. You have scattered the . . . of the ignited stove,

14. You have left the livestock (?) to the maw of the murderous storm,

15. You have cast discord among harmonious brothers.

16. Smash the eye! Send the eye away!

17. Make the eye cross seven rivers,

18. Make the eye cross seven canals,

19. Make the eye cross seven mountains!

20. Take the eye (*enu*) and tie its feet to an isolated r[ee]d stalk,

21. Take the eye (*enu*) and smash it in its owner's face like a potter's vessel!

(*fragmentary lines, then breaks off*)

(VAT 10018:1–21)[97]

Lines 1–4 identify the eye as hostile, as the human eye of woman and man, enemy and neighbor, and of a child's nurse.[98] Lines 5–15 spell out the damages inflicted by the Evil Eye. The desired destruction of this Evil Eye and its owner is stated in lines 16–21.

The Evil Eye is depicted here as both an independent entity (note its "feet" in line 20) that can be addressed (lines 1, 5–21) and as the eye of a human (lines 2–4). Possessors of this hostile Evil Eye involve both genders, and, besides enemies, also neighbors and an infant's nurse—that is, members of one's intimate circle (lines 1–4) where it can also sew discord (line 15).[99] The Evil Eye is thought to attack the thresholds of domiciles and invade homes (lines 5–7, 13). It also attacks the means of one's livelihood such as pottery kiln, boat, loom and one's domestic animals (lines 8–12, 14). The

97. Translation according to Foster 2005:962, IV.35; cf. 1993:848. See also Ebeling 1949:203–4; Thomsen 1992:24; Geller 2003; 2004; cf. Ford 1998:259. Ebeling 1949:176, 204 notes that VAT 14226 offers a partial parallel.

98. Instead of "eye," "evil eye," Geller (2004:52; cf. also Geller 2003), expressing an independent view, takes Sumerian *igi ḫul* to mean "'evil face' in most instances in the Sumerian incantations, rather than 'evil eye.'" "Sumerian incantations," he observes, "are distinctive. While generally the 'evil eye' is either treated as an abstraction for 'envy' or 'jealousy,' or as a demon, in Sumerian incantations of this type, the '*igi ḫul*' appears as an hallucination of the patient's feelings of persecution and paranoia, personified as the face (*igi*) of an enemy" (Geller 2004:52 n. 2).

99. See also BM 122691:5.

incantation concludes with an imprecation that the Evil Eye by destroyed, removed, bound, and then turned back against its owner and smashed in his face (lines 16–21). Several of these features (varied possessors of the Evil Eye; threat to family members, homes and thresholds, domestic animals, and occupations; its "return to sender") remained conventional and stable features of such Evil Eye features and anti-Evil Eye incantations over the centuries. The elaboration of Evil-Eyed persons (fascinators) (lines 3–4), as Ford has stressed, also reappears in Evil Eye incantations of the post-biblical period.[100]

A bilingual Sumero-Akkadian exorcism incantation from Babylon (c. 911–612 BCE) explicitly equates the roving Evil Eye with a marauding demon that has brought trouble and sickness to the land and illness to the wanderer:

> The . . . which binds,
> a demon which envelops the person,
> the . . . bringing trouble, which binds,
> the . . . . . . upon the land,
> bringing sickness upon people,
> the roving Evil Eye has looked on the neighborhood
> and has vanished far away,
> has looked on the chamber of the land
> and has vanished far away,
> it has looked on the wanderer;
> and like wood cut off for poles,
> it has bent his neck.
> Ea has seen this person and
> has placed food at his head,
> has brought food near his body,
> has shown favor for his life—
> You, O man, son of his god,
> may the food which I have brought to your head—
> may the food with which I have made an atonement for your body
> assuage your sickness, and you be restored,
> that your foot may stand in the land of life;
> You, O man, son of his god,
> The Eye which has looked on you for harm,
> the Eye which has looked on you for evil,
> which in . . .
>
> . . . . . .

---

100. For post-biblical Christian texts (Ethiopean, Syriac) see Ford 1998:238–40 and Vol. 4, chap. 2; for a Hebrew-Aramaic amuletic text, see Ford 1998:214.

May Ba'u smite [it] with flax,
may Gunura [strike(?) it] with a great oar (?).
Like rain that falls from the sky
directed to the earth,
so may Ea, King of the Deep, remove it from your body.

(CT 17, 33 "Tablet of the Evil Eye")[101]

Marie-Louise Thomsen offers a more recent translation of lines 5–14:

5. The eye of an evil, restless (man) (Akkadian: evil, restless eye),

6. when it looks into the corner, it makes the corner empty,

7. when it looks at the side (of the house), it makes it empty,

8. when it looks at the living quarters of the land, it makes the living quarters of the land empty,

9–10. When it looks at the restless man, he bends his neck like a cut (and) broken tree.

11. Enki saw this man,

12. placed bread on his (the patient's) head,

13. approached bread to his body,

14. prayed for him the prayer of life.[102]

---

101. CT 17, 33 = STT 179 = BM 54626 (Pinches 1901: 200). Texts and translation by Thompson 1904 2:113–17 (Plate 33), adapted by K. C. Hanson.

102. Thomsen 1992:24 (transliteration and translation):

5. [igi níg.h]ul dím-ma pap.hal.la-ke$_4$:
i-ni le-mut-tu$_4$ mut-tal-lik-tu$_4$

6. [ub-šè ab]-ši-in-bar ub im-sud:
a-na túb-qa ip-pal-lis-ma túb-qí ú-ri-iq

7. [da-šè ab]-ši-in-bar da im-sud :
ana šá-hat ip-pal-lis-ma šá-hat ú-ri-iq

8. [ama/ama$_5$ kalam-ma-šè] ab-ši-in-bar ama(/ama$_5$) kalam im-sud:
ana maš-tak ma-a-tú ip-pal-lis-ma maš-tak ma-a-tú ú-ri-iq

9. [lú.u$_{18}$.lu] pap.ḫul.la-šè ab-ši-in-bar ĝis kud-kud-da-gin$_7$ gú ki-a im-mi-in-gam:

10. *ana a-me-lu mut-tal-li-ku ip-pal-lis-ma ki-ma iṣ-ṣi nak-su še-eb-ri ki-šad-su liq-ṭa-du-ud*

11. ^{d}En-ki lú-bi igi ù-bí-in-du$_8$:
^{d}IDIM LÚ *šùm-*(var. *šu-ma-)a-tim i-mur-ma*

12. ninda saĝ-ĝá-na mu-ni-in-ĝar:
a-ka-lu ina qaq-qa-di-šú iš-kun

13. ninda su-na mu-ni-in-te:
a-ka-lu ana SU-šú ú-ṭah-hi

14. šùd-dè nam.tìl-la-ke4 mu-un-na-an-šùd:
ik-ri-bi ba-la-ṭu i-kar-rab-šú

A restless Evil Eye (Evil-Eyed person) wreaks havoc on homes and living quarters and injures the restless wanderer. Restoration of the victim's body is sought through the offering of food and prayer and petition for the Evil Eye's defeat and removal.

An Old Babylonian Sumerian incantation linked a harmful Evil Eye with an "evil man" and his damaging "evil mouth" and "evil tongue." The injury brought about indicates the presumed association of eye and mouth/tongue, looking and speaking:

> 5 (29) The evil man, evil eye, evil mouth, and evil tongue, (30) the evil ... worked woe in him. (31) They roared at him from the mountain like wind in a porous pot. (32) The destructive acts bound the mouth, (33) and the spells through their evil seized the tongue."
>
> (*Udug Hul,* Tablet 3, Text 1, CT 16, 31).[103]

A subsequent Akkadian text expands on the foregoing Sumerian incantation and associates "spirit, evil eye, evil god" with an evil human who lurks like a venomous snake, threatening humans and livestock alike:

> He that is evil is evil
> That man is evil
> That man among men is evil.
> In the midst of mankind
> They have let (him) lurk (like) a snake;
> That man is set among men as a cord that is
> Stretched out for a net
> He hath sprinkled the man as with venom,
> The terror of him stifling his cries.
> Where his evil pain [hath smitten]
> It hath torn his heart . . .
> Spirit, evil eye (*igi ḫul*), evil god . . .
> Hunting the sheep fold . . .
> Hunting the cattle-pen . . .
> His side the man . . .
> Unto his heart Shamash . . . hath spoken
> By this (incantation) may Shamash remove his hand
> O my lord Ea! Thine is the power to brighten and bless!"

---

103. Transliterated text and translation in Thompson 1903 1:113–15. Compare Thomsen (1992:21–22) on CT 16, 31: 105–8 (= *Udug.hul.a.meë*): "Evil man, evil eye, evil mouth, evil tongue, evil spell, witchcraft, spittle, evil machinations, go out of the house!" See also Geller 1985, 2007.

(*Utukki Limnuti/Utukkū Lemnūtu*, Tablet XVI, "Prayer of the Hair of the Yellow Goat [and] the Kid")[104]

The Evil Eye of man and spirit and deity strikes terror and causes illness and pain. The aim of the incantation is, with the aid of the gods, to effect relief and release from its power.

Writing on Mesopotamian spells as words used to control nature and evil, Beatriz Barba de Piña Chán observes:

> Later Assyro-Babylonian translations [of earlier Mesopotamian sources] make it seem that one of the most crucial concerns of these peoples was the evil eye, the evil that surrounds men on all sides and affects them especially in the form of envy of enemies. One spell against the evil eye went as follows:
>
> > Let the finger point to the evil desires,
> > the word of ill omen.
> > Evil is the eye, the enemy eye,
> > eye of woman, eye of man,
> > eye of rival, anyone's eye.
> > Eye, you have nailed yourself to the door
> > And have made the doorsill tremble.
> > You have penetrated the house . . .
> > Destroy that eye! Drive out that eye!
> > Cast it off! Block its path!
> > Break the eye like an earthen bowl!"[105]

Possessors of the Evil Eye are mentioned and its presence at the door and threatened invasion of the home is indicated, along with an imprecation that it be destroyed, driven away, blocked and broken.

An Akkadian incantation from the *Maqlū* corpus of texts (*Maqlū* I 1–36)[106] illustrates a witchcraft accusation. The speaker, considering himself falsely accused by a deceitful woman, accuses her of being a witch who has ruined his reputation and health with her "bewitchments, enchantments and charms." From the gods of Anu he seeks release from her spell, her

104. Text and translation in Thompson 1903 1:113–15. The Neo-Assyrian *Utukki Limnuti/Utukkū Lemnūtu* in sixteen tablets (Akkadian) "Evil Spirits" series [CT 16] is an expansion of the Sumerian exorcism canon *Udug-hul.*

105. De Piña Chán 1989:220. The source given is J. Garcia Font, *El mundo de la magica* (Madrid, 1963), with no indication of the date of the spell. The text is another illustration of the elaboration of Evil Eye possessors and its attack on thresholds and domicles.

106. The *Maqlū* corpus of texts involves nearly one hundred Akkadian incantations from the early first millennium BCE prescribing lengthy anti-witchcraft, or *kišpū*, ritual.

punishment as a witch, and destruction of the organs (mouth and tongue) of her witchcraft.[107] An Akkadian exorcism incantation linking the Evil Eye, Evil Mouth, and Evil Tongue as among the demonic and human causes of plague, fever, and illnesses is cited by Siegfried Seligmann:

> The plague and fever that devastate the land,
> the epidemic, the consumption that lay waste the land,
> injurious to the body, upsetting the entrails,
> the evil demon, the evil alal, the evil gigim,
> the Evil-minded person, the Evil Eye, the Evil Mouth, the Evil Tongue—
> may they leave the body of this person, son of his god,
> may they leave his entrails.
> They will nevermore cling to my body;
> They will nevermore cause evil in my presence;
> They will nevermore strut among my entourage;
> They will nevermore enter my home;
> They will nevermore wander through my chambers;
> They will nevermore find refuge in my residence."[108]

The incantation lists the Evil Eye among numerous other forces thought to bring illness to humans and their households and destruction to the land. The incantation was meant to drive away all noxious forces, natural, demonic, and human—including the Evil Eye, Evil Mouth, and Evil Tongue—from the speaker and his home. The association of Evil Eye and Evil Mouth and Tongue, harmful looking and harmful speaking, will reappear in later Greek and Roman sources.

An Assyrian conjuration, also cited by Seligmann, prays to the deity for protection of a residence and its inhabitants against the goddess Lamashtu,

---

107. See the text and discussion in Abusch 1987.
108. Seligmann 1910 1:6 (without further identification and dating); trans. JHE:
   "Die Pest und das Fieber, die das Land verherren,
   die Seuche, die Auszehrung, die das Land verwüsten,
   schädlich dem, Körper, verderblich den Eingeweiden,
   der böse Dämon, der böse alal, der böse gigim,
   der boshafte Mensch, der böse Blick, der böse Mund, die böse Zunge,
   dass sie des Menschen, Sohn seines Gottes, Körper verlassen mögen,
   dass sie seine Eingeweide verlassen mögen.
   Meinem Körper werden sie nimmer anhaften,
   vor mir werden sie nimmer Böses stiften,
   in meinem Gefolge werden sie nimmer einherschreiten,
   in mein Haus werden sie nimmermehr eintreten,
   mein Zimmerwerk werden sie nimmer durchschreiten,
   in das Haus meiner Wohnstätte werden sie nimmermehr einkehren."

slayer of newborn babies, and against the Evil Eye of mourning women: "O God, Protector, you who watch over the door of this mortal man . . . Protect him against Lamashtu. . . against the Evil Eye of the women mourning the dead![109] The juxtaposition of the demoness Lamashtu and the Evil Eye makes sense: both threaten the lives of the newborn infants.[110]

In addition to the incantations as evidence of Evil Eye belief and practice, mention might also be made of the Mesopotamian belief that the goddess of the Deep, Tiamat, was thought to have had an Evil Eye from which the deity Marduk sought to protect himself.[111] The Babylonian creation epic depicts Marduk, son of Ea, champion of the gods, armed heavily to fight Tiamat. He also "carried between his lips an amulet made of red paste, or red stone, in the form of an eye, and he held in one hand a bunch of herbs which was intended to protect him from a magical influence which would be hostile to him."[112] The story also indicates that the gods gave these powerful means of protection to humans while also using them themselves.[113]

J. N. Ford has traced the "thematic continuity in Mesopotamian Incantations against the Evil Eye from Sumero-Akkadian to Mandaic" texts.[114] He mentions four recurrent motifs: 1) the repetitive structure of the incantation expressing the pernicious roaming of the Evil Eye; (2) the pernicious effects of the Evil Eye (breaking cattle yokes, discord within families, disruption of weaving, destruction of food-bearing plants); (3) its functioning like an ensnaring net; (4) the Evil Eye as a sick, defective, or dimmed/blinded eye, and its being colored blue or red. He might have also included the conception of the Evil Eye as a demon, who is then later depicted in the Syriac and Coptic traditions as a demoness slain by the lance of a rider on a horse.[115]

---

109. Seligmann 1910 2:344: "O Gott, Beschützer, der du wachst über der Tür des sterblichen Menschen, Schütze ihn gegen den lamastuw (ein Schrenkgespenst),. . . gegen den bösen Blicke des Klageweibes der Toten. . . !" No identification or date given.

110. On Lamashtu with an Evil Eye linked with the excessive crying of babies, both threatening the tranquility of the household and the spirits of the ancestors dwelling there, see van der Toorn 1998.

111. As noted by Kötting 1954:473

112. Budge 1978/1930:xx, referring to Meissner 1917 2:41, 44, lines 61–62.

113. See Budge 1930/1978:xi–xxxix on Babylonian and Mesopotamian belief and practice and on amulets 1978/1930:82–126, with numerous illustrations from the British Museum. On Babylonian mosaics see Bernand 1991 for specimens and texts, and his notes for inscriptions and photographs.

114. Ford 1998:256–68 (Appendix 2).

115. Ibid., 213–14, figs. 1 and 2. For this motif see also Vol. 4, chap. 2.

Amulets

Among the numerous Sumerian, Babylonian, and Assyrian amulets for warding off the Evil Eye and other evil potencies, according to Budge,[116] is a very old cylinder seal of the Archaic Period (3300–2850 BCE) with a scene representing a row of horned animals with a protective eye above them[117] that "symbolized divine protection."[118] Among the Mesopotamian preventative amulets Georges Contenau also lists representations of the "horned hand" (*mano cornuta*) and the "fig hand" (*mano fica*).[119] Protective amulets also included hands with outstretched fingers and the colors red and blue.[120] The use of these colors for thwarting the Evil Eye suggest that the pronounced blue eyes on numerous Mesopotamian statues and on jewelry may also be evidence of protection employed against the Evil Eye.[121] Mesopotamians and Egyptians also thought the color red effective in terrifying demons and repelling hostile spirits.[122]

The prominence given to the human eye in art and on jewelry shows a fascination with the eye as an instance of beauty and power. Among the amulets from Mesopotamia are also "beads resembling an eye or pair of eyes,"[123] as well as "pieces of onyx or agate which, by their markings, resembled an eye or a pair of eyes. They were known in Akkadian times and in the first half of the second millennium, but the majority of those which have survived belonged to the Kassite [1700–1160 BCE] and Neo-Assyrian [c. 800–600 BCE] periods."[124]

116. Budge 1978/1930:82; 82–126.

117. Ibid., 89, Plate XI, no. 6, British Museum, no. 107390.

118. Ibid., 91.

119. Contenau 1947:244, providing, however, no further information. On these two apotropaics, so popular among the later Greeks and Romans, see Vol. 2.

120. Ebeling 1938:55.

121. See Strommenger 1964, Plate XVIII, for the skull and jewelry of a Mesopotamian court lady from the royal cemetery at Ur, Early Dynastic Period, c. 2685–2645 BCE, in the Iraq Museum; cf. also Plate XIX, 2685–2485 BCE and the blue eyes on many statues.

122. See Contenau 1947:142–43. On red and blue as apotropaic colors repelling the Evil Eye see also Seligmann 1910 2:246–59 (ancient and modern practice) and Vol. 2. On colors and their significance in the Circum-Mediterranean world see Hermann and Cagiano di Azevedo 1969; Borg 1999. On the color blue, its production and significance see Ball 2001:231–49; Pastoureau 2001; P. Brown 2009; Deutscher 2011; Sterman and Sterman 2012.

123. Thomsen 1992:26.

124. Van Buren 1945:18–23, esp. 18; for the prophylactic purpose of eyes and their symbolization of fecundity and fertility see also Contenau 1947:242–44.

An Aramaic incantation bowl from Mesopotamia (c. 300–600 CE), now in the Israel Museum,[125] has words written on it intended to safeguard the home and residents of a certain Khwaday, son of Pali, from the Evil Eye and other hostile forces:

> I. Bound are the demons, sealed are the devs, bound are the idol-spirits sealed are the evil liliths, male and female.

> II. Bound is the evil eye (*'yn' bishta*) away from the house of Khwaday, son of Pali, from this day to eternity. Bound is the evil eye (*'yn'*).

> III. Bound is the evil eye (*'yn' bishta*) from the house of Khwaday, son of Pali, from his house and from his . . . ,

> IV . . . and from Adur-dukh and from her sons from this day to eternity.

> Amen, Amen, Selah.

Summary

The common opinion of Assyriologists that Evil Eye belief and practice was widespread in Mesopotamia[126] has been challenged by Marie-Louise Thomsen (1992). She considers the number of texts mentioning the Evil Eye relatively meager, with the Sumerian term for Evil Eye, *igi ḫul*, occurring "rather rarely."[127] "Most sources," she insists, "are Sumerian, some of them with Akkadian translation, and there is one Akkadian incantation."[128] The present evidence, she states, consists of "[f]ewer than ten incantations, a few medical recipes, and only one fragmentary ritual directed against the evil eye."[129] "[I]t is doubtful whether this rather limited material allows us to speak of a widespread belief in the evil eye in ancient Mesopotamia."[130] She

---

125. Naveh and Shaked, Bowl No. 8, 2009/1985:172–73 and Plate 24; Israel Museum, N. 69.20.265; translation by authors; specific date and provenance not given.

126. Lenormant 1878:40–41; Fossey 1902:50; Jastrow 1905 1:285 (witch's Evil Eye causing great suffering); Kriss and Kriss-Heinrich 1962 2:17 (tracing Islamic belief in the Evil Eye back to the Sumerians and Assyrians); also Seligmann 1910 1:12. See also above, n. 9.

127. Thomsen 1992:20.

128. Ibid., 27–28.

129. Ibid., 20.

130. Ibid., 20. Brenk 1999:174 is among her few followers.

sees the Evil Eye as "harmless" in character, belonging to "everyday annoyances" that "did not affect the health of the person."[131]

The content of the incantations, however, tells a different story. The Evil Eye, it was believed, could wipe out one's family, one's means of livelihood, and one's life. It was no trivial matter. It is likely that the paucity of evidence—she discusses only texts but not artifacts, amulets etc.—is merely circumstantial. The seriousness with which the Evil Eye was viewed in the texts that are extant and the extent of the similarities between these and later evidence pertaining to the Evil Eye in the Greco Roman period support the majority view that fear of the Evil Eye was as widespread as it was long-standing in Mesopotamia just as was the case in Egypt, the biblical communities, Greece, and Rome.

For over two millennia of Mesopotamian culture and tradition, the Evil Eye appears to have been a constant object of fear and dread. Seen either as the malignant eye of a human being or animal[132] or as an independent demon-like entity or monster with face, eye, mouth, and feet roaming from earth to heaven, the Evil Eye was linked with dragons, serpents, and demons (similar to the later Greek *baskanos daimôn*) as a source of illness and death and as a force wrecking havoc on crops, cattle, one's domicile, family and infants, and means of livelihood. It ranked among the most evil of powers: "The eye is evil, the most evil thing" (YOS 11, 71:3), a sentiment echoed centuries later by an Israelite sage: "Remember that an Evil Eye is a wicked thing; what has been created more evil than an Evil Eye?" (Sir 31:13). An unstable entity, it roamed to and fro seeking victims and objects for destruction. It was linked with an Evil Tongue and Evil Mouth; it wrought evil by both glance and speech. It could stop rain and cause crops to wither. It could cause the milk of domestic animals to dry up and animals to die. It attacked birthing mothers, newborns and infants, vital and beautiful young men and women. It was linked with the Evil-Eyed demon Lamashtu, slayer of infants. It could devour flesh and blood. It was viewed in ancient Mesopotamia, as in later periods, as a significant cause of illness and death.

Some incantations describe the Evil Eye in terms of a "distinct demon" with a body and body parts (e.g., VAT 10018:20–21).[133] This could point to either a demon/demoness possessing an Evil Eye[134] or to a demon/demoness as hypostatization of the Evil Eye.[135] In either case, the association of

131. Thomsen 1992:28.

132. Ibid., 25–26.

133. Ford 1999:211, following del Olmo Lete 1992b:258.

134. Wasserman 1995, citing the similarity of BM 122691 and IM 90648,

135. Ford 1998:211.

the Evil Eye with a demon is attested early on in the tradition and continued over the centuries. The Greeks knew it as the *baskanos daimôn* ("Evil
Eye demon") and this Evil Eye demon appears still later in Mandaean and
Christian Coptic sources of the post-Biblical period.[136] Anti-Evil Eye amulets from this later period depict a cavalier lancing a prostrate demon(ess)
that on one occasion is explicitly identified as *Baskosynê*, the Evil Eye.[137]
In Israel's Evil Eye tradition, the demoness and night hag *Lilith* (Isa 34:14)
parallels the Mesopotamian demoness *Lamashtu*; both are linked with the
Evil Eye and both are killers of birthing mothers and their newborns.[138] In
an Aramaic incantation involving *Lilith* being adjured by Elijah, "wicked
Lilith . . . Foul One and Spirit of Foulness," declares to Elijah that she is
"going to the house of the woman in labor . . . to give her the sleep of death
and to take the child born to her, in order to suck his blood and to suck the
marrow of his bones and to destroy(?) his flesh."[139]

The living beings thought to possess and wield an Evil Eye include
humans and animals: men and women, various artisans, rivals, nurses,
neighbors, enemies, friends, oxen, and sheep.[140] Statements about the Evil
Eye "looking," "seeing," "gazing" with hostile intent and force[141] show that:
(1) an ocular action is in mind; "Evil Eye" is not an abstract force isolated
from the eye, but a form of ocular activity; (2) the eye is thought to be active,
not passive so that an extramission theory of vision is presumed, as generally throughout the ancient world;[142] and (3) the ocular glance of an Evil Eye
can injure and harm. All three remain salient features of the Evil Eye belief
complex down through Late Antiquity and beyond.

The Evil Eye here is closely linked with envy; the act of beholding
something beautiful or handsome prompts envy which then leads to violence.[143] The Evil Eye "saw its 'brother'—how lovely he was!, its 'brother'—
how very seemly" (KTU[2] 1.96, lines 2–3). The Evil Eye's fastening upon
the beauties of nature are described centuries later in a Mandaic text of

136. Ibid., 212–15.

137. See Vol. 4.

138. Ford 1998:215–216.

139. Published in Montgomery 1913:258–64 and cited by Ford 1998:215

140. For lists of Evil Eyes and Evil-Eye possessors see also VAT 10018:3–4; KTU[2]
1.96; AMB, 133 (cf. also Shachar 1981, no. 781); and a Syriac incantation (Gollanz
1912, Codex C §19 (p. 87); Ford 1998:238–41.

141. E.g., CT 17, 33, lines 25–26: "The Eye which looked at you to cause suffering,
The Eye which looked at you to cause evil")

142. On this extramission theory of vision see above, Chapter 1, and Volumes
Two-Four.

143. Ford 1998:213–14, 224–28, 252.

the postbiblical period, *Šapta d-Pišra d-Ainia*, a "Scroll for the Exorcism of (Evil) Eyes."[144] This association of Evil Eye and envy is one of the most pronounced and constant features of the Evil Eye belief complex over time and across cultures.[145]

The *damage* done by an Evil Eye is varied and devastating: devouring of a kinsman's flesh and blood (KTU[2] 1.96, lines 2–4), abducting or strangling infants (BM 122691: 7), causing illness (CT 17, 33:4); causing rain to cease, herbs from growing, oxen to be lost, cheese to be destroyed, the rotting of vegetables and fruits, loss of or damage to garments of youth, and harm to a nurse and child (TCL 16, 89). Centuries later, a Mandaic text presents a similar listing of Evil Eye damage: objects admired by an Evil Eye for their beauty withered and died; fruit trees, grapevines, and nut trees withered; sheep refrained from grazing and their young from suckling; Pharoah's bulls also stopped grazing and their young from suckling; and their herdsmen all died.[146] The Evil Eye "strikes, slays, and makes ill."[147] In this post-biblical period, Jewish rabbis as well continued to attribute illness and death to the Evil Eye. Concerning the biblical statement, "And the Lord shall take away from you all sickness (Deut 7:15a), the Talmud states: "Rab said: 'By this the [evil] eye (*'yn*) is meant. This is in accordance with his opinion [expressed elsewhere]. For Rab went up to a cemetery, performed certain charms [literally, "did what he did"], and then said; 'Ninety-nine [have died] through an evil eye [*b 'yn r'h*] and one through natural causes.'"[148]

Features of Evil Eye possessors involved unusual ocular features or defective eyes—a notion that recurs in later Evil Eye material as well.[149] The objects and victims, which also included field crops, domestic animals, tools of production, kiln, loom, and boat, were vital to familial survival. Thus the danger posed by the Evil Eye was of major proportion and concern. Defense, however, against the Evil Eye was possible. The vulnerability of the many valued objects explains the numerous amulets and protective strategies employed to defend against and ward off the Evil Eye. In addition to the incantations and amulets already discussed, mention should be made of

144. Drower 1937:590, line 12 to 591, line 10, cited in Ford 1998:225–28.

145. On connection of the Evil Eye and envy see Schoeck 1970; Maloney 1976 passim; Stein 1976; Elliott 1988; 1990; 1991; 1994; 2005a; 2007a; 2007b; 2008; Pocock 1992; Gravel 1995:7–8, 42–44; Malina 2001:108–33.

146. *Šapta d-Pišra d-Ainia,* Drower 1937: 590–91; Ford 1998:225–27, esp. 227.

147. Drower 1938:2, line 8.

148. *b. Bava Metzi'a* 107b, Daiches-Freedman 1962 translation (Soncino edition); cf.also Ulmer 1994:24–27, and Vol. 4, chap. 1.

149. See Ford 1998:238–42 for types of possessors, varieties of ocular defect and colors of eyes.

the regard of the falcon as "the chief bird against the Evil Eye,"[150] the use of saliva, which was associated with the power of sexual reproduction,[151] and the employment of the colors of red and blue for protection. In Mesopotamia, the color red was employed to defend against, and terrify, spirits and demons and the Evil Eye.[152] Blue eyes, which in the Near East, Contenau comments, are a rarity and which in the West are highly prized, were associated with Evil-Eyed fascinators.[153] The color blue, at the same time, was also used to ward off the Evil Eye[154] in accord with the ancient principle of *similia similibus*, "like influences like."[155] The manual gesture of the *mano fica* (thumb inserted between the index and third fingers of a fisted hand) and the gesture of the *mano cornuta* (fisted hand extending the index and little fingers to form horns), Contenau asserts, likewise served to avert the Evil Eye, along with tortoises, pomegranates, horns, apotropaic eyes and other items associated with fertility and fecundity.[156] The remedies, rituals, and prayers to the gods for aid indicate the hope that the Evil Eye could be resisted, warded off, or overcome. Incantations were considered an especially effective means of protection and cure. Curses against the Evil Eye were also uttered. Often the Evil Eye was commanded to return to the one casting the Eye, so that the caster would be hurt by his own evil.[157] As already mentioned, this motif of "return to sender" recurs in the later Greek and Latin amuletic inscriptions.[158] Reference to the Eye alone as subject appears to be *pars pro toto* for the entire human being, whose most distinctive feature was his/her Evil Eye. Concentration on the eye would be consistent with later amulets depicting only a threatening eye or eye under attack.[159] Underlying these notions of the power of the Evil Eye and glance was a notion of the eye as an active, rather than passive, organ of sight and one whose mere glance could injure that upon which it fell, a notion likewise underlying biblical Evil Eye texts. The contours of this theory were eventually laid out in later Greek sources (Plutarch, Heliodorus). Virtually all these features, as

---

150. Contenau 1947:142.

151. Ibid., 140–41.

152. Ibid., 142–43, 260.

153. Ibid., 260.

154. Seligmann 1910 2:246–47; on blue and red see also Ford 1998:262, 265–68.

155. On this principle, see Vol. 2.

156. Contenau 1947:244, 262–63.

157. See Ford 1996:248–51 for texts.

158. See Vol. 2.

159. On these amulets, see Vol. 2.

we shall see, are found in texts or materials of later periods and cultures of Circum-Mediterranean antiquity.

Motifs associated with the Evil Eye in Mesopotamian incantations, Ford amply demonstrates, recur in sources from much later periods. This point is reinforced in his conclusion[160] with two contemporary anthropological field reports concerning the Evil Eye belief and practice among the Amhara of Ethiopia (Reminick 1976) and among the Gusii of Kenya (Matsuzono 1993). Here too, Evil Eyed persons are thought to roam about, to be envious of beautiful persons, to fix victims with their gaze and devour them, and to have returned to them their own noxious evil.

In the post-biblical period, incantations of the Mandaean community in Mesopotamia echo many motifs of the ancient Mesopotamian incantations. Thus a Mandaic incantation of the late Roman period in the *Šapta d-Pišra d-Ainia,* ("Scroll for the Exorcism of [Evil] Eyes") reads:

> And he said: 'As for the eye of your neglected (?) father, and the eye of evil neighbours against (?) their sons, and the eye that goes, and the eye that comes, and the eye of those who are far away , and the eye of those who are near, and the eye of little boys, and the eye of little girls, and the eye of a whoremonger (?), and the eye of a male prostitute (?), and the eye of the entire world, and the eye that struck N. son of N.—may a raven take it and ascend to a lone palm tree, may it sit on a branch and rip it into piece(s), may it shake what it rips off from it; during the shaking?) some of it will drop (down) among the flock, so that the bulls shall trample it, and ewes shall trample it."[161]

Here too the Evil Eye can be possessed by a wide variety of persons and can inflict harm even on family members and neighbors. A Syriac incantation of the same late Roman period illustrates the same breadth of fascinators, including neighbors and strangers, insiders and outsiders ("barbarian," "heathens," "infidel"). This incantation, published by Hermann Gollancz in *The Book of Protection,* reads:

> I bind you and ban you and overthrow (you), O evil and envious eye (*'yn' byš t' wḥsmt'*), eye (*'yn'*) of seven evil and envious neighbors, eye (*'yn'*) of every sort, eye (*'yn'*) that strikes and does not pity, eye (*'yn'*) of a father, eye (*'yn'*) of a (text: her) mother, eye (*'yn'*) of a barbarian, eye (*'yn'*) of heathens, eye (*'yn'*) of a barbarian, brownish/tawny eye (*'yn' šhlnyt'*), jealous [JHE: more

160. Ford 1996:252–53.

161. Drower 1937:592, lines 30–36; Ford 1998:238 provides a transliteration of the original.

accurately, *envious*] eye (*'yn' ṭnnyt'*), blue eye (*'yn' zrq'*), {eye}
eye of those who are far away, eye of all evil people, eye of those
who are far away, eye of those who are near, eye of every sort,
{eye} eye of men and women, eye of old men (and) old women,
eye of evil and envious people (*'yn' dbnynš' byš' wḥsm'*), eye of
an infidel . . .[162]

The Evil Eye here is explicitly identified as "envious," a point also stressed
in the Mandaic *Šapta d-Pišra d-Ainia*, ("Scroll for the Exorcism of (Evil)
Eyes"): "The eye that envies (*aina d-hasma*) children, male and female, envies it (sc. the child), strikes it and torments it."[163] This association of the
Evil Eye with envy is one of the most prominent and enduring features of
Evil Eye tradition down through the centuries and across cultures. In this
list of fascinators and types of eyes, the *blue eye* (*'yn' zrq'*) is notable.[164] Blue,
as already noted, is one of two colors, the other being red, that are most
often associated with the Evil Eye across cultures and down through the
centuries.[165]

An anti-Evil Eye incantation appearing on an Aramaic Magic Bowl of
the Late Roman period adjures the Evil Eye along with other threatening
forces, delineating various types of fascinators, Evil Eyes and their colors,
among which again are blue and green eyes:

I adjure you, every sort of evil eye (*'yn' byšt'*) and every sort of
plague and pestilence and demons and spirits and liliths, black
eye (*'yn' 'wkm'*), brownish/tawny (lit. 'yellow') eye (*'yn' šhwb'*),
blue eye (*'yn' tklt'*), green eye (*'yn' yrwq'*), long eye, short eye,
narrow eye, straight eye, crooked eye, round eye, sunken eye,
bulging eye, eye that sees (*'yn' rw't'*), eye that gazes (*'yn' mbṭt'*),
eye that bursts, eye that sucks up, eye of a male, eye of a female,
eye of a man and his wife, eye of a woman and her daughter, eye

162. Gollancz 1912:87 (Codex C §19); cf. lxxxii–lxxxiii; transliterated text and
translation according to Ford 1998:239–40.

163. Drower 1938:2, lines 2–23; Ford 1998:224. See also the phrase "envious Evil
Eye" (*aina bišta] hasumtia*), Drower 1938:4, line 16; Ford 1998:224 n.75.

164. Translated "the caerulean eye" by Drower (Ford 1998:239, n. 135).

165. See Seligmann 1910 2:246–59 (ancient and modern practice). Ford (1998:239,
n. 135) finds the expression "more or less synonymous with *'yn' zrwqt'*" (translated 'the
blue-coloured eye' by Gollancz), which occurs in the parallel incantation in Codex B
§9, pp. 69–70, where "green eye" (*'yn' yrwqt'*) and blue eye (*'yn' zrwqt'*) are paired. Ford
traces this combination to the fact that "blue and green physiological eyes are similarly
classed together in the Arabic physiolognomical treatise;" see Mourad 1939: 64, lines
7–8. For Syriac, Greek, Aramaic, and Arabic texts mentioning blue and other colors
associated with the Evil Eye see Ford 1998:239–42, 261–68. For the apotropaic function
of blue in Egypt see Abd el-Azim el-Adly 1994.

of a woman and her sister, eye of a woman and her female relative, eye of a young man, eye of an old man, eye of a virgin, eye of a non-virgin, eye of a widow, eye of a married woman, every sort of evil eye (*'yn' byš'*) that exists in the world that desires to burn (people) by gazing upon them with a strengthening of the element fire from the east, west, south and north . . . (*AMB* 113)[166]

Beside the human possessors of the Evil Eye, its actions are also mentioned: the Evil Eye "sees," "gazes," "bursts," "sucks up," and "desires to burn (people) by gazing upon them." This last action implies a conception of the eye as active and emitting burning rays. This is another recurrent feature of the Evil Eye over times and cultures.[167]

Among the ancient sources from Sumero-Akkadian to Mandaic, Ford has found a number of common motifs: (1) the repetitive structure of Evil Eye incantations, including its "roaming;" (2) the pernicious effects of the Evil Eye (breaking yokes, sewing discord in families, disruption of weaving, and of food-bearing plants); (3) the Evil Eye conceived as a net; and (4) as sick and defective (blinking, squinting, glowing, inflamed, bloodshot, bruised, blue, blurred, black/dimmed, ulcerated, tearing, having a cataract). The Evil Eye is linked also with blindness ("dimmed eye"). An as yet unpublished text of a Jewish Babylonian Aramaic incantation bowl reads: "Spirit whose name is 'Agag, daughter of Brwq, daughter of Brwqt,' daughter of Nqwr, daughter of Nmwn, daughter of the Evil Eye (*bt 'yn r'h*); they call you 'the blinded one, the one who(se eye) is poked out, the blind one . . ."[168] This association of Evil Eye and blindness is relevant to the accusation directed against the apostle Paul in Galatia that he possessed an Evil Eye. Blindness was among the tell-tale features of an Evil Eye attributed to the apostle.[169]

Ford's instructive study identifies and cites numerous "thematic parallels" between the Mesopotamian anti-Evil Eye incantations and later texts in Aramaic, Hebrew, Mandaic, Syriac, and Coptic. This includes references to the Evil Eye in the writings of the Mandaeans, a Semitic people that emerged as a baptismal sect in first-century Palestine (eastern Jordan region). The sect revered the biblical figures of Adam, Abel, Seth, Enosh, Shem, and especially John the Baptist. Gnostic in religious orientation, the sect fled in the

---

166. Transliterated text and translation in Ford 1998:241, citing Naveh and Shaked 1985:133.

167. See Vol. 2.

168. MS 1927/8:6–7, transliteration and translation by Ford 1998:265.

169. See Vol. 3.

second century CE to Mesopotamia and settled there in the third century. Mandaeans spoke a dialect of Eastern Aramaic known as Mandaic.

Among the devices the Mandaeans used for driving off demons and evil spirits, and in all likelihood, the Evil Eye, from their homes were inscribed terra-cotta bowls that were placed by or under the foundations of their residences.[170] Many such bowls were discovered at Nippur and were described, translated and analyzed by J. A. Montgomery (1913). Two of the bowl amulets discussed by Montgomery and reported by Budge[171] have inscriptions against "Liliths that haunt the house," "evil Lilith," "all species of Liliths,"[172] and "Liliths male and female that attach themselves to Adak bar Hathoi and Ahath bath Hathoi. . . and dwell in their archways and lurk in their thresholds and appear to them in one form and another, and that strike and cast down and kill."[173] This dread of Lilith, scourge of infants and mothers, along with the concern for protecting the dwelling recall similar motifs of the much older Mesopotamian anti-Evil Eye incantations.[174] Ford's 1998 study, moreover, points to several passages of Mandaic texts, especially the "Scroll for the Exorcism of (Evil) Eyes" (*Šapta d-Pišra d-Ainia*),[175] that illustrate the thematic continuities between the Sumero-Akkadian incantations and the much later Mandaic literature: roaming of the Evil Eye;[176] pernicious effects of the Evil Eye;[177] the net motif;[178] and the Evil Eye as sick or defective eye and blue in color.[179] When the comparison is extended to include Hebrew, Greek and Latin texts as well, the picture of similarity and continuity is most remarkable.

170. Budge 1978/1930:246–47.

171. Ibid., 247–49

172. Montgomery 1913:117, no. 1.

173. Ibid., 141, no. 6.

174. On Lilith see Gordon 1957; Scurlock 1991.

175. For a critical reassessment of this text see Tarelko 1999–2000.

176. Ford 1998:257–58.

177. Ibid., 258–60.

178. Ibid., 260–61.

179. Ibid., 261–68. For the Mandaic texts see Drower 1937; 1938; 1943. On the Mandaic amulets see Budge 1978/1930:239–49; Naveh 1975; Tarelko 2000. On the Aramaic incantation bowls see Montgomery 1913; Gordon 1937; Yamauchi 1967; Isbell 1975; Budge 1978/1930:283–90, 446–47 ("Babylonian terra-cotta Devil traps" =Aramaic incantation bowls); Duling 1983:947–48; D. Aune 1986:217; Naveh and Shaked 1985:172–73 (bowl 8); 1993; Schiffman and Schwartz 1992; Naveh 1998; Ford 1998:212 n. 30. For a photograph of one such incantation bowl see *ISBE* 3 (1986) 218. On these Aramaic incantation bowls see also Vol. 4, chap. 1.

THE EVIL EYE IN EGYPT

Introduction

Egypt, the land of the Nile at the western end of the Fertile Crescent, like Mesopotamia to the East, had a vibrant and long-standing tradition of belief in the deadly Evil Eye. Egypt, like Sumer and Babylonia, derived its power and wealth from agriculture. Here too farmers and herders lived in a tenuous relationship with the forces of nature and with each other, facing the extremities of flood and drought, feast and famine, on a regular basis. Humans in general contended with a precarious existence, exposed on all sides to the unpredictable forces of nature and the caprice of mysterious spirits and powers causing illness, calamity, and death. This, of course, is in addition to the everyday struggle over access to those scarce and limited resources upon which survival depended. These are among the conditions, anthropologists have noted, in which Evil Eye belief and practice traditionally has thrived.[180] Throughout the long history of Egypt, with all of its political and cultural undulations, dread of the Evil eye has always been a constant, even down to the present.[181] The two main periods of Egyptian history for tracing Egyptian aspects of this belief are Ancient Egypt (3000–332 BCE, comprising the thirty dynasties of pharaohs ending with the conquest by Alexander the Great in 332 BCE), and second, Egypt under Greek and Roman Rule (332 BCE to Late Roman Antiquity).[182]

---

180. See Roberts in Maloney 1976: 223–278; Garrison and Arensberg in Maloney 1976:294–97.

181. On the Evil Eye in ancient Egypt see Elworthy 1958/1985:6, 126; Seligmann 1910 1:18, 2:157–58 and passim; Spiegelberg 1924; Meisen 1950:144–45; Saueron 1966:51, 63 and nn. 77–78; Budge 1978/1930:141–42, 360–62; Cahill 1984; Quirke 1992:112; Pinch 1994:39, 58, 73, 107, 117, 123; Ulmer 2003.

182. Egyptian chronology: Early Dynastic Period (Dynasties 1–2, c. 3100–2686 BCE; Old Kingdom (Dynasties 3–6, c. 2686–2181 BCE, the *Pyramid Texts*); First Intermediate Period (Dynasties 7–10, c. 2181–2040 BCE); Middle Kingdom (Dynasties 11–12, c. 2133–1786 BCE, the *Coffin Texts*); Second Intermediate Period (Dynasties 13–17, c. 1786–c. 1590 BCE); New Kingdom (Dynasties 18–20, c. 1550–1070 BCE; the *Book of the Dead* on papyrus [c. 1550–50 BCE]); Third Intermediate Period (Dynasties 21–25, c. 1069–702 BCE); Late Period (Dynasties 26–30 and Nubian, Saite, and Persian rule, 664–332 BCE).

Ancient Egypt (3000—332 BCE):
from the Pharoahs to the Ptolemies

Mesopotamian influence reached Egypt quite early (2500 BCE or earlier), bringing with it the cylinder seal, a stimulus to develop a system of writing, and also various features of monumental architecture and artistic motifs.[183] It is quite likely that this influence from East to West also brought with it elements of Evil Eye belief and practice, which were then recast in distinctively Egyptian dress. "Egyptian gold and Mesopotamian silver were the lifeblood of Mediterranean trade, which reached significant levels in the second millennium B.C."[184] and both metals were used in the production of anti-Evil Eye amulets. The chief and most widely attested scripts of the Egyptian language in this initial period were hieroglyphic and hieratic. These were followed by Demotic (c. 650 BCE), with the last phase of Egyptian being Coptic (third–eleventh cents. CE).

The second major period of Egyptian history, Hellenistic-Roman Egypt (332 BCE—641 CE), extended from the reign of Alexander the Great (332–306 BCE) through the rule of Alexander's successors, the Ptolemies/Lagids (306-30 BCE), to control by Rome from 30 BCE onward. The lingua franca of this Hellenistic period was Greek. This time frame saw an extensive merging of Egyptian, Greek/Macedonian, and Roman cultures and, with it, a blending of Egyptian, Greek, and Roman Evil Eye belief and practice.

When the concept of the Evil Eye first emerged in Egypt is difficult to say, since its *explicit* mention in ancient Egyptian sources is infrequent and mostly in later sources. Egyptologist Wilhelm Spiegelberg insisted that clear attestation of the belief occurs only in later Egyptian texts of the Saitic (663–525 BCE), Persian (525–332 BCE), and Ptolemaic (301–30 BCE) periods. He mentions only two literary texts:[185] (1) a segment of the library catalogue from Edfu in Upper Egypt (Ptolemaic period) containing "Sayings for driving away the Evil Eye"; and (2) a fragmentary text[186] in which reference is made to the goddess Sekmet loosening/dispelling/slaying the Evil Eye.[187] Spiegelberg considered personal proper names containing the expression "Evil Eye" to be the best evidence available.[188] These names, mostly of women, refer to

183. On the relations of Egypt with the Near East and Canaan, see Openheim in *IDB* 1962:303; Wilson in *IDB* 2: 44; Helck 1971; Ward 1963, 1971, 1992.

184. Braudel 2001:74.

185. Spiegelberg 1924:153.

186. Catalogue du Musée Guimet (Paris), Plate 64, no. 72.

187. On the catalogue see also A. Erman 1934: 311–12, and on the Evil Eye, 147, 395.

188. Spiegelberg 1924:150–53.

some deity taking destructive action against the Evil Eye: "deity NN protects against/slays/rips out the Evil Eye (*St3–jr.t–b'n.t)*": "Nut slays the Evil Eye";[189] "Neith slays the Evil Eye";[190] "Chons slays the Evil Eye";[191] "Sekhmet slays the Evil Eye."[192] Spiegelberg plausibly compares such Egyptian proper names with the Greek adjective *abaskantos* ("safe from the Evil Eye"), which likewise was employed as a proper name in later Ptolemaic times.[193] The names, given by Spiegelberg in hieroglyphic and demotic, were believed to possess apotropaic power.[194] On the basis of these sources, dating from mid-first millennium BCE onward, Spiegelberg concluded that the Evil Eye belief itself arrived late on the Egyptian scene and was possibly borrowed from the neighboring Libyans or Nubians.[195]

Other scholars, however, trace the belief in Egypt to earlier times. This includes E. A. Wallis Budge in his classic study on *Amulets and Superstitions* (1978/1930),[196] Albert Potts (1982), and, more recently, Egyptologist Geraldine Pinch (1994). "In the first millennium BC," Pinch observes, "it became common to attribute problems to the envy or spite of people who possessed the Evil Eye."[197] It would be extraordinary if Egyptian belief and practice associated with the Evil Eye had not undergone change and variation over the centuries from archaic times to the Roman conquest. The period of the New Kingdom (c. 1550–1070) and thereafter, for example, was permeated by a mood of pessimism and fatalism accompanied by increased resort to means for warding off evil, protecting oneself against snakes and scorpions, or hexing one's enemy, or gaining the aid of the gods in everyday affairs. Although *explicit* mention of the Evil Eye is first attested only from 663 BCE onward, the Horus myth and material evidence of amuletic Eyes of Horus (*wedjat* eyes) point to a far earlier date of origin.[198] Traces of the Horus myth in the *Book of the Dead* (c. 3100 BCE) and *The Pyramid Texts* (2613–2345 BCE), together with Eye of Horus amulets buried with the dead in tombs of

189. Stele of Apis, Louvre 379.

190. Canope Saqqara, 26th Dynasty (663–525 BCE); Spiegelberg 1924:152.

191. Spiegelberg 1924:152.

192. Stele Serapeum, Louvre 4108; Spiegelberg 1924:153.

193. Spiegelberg 1924:153; see also Vol. 2.

194. See also Meisen 1950:144; Ford 1998: 212 n. 28.

195. Spiegelberg 1924:153–54. Meisen 1950:144–45 appears to concur.

196. Budge 1978/1930:141–42, 360–61.

197. Pinch 1994:73.

198. Budge 1978/1930:141–42; Meisen 1954:144.

the Fourth Dynasty (c. 2600 BCE), attest the great antiquity of Egyptian Evil Eye belief and practice.[199]

One recent author, Thomas Rakoczy, in his excellent 1996 study of the Evil Eye in the Greek world, allows, on the basis of the early prominence of the eye and the Eye of Horus in Egyptian mythology and art, that Egypt, rather than Mesopotamia, even may have been the birthplace of the belief.[200] Racokzy adds that words of similar sounding consonants were thought to have an essential connection, with the hieroglyph for "eye" (*i.r.t*) also standing in for the verb "to do, make" (*i.r.j*). The Egyptian language thus enables the conception of the eye as an active agent, which, in turn, provides the basis for the notion of an injurious Evil Eye.[201]

The case for a Mesopotamian origin is stronger, however, and so we have begun with Mesopotamia rather than Egypt. The economic, social, and cultural linkage between Mesopotamia and Egypt, nevertheless, was close and long-standing. This contact, and the Egyptian evidence to follow, make it likely that Evil Eye belief and practice appeared in Egypt at a relatively early date, perhaps as far back as the Middle Kingdom (2133–1786 BCE). Mesopotamian cultural influence reached Egypt quite early (2500 BCE or earlier), bringing Egypt the cylinder seal, a stimulus to develop a system of writing, and features of monumental architecture. Pinch, observes that "During the late fourth/early third millennia BC, certain aspects of Mediterranean culture seem to have been imported into Egypt."[202] Foreign cultural influences due to alien invaders or captives settling in Egypt continued over the centuries through Roman times and beyond.[203]

It is quite likely that this flow of influence from East to West also brought with it elements of Evil Eye belief and practice, which were then recast in distinctively Egyptian features. In Egyptian art, sculpture and myth and even personal jewelry, interest in the eye has always been apparent. It

199. So Potts 1982:17.

200. Rakoczy 1996:17 n. 19; 272.

201. On the eye in Egyptian culture see Otto 1975 1:559–661; Seawright 1988. On the eye of the sun myth, see Sethe 1912; Spiegelberg 1915; 1917; De Cenival 1988. On the Evil Eye and *wedjat/udjat* Eye of Horus in Egyptian culture, see Seligmann 1910 1:18; 2:476 (index: Egypt); Gardiner 1916; Spiegelberg 1924; Lexa 1925 1:90–91; Blackman 1927:71, 218; Schott 1931; Erman 1934:311–12; Contenau 1947:96–97, 259–63; Bonner 1950; Rudnitsky 1956; Sainte Fare Garnot 1960; Sauneron 1966:51, 63; Bourgouts 1973; Budge 1978/1930:141–42; 360–61; Rundle-Clark 1978:218–30; de Wit 1979; Bonneau 1982; Lewis 1983:78–79; Cahill 1984; Vittmann 1984:74; Cauville 1989; Abd el-Azim el-Adly 1994; Hermann 1994, 2002; Pinch 1994:39, 58, 73, 107, 117, 123; Darnell 1997; Bonnet 2000:122; Bryen and Wypustek 2009.

202. Pinch 1994:161.

203. Ibid., 161–77.

is likely that this general interest in the eye sustained a belief in the Evil Eye as well. In art and statuary, human eyes were particularly accentuated and strikingly colored. Representations of eyes appear everywhere and in various sizes—on sarcophagi, doors, stelae, tomb walls, model boats, papyri, and amulets.

Heaven too was thought to have eyes, the chief of which were the sun and moon. As early as the Fifth Dynasty (2500–2350 BCE), twin eyes were painted side by side on tomb walls and coffins to "represent the Eye of the sun and the Eye of the moon, i.e. the two Eyes of the very ancient Sky-god Ḥer," and also "were painted on articles of funerary equipment throughout the dynastic period."[204] At this time, worship of the sun was introduced at Heliopolis and the specific sun god Ra/Re, ruler of the universe, was declared to be the celestial father of the ruling pharoah. In *The Book of the Dead* frequent reference is made to "the eye of Ra/Re" as benevolent and source of sustenance: "Your cakes will come from the Eye of Ra, your beer from the Eye, your meals of the dead from the Eye."[205] The eye of Ra, alias Atum Ra, the creator deity, was identified with the disc of the sun and could take the form of various goddesses, among them Hathor, Sekhmet, Wedjat (in the form of a cobra), and Tefnut (in the form of a lioness).[206] The eye of Ra lit up the darkness and could serve as an agent of Ra in the form of an independent eye goddess.[207] The eye of Ra was thought to wreak revenge on Ra's enemies and bring about illness, destruction and death. Pharaohs from the Fifth Dynasty onward claimed for themselves the title "Son of Ra" and on the front of their crowns displayed a uraeus, image of an upright cobra and symbol of the ancient goddess Wedjat. The image of a winged solar disk likely functioned as representation of the solar eye. This celestial solar eye symbolized both beneficial and destructive power,[208] a significance that was attributed to the human eye as well.

Paired with the major celestial "eye" of heaven, the sun, was heaven's other main "eye," the moon. Sun and moon also could be viewed either as the two eyes of Ra/Re, or the two eyes of the falcon-god Horus, son of Ra/Re, or the eye of Ra/Re (right eye) and the Eye of Horus (left eye). Eventually both celestial eyes were linked with the falcon god Horus, with his right eye

204. Budge 1978/1930:141, 360. On the Eye of the sun in the Pyramid Texts see Anthes 1961.

205. *The Book of the Dead,* chapter 125 (1979 ed.).

206. Pinch 1994:24.

207. Ibid., 24–26.

208. For its healing power see Weinreich 1909.

representing the sun and his left the moon.[209] The two eyes of heaven, the sun and the moon, also could be called the "children of Horus."

Other deities were also linked with the sun and called "eyes of Ra." The eyes of these deities were also a focus of concern.[210] The goddess Hathor, depicted as a human with the head of a cow between whose horns was a disk representing the sun, was called "the eye of Ra." The goddess Isis also was known as the "eye of Ra" and in the Nineteenth Dynasty (1345–1200 BCE) was the divinity representing the unity of the two regions of Lower and Upper Egypt. According to one ancient myth, it was from the tears of the sun-god that humans originated. "Ptah, the father of the gods," so goes the myth, "brought forth all the other gods from his eye, and men from his mouth—a practical rendering of the ancient belief that, of all bodily emanations, those from the eye were the most potent."[211]

The "divine eye" in the mythological tradition thus could refer to the eye of Ra or that of Horus or other deities.[212] The image of a sacred eye was depicted on obelisks, temples and monuments.[213] A distinct "Eye Goddess" likewise enjoyed a prominent role in ancient Egyptian Memphite creation mythology.[214] In all these aspects of the eye's symbolism, the eye was a doubled-sided image of both life and death, bane and blessing. Conceiving of the sun as a celestial eye in turn supported the notion that the human eye, like the sun, is active and projects rays that can harm and destroy.[215]

Significations of the eye, in sum, varied over time, with the Eye of Horus eventually emerging as the most potent agent for warding off the damaging effect of the Evil Eye and other injurious forces. The "all-seeing eye of Horus," as a *Coffin Text* indicates, "strikes terror . . . a Mighty One of Frightfulness," while it was also considered a source of health, strength, protection, and well-being.[216] Belief in the power of the Eye of Horus was expressed and sustained by a tradition of myths concerning Horus, which

209. Pinch 1994:27

210. Deonna 1965:100

211. Elworthy 1912:608–9.

212. On the divine eye in Egypt and eyes symbolizing deities see Deonna 1965:100, 183, 265, 268–69, 292.

213. See Cavendish 1983:889 for an illustration of the sacred eye on an Egyptian obelisk now in Istanbul.

214. Pinch 1994:24–26.

215. On Egyptian eye symbolism and the Evil Eye see also Rundle 1978, esp. 218–30.

216. In its apotropaic function, the Eye of Horus overlaps with the similar capacity of the Eye of Ra; cf. Darnell 1997:35–37. For changing aspects of the divine eye in ancient Egypt see, in addition to Budge 1978/1930 and Pinch 1994 passim; Ulmer 2003. On the Eye of Horus, see Rudnitzky 1956.

were complex and which varied over time. In his cosmic form, Horus was thought to be a sky falcon whose right eye was the sun and whose left eye was the moon. Another highly influential myth told of Horus as son of Isis and Osiris, and heir to Osiris's throne. In a momentous battle for this throne, Seth, his uncle (or, alternatively, brother), ripped out Horus' left lunar eye. This eye, however, was restored to wholeness by the god Thoth and was known thereafter as the *wedjat* (or *udjat*), meaning "sound eye."[217] With this restored powerful eye, Horus helped establish his father Osiris as lord of the underworld where he reigned eternally as judge of the dead.[218] We shall return to this myth shortly.

Sharing with the Mesopotamians a belief in the existence of demons and transhuman forces threatening life and health at all times, the Egyptians also had a dread of the Evil Eye of both humans and demons. They too saw it as a threat to health, family, and especially children, and employed incantations, spells and amulets to repel it. "Within Egypt itself," Pinch notes, "evidence for a belief in witches is remarkably lacking. The nearest equivalents were possessors of the Evil Eye. This power of 'ill-looking' people was usually attributed to persons of malicious or envious temperament. 'May you not meet with an Evil Eye' became a standard greeting by the end of the period of Greek rule."[219]

For the earlier period of Egyptian history (Old, Middle, and New Kingdoms (c. 3000–1070 BCE), evidence of Evil Eye belief and practice is less in texts than in art and the myriad of Eye of Horus amulets uncovered in archaeological digs. There were, however, spells and incantations concerning the Evil Eye and other noxious forces that originally were spoken or chanted. Thereafter they were also written on papyrus, and inscribed on stone slabs, potsherds, wood, wax, wooden tablets, large stone stelae, and on walls of houses and tombs. The Temple of Edfu dedicated to Horus has several incantations against the Evil Eye.[220] Eye of Horus amulets were found in tombs dating from the Fourth Dynasty (c. 2613–2494 BCE). The antiquity and ubiquity of *wedjat* amulets against the Evil Eye attest a widespread fear of the Evil Eye against which the Eye of Horus was deemed a potent protection.[221] "Tomb findings from the Fourth Dynasty onward include Eye of Horus amulets buried with the dead. Thus the set of concepts encompassed

217. For a gold amulet showing the god Thoth in his ibis-headed form displaying the divine *wedjat* eye (c. tenth cent. BCE) see Pinch 1994:27, fig. 10

218. Pinch 1994:26–27.

219. Pinch 1994:58.

220. Budge 1978/1930: 361.

221. So ibid., 141–42, 174; cf. Watterson 1984:103; Pinch 1994:109–11.

by an eye amulet had to have been established by 2600 B.C., some forty-five centuries ago."[222] "My belief," Budge states, "is that the Egyptians, like the Chinese, were terrified by their fear of the Evil Eye, and that the Udjat [aka *wedjat*] was worn or carried universally as a protection against it."[223] The extensive fear of the Evil Eye attested by Ptolemaic Egyptian evidence (332–30 BCE) and from the Roman period (30 BCE—323 CE), moreover, cannot have arisen out of thin air. It more likely continued a long-established dread of the Evil Eye. Even though direct mention of the Evil Eye in Egyptian literature appears only midway through the first millennium BCE, the antiquity and virtual ubiquity of interest in the Eye of Horus and its use against the Evil Eye argue strongly for the existence of a belief in the Evil Eye prior to the first millennium BCE. Budge insists, "that *iri-t ban-t . . .* means the Evil Eye, and it is equally clear from the text on the wall of a chamber in the temple of Edfû that books of spells, which were intended to destroy its existence, were recited in the temple." Moreover, he notes,[224] "the word *siḥu* seems undoubtedly to mean fascination, or the influence of the Evil Eye."[225] A text from the Sixth Dynasty (c. 2350–2180 BCE) collection of ancient Egyptian wisdom sayings, *The Instruction of Ptah-hotep* (a vizier during the reign of Pharoah Isisi [Fifth Dynasty]), gives advice to a husband concerning his wife's "stormy gazing eye" that wrecks havoc:

> When you prosper and found your house,
> And love your wife with ardor . . .
> Do not contend with her in court,
> Keep her from power, restrain her—
> Her eye is her storm when she gazes—
> Thus will you make her stay in your house.[226]

A reference to a demon with the Evil Eye is contained in a *Coffin Text* of the Middle Kingdom (2133–1786 BCE).[227]

Evil Eye belief, as already noted, is connected primarily with the sky god Horus, who was portrayed as a falcon and who had a prominent place in the Egyptian pantheon. Kings and pharaohs identified themselves with

222. Potts 1982:17.

223. Budge 1978/1930:142.

224. Budge 1978/1901:361.

225. Seligmann (1910 1:18) also assumed the antiquity of the belief, noting that ancient Egyptian inscriptions and papyri often refer to *benen* (Evil Eye) or *sih* (strike with the Evil Eye/glance).

226. *The Instruction of Ptah-hotep*, proverb 21, lines 325–338, from Papyrus Prisse, translated in Lichtheim 1973 1: 69.

227. Borghouts 1973:143.

Horus, who spread his protective wings over the world and held back the forces of chaos and evil. In one of the several mythological traditions concerning Horus, his eyes were identified with the sun and the moon. Another tradition identified the sun as the solar eye of Ra-Amun and the moon as the Eye of Horus. The winged sun disk, once symbol of the king, later became an image of Horus of Edfu. Like the celestial "eyes" of sun and moon, the eye of Horus was thought to emit rays that could benefit or destroy all life on earth. In Edfu, a salutation of Horus of Behdet at break of day stated, "Thy living eyes which emit fire, thy healthy eyes which lighten darkness, awake in peace, so thy awakening is peaceful."[228] The "Protestation of Innocence" contained in *The Book of the Dead* has the deceased declaring his innocence to "Thou of the Pair of Eyes . . . thou [deity] whose eyes pierce like swords."[229] This analogy was consistent with the understanding of the working of the human eye and of the Evil Eye as well. As we shall discuss in further detail below, the human eye was thought of as an active, not a passive organ. It projected light, similar to the rays of the sun and the light of a lamp. This was the prevalent understanding of the eye and vision in the ancient world, and shared by the biblical communities as well.

Myths involving Horus, as told in *The Book of the Dead* and *The Pyramid Texts*, represent fluid funerary traditions from 3100 BCE onward. They provide the background for the association of the god and the Eye of Horus with the Evil Eye. *The Book of the Dead* "is certain to have existed in some form during the First Dynasty (3100–2390 B.C.)."[230] "The *Pyramid Texts* were engraved on the walls and corridors of the pyramids at Saqqara, which belong to the Fourth and Fifth Dynasties (c. 2613–2345 B.C.)."[231] Recounted in numerous variations, the core of the myth (explaining the cycles of the moon) told of the animosity of two divine brothers, Seth, the storm-god, and Horus, the moon-god. Once, as they battled, so the story went, Seth ripped out Horus' (left) eye and Horus ripped off Seth's testicles. Horus's eye, however, was restored and returned to him by the sky-god Thoth, the "carrier of the eye."[232]

228. Ulmer 2003, citing Piankoff 1964:47.

229. *The Book of the Dead* (1979 ed.):91, 93.

230. Potts 1982:17, following Budge 1914.

231. Potts 1982:17.

232. See Pinch 1994:27 and fig. 10 for a gold amulet statuette of Thoth carrying the *wedjat* Eye of Horus, c. tenth cent. BCE. In later time, the figure of Horus was absorbed into the Osiris myth as son of Osiris and Isis (similar to the other son, Harpocrates). Seth and Osiris were the contending brothers for supremacy in the universe. Seth, representing the forces of destruction and chaos, slew his brother Osiris, the god of agriculture and grain, and hacked him to pieces. Osiris's sister consort and wife, Isis, gathered Osiris' pieces, restored him to life, and bore him a son, Horus (also identified with Harpocrates). On Horus see Helck 1979; Brashear 1994; on the conflict of Horus

Horus's survival of Seth's attack and the restoration of his eye endowed this eye with extraordinary regenerative power. This potent restored Eye of Horus was depicted artistically as a human eye combined with the facial markings and outstretched wing of a falcon, representing Horus, the falcon god. It was

Illus. 2.1
Eye of Horus with falcon wings, painted on
outer coffin of Masaharta, High Priest of
Amon-Ra at Diospolis Megale/Thebes, Egypt ,
c. 1055–1045 BCE

called *wedjat* (*wd3–t*), written otherwise as *udjat*, which means "sound eye" or "whole eye," referring to the healed and restored Eye of Horus.[233] "*Udjat/wedjat*" is attested from the New Kingdom onward (1550 BCE), but the Horus myth is much older.[234] More generally, the *wedjat* "typified good health, soundness, safe protection, and physical comfort and well-being generally."[235] Representations of this Eye of Horus/*wedjat* were used as amulets for warding off or destroying evil forces, particularly the Evil Eye, and as a medium of healing.[236] Images of the *wedjat* have been found in tombs and on coffins, stelae, statues as well as in the form of amulets to be worn or carried. The Eye of Horus/*wedjat*/*udjat* was a human eye combined with features of a falcon,

---

and Seth see Kees 1923; Rudnitsky 1956; Griffiths 1960.

233. Cahill 1984:293.

234. See Spell 335 in the *Coffin Texts* (Middle Kingdom, 2133–1786 BCE).

235. Budge 1978/1930:141; Pinch 1994:27.

236. Pinch 1994:109–11, 115, 135 and figs. 56, 57. For Horus as protector and healer see the cippus with a standing figure of Horus protecting against surrounding attacking creatures (24th–25th Dynasties, c. 700 BCE, Oriental Institute, University of Chicago), see Aune 1986:215. The depiction of a figure surrounded by attacking creatures is similar to later Greek and Roman anti-Evil Eye amulets showing an Evil Eye attacked by the same creatures (scorpions, snakes, crocodiles) and used to afford protection from the Evil Eye.

rather than being a representation simply of an eye, as in later Greek and Roman amulets. It did, however, like the latter amulets, illustrate the principle of *similia similibus* ("like influences like"): eye against eye—in this case Horus's powerful restored eye against the Evil Eye.[237]

This protecting action of Horus and his eye(s) was a venerable theme of Egyptian lore. A spell from *The Pyramid Texts*, the oldest surviving collection of funery literature (24th–22nd cent. BCE)[238] mentions a blue-eye Horus and a red-eyed Horus, the two colors most often used through modern time to ward off the Evil Eye and so prominent among *wedjat* amulets:

> The blue-eyed Horus comes against you,
> beware of the red-eyed Horus, violent of power,
> whose might none can withstand![239]

The *Pyramid Texts of [King] Unas* (2350 BCE) refer repeatedly to the Eye of Horus "that Seth has pulled out," that accompanies offerings, and that nourishes and protects Osiris King Unas. In scene nineteen of the Ramesseum papyrus (c. 1980 BCE), the oldest known surviving illustrated papyrus roll, Horus declares to his children, "You shall fill my house upon earth with my eye . . . I have protected you."[240] The Eye of Horus is mentioned in a food offering ritual as a designation for an offering (of bread or bread and beer) to Osiris King Nefer-ka-Re. According to yet another myth, Horus, the dutiful son, gave his eye in fighting on behalf of his father Osiris so that to be a dutiful son was "to give the eye of Horus."[241] By extension, "the Eye of Horus became the symbol of all sacrifices and thus one of the holiest symbols of the ancient Egyptian religion."[242]

The *Book of the Dead* (in circulation since c. 1550 BCE) contains a spell uttered by the deceased who seeks to identify with the gods so as to pass the dangers of the Underworld:

> I am the god Unen . . . I am the Dweller in the Eye; no evil or calamitous things befall me . . . I am he who fashioneth with his eye, and who dieth not a second time . . . I am Horus, prince of eternity, a fire before your faces . . ."[243]

237. Elworthy 1958/1895:127.

238. Pinch 1994:21.

239. *The Pyramid Texts*, Spell 246 (PT 2531–b); Falkner 1969:59.

240. Bouquet 1954:57. The illustrations show the Pharoah appearing in the role of Horus multiple times.

241. Ibid., 63–64.

242. Potts 1982:17.

243. *The Book of the Dead* (1979 ed., 110, *Anhaï Papyrus)*; for *Dweller of the Eye and*

A later spell invokes Horus and his lance, among a host of armed deities, as protection against any who might cast an Evil Eye against a person named Pediamunneb-nesuttowi:

> Sakmet's [Sekhmet's] arrow is in you, the magic of Thoth is in your body, Isis curses you, Nephthys punishes you, the lance of Horus is in your head. They treat you again and again and again, you who are in the furnace of Horus in Shenwet, the great god who sojourns in the House of Life! He blinds your eyes, oh all you people, all nobles, all common people, all the sun-folk and so on, who will cast an evil eye against Pediamunneb-nesuttowi born of Mehtemwesket, in any bad or ominous manner! You will be slain like Apap, you will die and not live forever."[244]

A large figure of Horus appears on the famous Metternich stele or "Cippus of Horus" (370–360 BCE) in the British Museum, with Horus accompanied by twin *wedjat* eyes and figures of many deities, animals and spells designed to ward off hostile forces and attacks of scorpions.[245]

Eventually *wedjat* eyes were depicted as either left or right eyes, and so could symbolize the moon (lunar Eyeof Horus) or the sun (solar Eye of Ra), or Horus's left or right eyes; or both eyes could also be combined as twin eyes.[246] One spell that intended to provide protection of a person from head to foot, identifies the patient's right eye with the solar eye of Ra-Atum and his left eye with the lunar Eye of Horus.[247] A *wedjat* amulet of green and black faience (c. 500 BCE), depicts two stacked pairs of left and right *wedjat* eyes separated by papyrus columns symbolizing vitality and growth.[248]

Iterations of the myth of the conflict between brothers Seth and Horus, Seth's destruction of Horus's eye, and its restoration by Thoth illustrate the enormous interest of the Egyptians in this restored Eye of Horus (*udjat/wedjat*) and its assumed power to heal and ward off evil. This power of Horus's eye was attributed to apotropaic representations of his eye as well. From the

---

Horus see also *The Book of the Dead* (1979 ed., 59, *Ani Papyrus*).

244. Borghouts 1978:2, citing the text given by Schott 1931.

245. See Budge 1978/1930:165–71 and depiction of the obverse and reverse of the stele, pp. 166–167. See also Budge 1971/1901:147–56; for the Metternich stele, see 149, 153.

246. Budge 1978/1930:141. Budge (1971/1901:56) took the combination of *wedjat* eyes to represent the two eyes of Horus, "one of which, according to an ancient text, was white [right eye] and the other black [left]."

247. P.Leid. 1. 348; Pinch 1994:142.

248. Pinch 1994:109, fig. 56. On the mythology of the solar and lunar eyes and the association of the eye of Ra with the Eye goddess, his daughter, see Pinch 1994:18–32. On the Eye-God, Eye-Goddess see Crawford 1957; Riemschneider 1953;

Eighteenth Dynasty (1550 BCE) onward, the *wedjat* Eye of Horus adorned tomb walls and coffins to protect the dead and guide them in their underworld journey.[249] The Turin Papyrus of *The Book of the Dead* (1600s BCE onwards), chapter 167, contains a spell, the reciting of which was thought to cause the god Thoth to bring the *wedjat* to the deceased during his journey to the realm of Osiris. A papyrus of the Twentieth Dynasty (c. 1186–1070 BCE) in the Turin museum includes the statement, "you forced her with two chains, and [you forced] him with your eye."[250] Another papyrus contains the words, "We protect her from the Evil Eye in order to get back the Evil Eye."[251]

In various colors and sizes, representations of the *wedjat/udjat* Eye of Horus were depicted on papyri and deployed in temples, on stelae, and at door posts of houses. The image also appears on each of two apotropaic wands made of ivory (nineteenth–seventeenth cent. BCE).[252] Boats and ships also had an Eye of Horus painted on their prows to protect their cargo and personnel—a practice that continued in the Mediterranean world through later time and down to the present.[253] It was painted on coffins as early as the Sixth Dynasty (c. 2345 BCE) and displayed prominently in tombs.[254] "On the person of Tutankhamen there were no less than fourteen pieces of jewelry containing the Eye of Horus."[255] The enormous number of *wedjat*s found in tombs shows their vital importance for the Egyptians and the special service they provided to both the dead and the living.[256]

249. On Egyptian funery custom and art see also Pinch 1994:147–60.

250. Seligmann 1910 1:18.

251. Ibid.; cf. Goodenough 1953 2:240.

252. Pinch 1994:41, fig. 20.

253. Numerous depictions of Egyptian boats with *wedjat*s painted on their prows appear in the vignettes of the *Book of the Dead* (1979 ed.): see 36–37, 52, 67, 84; see also 115 (replica of a funery boat with *wedjat* on prow); also Potts 1982:20, fig 31 (*Papyrus of Ani*). Braudel (2001:80) praises the accuracy of Egyptian depiction while also mentioning a catalogue of sixty-nine drawings of ancient ships of the Aegean by Spryridon Marinatos in 1933, and a reproduction by Diana Woolner of thirty-eight graffiti showing ships carved on a pillar in the temple of Hal Tarxian in Malta; see also Seligmann 1910:2, figs. 105–16. On ancient ships and boats, see Cassib 1971, Johnstone 1980, and Rougé 1981; for apotropaic eyes on ships in the Hellenistic and Roman periods see Nowak 2006.

254. Budge 1978/1930:141.

255. Potts 1982:17.

256. Budge 1978/1930:142. For illustrations see Budge 1978/1930:141, 166, 174; Elworthy 1958/1895:126, fig. 10; Seligmann 1910 2, figs. 127–132; Potts 1982:17–20; Höbl 1986, Plates 80–89; Hermann 2002:48–54, 85–91, 11–112, 115, 150–51. On the *wedjat/udjat* Eye of Horus see Pinch 1994: 27–29, 41, 79, 109–10, 115, 135, 180; figs. 10, 56; on the Evil Eye more generally, Pinch 1994: 39, 58, 73, 107, 117, 123.

The Eye of Horus (wedjat) as Amulet

Representations of the *wedjat* (or variously written *udjat*) Eye of Horus were also worn as personal amulets for protection against the Evil Eye. This Eye of Horus was for Egyptians "the archetypal amulet,"[257] and chief means for countering the Evil Eye.[258] Archaeological digs have turned up myriads of amuletic Eyes of Horus, not only in Egypt but throughout the Mediterranean world. "Historically, the oldest amulets come from Egypt," dating as far back as the fourth millennium BCE.[259] In following centuries, "Egyptian amulets were exported or copied all over the ancient world."[260] Amulets worn regularly for protection "were likely to be in the form of jewellery . . . most Egyptian jewellery had amuletic value."[261] The first half of the second millennium BCE saw a great expansion of amulet types. "Much amuletic jewellery of fine quality survives from this period."[262] Amuletic eyes of Horus provided both adornment and protection. Appearing from the Old Kingdom onward

Illus. 2.3
Eye of Horus image from
porticus of the temple of
Dendera, Egypt
(from Seligmann 1910
2:127, fig.129)

Illus. 2.2
Eye of Horus amulet,
Egypt (from Elworthy
1895/1958:126, fig. 10)

257. Pinch 1994:109.

258. For representations of the Eye of Horus/*wedjat*/*udjat* see illustrations 2.1, 2.2, 2.3; also Seligmann 1910:1, fig. 55; 1910:2:, figs. 127–132; Budge 1978/1930:141, 174; Ulmer figs. 1, 2, 3, 8; Pinch 1994:27, fig. 10; 109, fig. 56; Herrmann 2002 passim; see also the large collection of *wedjat* amulets of various shapes, sizes and colors in the Bologna Museum, Egyptian Section.

259. Gaster 1989:147; see Pinch 1994:9. On Egyptian amulets see Reitzenstein 1904:291–303; Naville 1910; Wiedemann 1910; Petrie 1914; Bonner 1950; Budge 1978/1930: 133–76; Andrews 1994; 2001 vol. 1:75–82; Hermann 1994, 2002; Pinch 1994:104–19.

260. Pinch 1994:104.

261. Ibid., 105; see also Naville 1910; Andrews 1996.

262. Pinch 1994:115. On amulets in general see Vol. 2.

(2400 BCE) or earlier,[263] this amuletic eye was made in various sizes and colors and of various substances (gold, silver, copper, granite, hematite, carnelian, lapis-lazuli, porcelain, wood, wax, faience,[264] with turquoise[265] being especially frequent).[266] It appears in a circular piece of gold and silver jewelry (c. 2000–1800 BCE) as one of several protective symbols.[267] Miniature *wedjats* were worn as pendants on necklaces, especially by children, whom Egyptians, like their neighbors, deemed particularly vulnerable to the Evil Eye. It was one of the most common amulets employed by the ancient Egyptians and then their successors in all periods of their history. Budge lists the *udjat/wedjat*/Eye of Horus among the principal twenty-five Egyptian funerary amulets employed to protect the deceased in the Hall of Judgment.[268] A small gold pendant amulet (c. tenth cent. BCE) depicts the god Thoth holding the *wedjat* eye.[269] "My belief," Budge states, "is that the Egyptians, like the Chinese, were terrified by their fear of the Evil Eye, and that the Udjat was worn or carried universally as a protection against it."[270]

When the Evil Eye eventually was linked conceptually with the vice of envy, the Eye of Horus was employed to protect against both. In Egypt of the first millennium BCE, Pinch has observed,[271] "it became more common to attribute personal problems to the envy or spite of people who possessed the Evil Eye." On a wooden "spell board" from Akhmim (fourth cent. BCE) is inscribed a spell meant to protect against any potentially harmful person or force.[272] On the reverse side, the seven carved *wedjat* eyes that join six

263. Potts 1982:17.

264. Budge 1971/1901:55.

265. Turquoise, mined at Sinai, was blue in color, symbolizing fertility and the heavenly realm of the gods.

266. The Museo Civico Archeologico of Bologna, Egyptian section, is one among many museums worldwide housing vast collections of *wedjat* Eyes of Horus. See also the faience plate of turquoise color with seven udjat eyes, Louvre Museum E17358, Department of Antiquities, Paris. A painted terracotta cup with two udjat eyes on the bottom from Ugarit (Minet-el-Beida), Syria (fourteenth–twelfth cent. BCE), is in the Louvre (AO 15727).

267. Pinch 1994:111 and fig. 57.

268. Budge, *Amulets* 1978/1930:135–49. These also include the Tjet amulet whose red color and symbolization of the genitalia of the goddess Isis and her blood (Budge 1978/1930:137; Andrews 1994) are identical with features of later Greco-Roman Evil Eye amulets. For a photograph of a Horus amulet for healing with surrounding beasts similar to those of all-suffering eye see *ISBE* (1986) 3: 215.

269. Pinch 1994:109 and fig. 10, p. 27.

270. Budge 1978/1930:142

271. Pinch 1994:73. See also Vittmann 1984.

272. Pinch 1994:73–74 and fig. 36.

images of gods suggest that the Evil Eye of envy was included among these hostile forces.

The protective and blessing Eye of Horus was worn and carried as a personal amulet far into the Hellenistic age and was popular far beyond the borders of Egypt. "The Udjat-eye was the most popular Egyptian amulet found in Palestine/Israel," Christian Herrmann has noted.[273]

A custom linked with the Eye of Horus, and which extended far beyond Egypt, is the use of the sign RX by medical physicians worldwide as a symbol for "prescription" or "as directed." This sign, it has been proposed, derives from details of the Egyptian artistic representation of the Eye of Horus, the *wedjat* or "sound eye, the life-giving eye, according to ophthalmologist George Bohigian."[274]

Illus. 2.4
Eye of Horus as basis for medical symbol of RX

The vertical line below the eye, which is usually accompanied by a wing of a falcon, resembles the mark below the eye of a falcon, Horus's animal representation. The accompanying elongated curved line beneath the eye resembles the tail of the cheetah, another animal revered by the Egyptians. The combination of lines resembled the letter R. The symbol RX, medical students today are taught, stands for *recipe*, the Latin verb meaning "take," in reference to drugs and their quantities in a prescription. This, however, was not the origin of the symbol, which rather was "another abstraction of the falcon-headed god, Horus."[275] It was used by physicians in ancient Rome in a prayer for healing directed to Horus. It also was placed above medical formulas to enhance their effects. Jupiter, king (*rex*) of the Roman deities, was thought to be the most powerful heavenly body for curing illnesses. RX was a symbol used by Roman physicians to call upon the healing powers of Jupiter, with RX likely an abbreviation of REX ("king" [Jupiter]). It has been suggested that in the Middle Ages the merger of the Eye of Horus image with the RX signifying Jupiter—both healing forces—resulted

273. Hermann 2002:48. For depictions of Egyptian anti-Evil Eye amulets found in Palestine see Herrmann 2002; for amuletic Eyes of Horus see Hermann 2002:48–54, 49–54, 85–91, 111–12, 115, 150–51; 168, 171, 186, 192 (Catalog numbers 22, 23–25, 26, 27, 89, 115, 117 [little man with large phallus], 125–26) and for figures of Bes, 19–26, 69–74, 113, 137–139, 163–64. 186 [Catalog Numbers 7–11, 114]). For photographs of the numerous *wedjats* found in Sardinia see Höbl 1986, Plates 80–89.

274. Bohigian 1997:92–94, figs. 1–33, 1998:44, listing also other derivative customs.

275. Moss and Cappannari 1976:2.

in the RX as a powerful healing symbol now used by physicians worldwide. Ironically, many may be unaware of its actual origin.[276]

The Evil Eye of Apopis/Apophis

Among living beings ascribed the Evil Eye, serpents were prominent in ancient Egyptian texts. Apopis/Apophis, alias Apep, was, in Egyptian mythology, the primeval chaos serpent and arch-demon, the most dangerous inhabitant of the underworld.[277] It possessed an Evil Eye that could endanger the sun and bring on darkness. A scene from the interior of a painted coffin from Thebes (eleventh cent. BCE) shows the deceased spearing the chaos monster Apep.[278] Rituals counteracting the Evil Eye of Apopis invoked an array of powerful deities including Thoth, Isis, the Eye of Ra, the spear of Seth, and the solar and lunar Eyes of Horus.[279] Another rite involved using a stick or club to hit a ball probably symbolizing the eye of Apopis.[280] This Apopis serpent may explain the prominence of serpents in Evil Eye representations.[281] Serpents were also said to have blue eyes,[282] which may have been thought to equip them with the protective color

Illus. 2.5
Sri Lanka anti-Evil Eye masks (John H. Elliott collection)

276. See Gifford 1958:67; Bohigian 1997:93, 1998:44; also Budge 1901:55–58.

277. Pinch 1994:35 and Borghouts 1973

278. Pinch 1994:159 and fig. 86.

279. Ibid., 86 describing a ritual mentioned in the *Book of Overthrowing Apep*, part of the fourth-cent. BCE Bremmer-Rhind Papyrus. Apophis also appears in *The Book of the Dead* (ch. 108.13; see also ch. 149.105).

280. So Brenk 1998:14, noting nineteen examples of this iconography found in temples; see also Borghouts 1973:122, 128, fig. 2, 3, and Plate 39.

281. So Brenk 1998:41; see also Borghouts 1973.

282. Rakoczy 1996:174 n. 631.

against an Evil Eye. Modern wooden brightly-painted amuletic masks used in Sri Lanka to protect houses against the Evil Eye involve a gorgon-like or Medusa-like head with fearsome visage, bulging bloodshot eyes, open teeth-baring mouth, extended tongue, and serpents for hair as typical of the Greek Gorgo/Medusa figures of two millennia ago. The serpents, however, are cobras with added *smiling* faces—a feature meant to signal the serpents as not hostile but friendly to the owner and protective of his possessions. Like the ancient serpents with the blue eyes, these modern snakes afford anti-Evil Eye protection, along with the rest of the details of the masks.

Other Defenses against the Evil Eye

Ancient defense against the Evil Eye, in addition to that afforded by the *wedjat* Eye of Horus, was attributed to other figures and objects as well. Prominent among the protective deities, beside Horus, was the god Thoth. A greeting of a statue of Thoth (sometimes portrayed as a squatting ape) includes the words, "O Thoth, if thou wilt be to me a champion, I will fear not for the [Evil] eye."[283] The deity is part of the Horus mythology and his name appears frequently on apotropaic devices. Appeal for protection was also made to Serapis.[284] Other protecting deities included Nut, Neith, Chonsou, Amon, and Sekhmet, as mentioned above. The dwarf demon Bes and the cat-goddess Bast also were linked with the Eye of Horus in providing protection against the Evil Eye. A medallion of the Persian period (525–332 BCE) found in Egypt, has a head of the god Bes on the obverse and a blue *wedjat/udjat* eye on the reverse.[285] The cat goddess Bastet, identified with the sun-god Ra, was viewed as the twin sister of Horus and privileged possessor of his restored eye. In the British Museum is a bronze statue of a seated Bastet from Saqqara, Egypt, c. 664–332 BCE. Named the "Gayer-Anderson Cat" after its donor, it wears an anti-Evil Eye *wedjat* (Eye of Horus) amulet on a necklace. It has also been argued that the numerous beads bearing representations of eyes (the earliest datable to the thirteenth cent. BCE) and frequently appearing with Eyes of Horus, often on the same necklace, also served to ward off the Evil Eye.[286] A rare replica of what could be a human eye, free standing and blue in color, displayed in the Egyptian section of the

283. *Papyrus Anastasi* 3.4.12 ff (c. 1200 BCE).; cf. Ehrman, ed. *Ancient Egyptians*, 306–7; on the Eye of Horus, see also ibid. 11, 12, 304.

284. On Serapis, see also Vol. 2.

285. Herrmann 2002:138–39, Cat. No. 115, p. 186. On Bes see also below.

286. So Eisen 1916; Pott 1982:17–25, with illustrations of ancient and modern eye beads.

Hermitage Museum, St. Petersburg, Russia, likewise may have served as an anti-Evil Eye amulet. The omnipresent blue glass eye replicas used and sold today in Greece, Turkey, and Russia and the *ojo de venado* ("Deer's eye"), an anti-Evil Eye amulet native to Mexico, are amuletic cousins of this eye and the *wedjat* Eye of Horus.

Illus. 2.6
Replica of blue eyes, Egyptian section,
Hermitage Museum, St. Petersburg,
Russia (Photo by John H. Elliott)

Illus. 2.7
Evil Eye bead amulets, St. Petersburg, Russia
(Photo by Alexander Schmidt, by permission)

Other anti-Evil Eye amulets were also employed in Egypt, as they were elsewhere, to protect women in childbirth and newborn babies.[287] Strings of *cowrie shells* were worn as girdles by women to ensure fertility.[288] The shape of these shells was thought to resemble the female genitals as well as the eye.[289] Accordingly, actual cowrie shells or imitations in faience, silver

287. Pinch 1994:106–7, 117, 123, 126.

288. Ibid., 107, fig. 55 (female figure with cowrie shell girdle, nineteenth–eighteenth cent. BCE); 126 and fig. 65 (faience fertility figurine with girdle, c. 1900–1800 BCE); also p. 115.

289. Pinch 1994:107; see also Andrews 1994.

or gold, also became a popular amulet of adornment for protecting birthing mothers against the Evil Eye.[290]

Similar to cowrie shells, images of the *phallus and testicles* also symbolized fertility and also were deployed to off the Evil Eye. The *Turin Erotic Papyrus* (c. 1520 BCE) found at Deir el Medina, Egypt, and now in the Egyptian Museum, contains twelve tableaus, perhaps for a brothel. Included is a bas relief of a phallus and testicles, a symbol that in later Roman time becomes a prevalent apotropaic against the Evil Eye. Among the Egyptian amulets found in Palestine was one of a squatting male equipped with a huge phallus (c. 664–30 BCE).[291]

The *eye makeup* and cosmetics of ancient Egyptian women, as of modern Egyptian women, particularly the heavy coloration with kohl and mesdemet (made from Galena or Stibnite) may also have been employed not only to enlarge the appearance of the eye, reduce sun glare, and avert eye infection. The makeup may also have been intended to protect against an Evil Eye.

The *hand*, also viewed as a symbol of power and creative energy, likewise appears on amulets. The goddess Hathor was given the epithet, "Hand of Atum." A pair of ivory clappers from Thebes (c. 1300 BCE) shows each clapper topped by a hand above a face of Hathor.[292] An amulet of a miniature open hand likely symbolized the gesture of liberality and generosity made by an open right hand, palm outward and held vertically.[293] An image of an open hand was placed on buildings to protect against an Evil Eye. In modern Spain this practice is also found. An amuletic open hand with an eye drawn in its center, alternatively, was worn on a pendent. This hand-with-eye-in-palm design continued to appear in anti-Evil Eye amulets down through the centuries in both Jewish and Muslim cultures as the Hand of Miriam (Hamesh) or Hand of Fatimah (Hamsa) respectively. The cover of Dundes's 1992 study, *The Evil Eye*, paperback edition, shows a photograph of an Israeli anti-Evil Eye amulet consisting of an open right hand with an eye in its palm.[294] This amulet is also current in the contemporary Southwest United States.

290. On cowrie shells as anti-Evil Eye amulets see also Vol. 2.

291. Hermann 2002:141–42 and p. 186 (Cat. no. 117). On the apotropaic phallus against the Evil Eye in Hellenistic Egypt see Licht 1971:369–70 and Vol. 2.

292. Pinch 1994:85, fig. 42.

293. So Budge 1978/1930:172–73 and fig. 11.

294. The amulet is from the private collection of Barry and Renée Ross. For representations of the apotropaic hand against the Evil Eye found in early Etruscan tombs see Elworthy 1958/1895:241–47 and figs. 96–101. On the apotropaic hand in Greco-Roman Evil Eye tradition see Vol. 2; on the Jewish "Hand of Miriam" and the similar Islamic "Hand of Fatimah," see Budge 1978/1930:467–71, and Vol. 4, chaps. 1 and 2.

Illus. 2.8
Sketch of an open
hand on a Tunesian
drum (from
Seligmann 1910
2:180, fig. 157)

Illus. 2.9
Replicas of open hands
(Hand of Fatima) on
modern building, Spain
(Photo by John H. Elliott)

Illus. 2.10
Amulet of hand with
eye in palm from El
Santuario de Chamayo,
New Mexico (John H.
Elliott collection)

The use of *divine decrees*, issued in the name of deities who gave oracles, "is peculiar to the late second/early first millennia BC."[295] These decrees
were written on tiny pieces of papyrus that were rolled up and placed in an
amulet case (*bulla*) worn by the recipient. Children named in these amulets
were promised protection against harmful deities as well as against demons,
foreign sorcerers, and the Evil Eye.[296]

Spells and incantations against the Evil Eye and other noxious forces
originally were spoken or sung/chanted. Then they were written on papyrus
and inscribed on stone slabs, potsherds, wood, wax, wooden tablets, large
stone stelae, and walls of houses and tombs. Spells written on wooden "spell
boards," as mentioned above, threaten anyone casting an Evil Eye on the
magician's client with a host of fearsome powers including seven Eyes of
Horus.[297] "In one such spell, the aggressor is to be struck with the arrow
of Sekhmet, penetrated by the *heka* [power] of Thoth, cursed by Isis and
blinded by Horus."[298]

Spells written on papyri or slabs of stone or potsherds also were used
to protect newborn infants from female ghosts or living women casting

295. Pinch 1994:116–117.

296. Ibid., 117 and figs. 16a and 16b (pp. 36–37) of a decree from the eleventh to
the ninth centuries BCE.

297. Ibid., 73–74 and fig. 36; cf. also Borghouts 1978:148.

298. Pinch 1994:73; see also Vittmann 1984. On Egyptian "magical" techniques in
general see Ritner 1993.

an Evil Eye. Childbirth in antiquity was a dangerous time for mothers and newborns. "In modern Egypt and Sudan, protection from the Evil eye is one of the main reasons given for keeping a mother and child in isolation of up to forty days after the birth."[299] For most of human history, between twenty and fifty percent of babies have not lived through their first year. Even in the later Roman period, about one-third of those surviving the first year of life were dead by age 6. "Nearly 60 percent of these survivors had died by age 16 . . . by age 46, 90 percent were gone. Less than three percent of the population made it to age 60."[300] Many mothers were lost in childbirth; widowers and orphans were commonplace. Among the causes of illness and death were infectious diseases, malnutrition, nonexistent sanitation, poor housing, bad diet, inaccessible medical care, and, in the common mind, the ubiquitous Evil Eye. Hence the imperative to provide these newborns and infants with anti-Evil Eye protection. The *personal names* given to children also were intended to provide this defense.[301]

The lion dwarf deity/demon Bes was thought to protect mothers at childbirth and newborns from the Evil Eye.[302] A relief of Bes appears on a block in the forecourt of the temple of Hathor at Dendera.[303] A free-standing limestone stela with three threatening Bes figures in a row (c. 100 BCE–100 CE) serves to protect a building and its area from dangerous forces including the Evil Eye.[304] Over a millennium earlier, a frightening image of Bes appears in relief on a limestone headrest from Deir el-Medina (thirteenth cent. BCE) owned by a royal scribe. Snakes gripped in his hand symbolize his power over the demons of the night.[305] Bes amulets are frequent among the Egyptian amulets found in Palestine.[306] One medallion combines the *wedjat/udjat* eye and Bes, with a head of Bes on the obverse and a blue *wedjat*-eye on the reverse—an interesting combination of anti-Evil Eye mo-

299. Pinch 1994:123.

300. Rohrbaugh 1996:4–5, citing the seminal work of Carney 1975:8.

301. On the assumed apotropaic power of certain personal names see Sainte Fare Garnot 1960; Sauneron 1966:51, 63 and notes 77–78; Bernand 1991:103.also Spiegelberg 1924:150–153.

302. Pinch 1994:122–123, 128–132.

303. Ibid., 129 and fig. 69. On Bes see ibid., 40, 43–45, 78, 84, 86 (and fig. 43, painted wooden figure of Bes from Thebes, c. 1300 BCE), 100, 101 (and fig. 53), 102, 115–116, 121 (and fig. 63), 122, 127, 129, 131–132 (and fig. 71), 157, 162, 164, 170, 171(and fig. 92), and the cover illustration.

304. Ibid., 171, fig. 92.

305. On Bes holding serpents, see also ibid., 40–43 (figs. 19–21).

306. For depictions see Hermann 2002:19–26, 69–74, 113, 137–39, 163–64, 186 [catalog numbers 7–11, 114]).

tifs.[307] Bes often is depicted displaying his genitals against the Evil Eye. The most powerful phallus protecting against the Evil Eye among Egyptians, Andrè Bernand proposes,[308] however, was associated with the god Min,

Illus. 2.11

Bes, Egyptian deity/demon, Egypt, 1550-1070 BCE. (Line drawing by Dietlinde Elliott)

whom the Greeks assimilated to their god Pan. Ithyphallic in form, he ruled in the desert regions as a symbol of fecundity in the face of infertility. Similar to the apotropaic function of Greek herms, and like Bes, Min too averted *baskania*/Evil Eye.[309]

307. Ibid., 138–39.

308. Bernand 1991:104. On Min as provider of the fertility of crops, animals and humans see Pinch 1994:120, and as protector of birthing mothers, ibid., 130.

309. An abundance of Egyptian amulets is housed in the Museo Civico Archeologico di Bologna. This includes the Room of Glass Exhibition, Case 9C: Eyes (Late Dynastic Period, 1075–332 BCE, nos. 242–243); ring with *wedjat* (Eye of Horus, Eighteenth Dynasty, 1400–1292 BCE, no. 245); necklace with various pendants, including the mano fica and blue beads, no. 252; another necklace with blue beads, no. 251. The Egyptian collection (lower ground floor) is arranged historically:

- Middle Kingdom: Double Eyes of Horus on sarcophagus of Irinimenpu, XII–XIII Dynasty, 1938–1640 BCE; Double Eyes of Horus on several stelae [no. 5, Stele of Ipi, XII–XIII Dynasties; no. 6, Stele of Bibi, XIII Dynasty (1759–1640 BCE, with ahnk between two eyes); no. 7, Stele of Iki (XII–XIII Dynasties);
- New Kingdom: Part One: no. 2, Double Eyes of Horus on funeral stele of Menkheper XVIII Dynasty, 1539–1292 BCE; also nos. 5, 7, 8, 10, 11. Part Two: Double Eyes of Horus on no. 1 (XVIII Dynasty); no. 5 (XIX Dynasty,

Fear of the Evil Eye showed no letup with the advent of Greek rule over Egypt. The evidence rather reveals a continued concern for protection and a merging of Egyptian and Greek Evil Eye traditions.

Egypt under Greece and Rome
(332 BCE to Late Antiquity)
Egyptian–Greek–Roman Syncretism

Alexander's conquest of Egypt (332 BCE) was followed by the imposition of Macedonian/Greek rule through Alexander's successor, Ptolemy and the Lagid dynasty (306–30 BCE). This resulted in Greek (Macedonian) political and cultural hegemony over Egypt and the further Hellenization of this corner of the Circum-Mediterranean world. In the process, Macedonian/ Greek and then subsequent Roman control of Egypt produced a syncretistic blending of native Egyptian with foreign Macedonian-Greek and then Roman cultures. Egypt, along with Persia, is now viewed by outsiders as one of "the two great magical cultures" and source of abundant occult wisdom.[310] At this time, however, there remained an extensive influence of Egyptian culture throughout the Circum-Mediterranean, including dread of the Evil

---

1279–1213 BCE, Ramses II).
- Late Period (664–332 BCE): three gold Eyes of Horus (no. 22); Eye of Horus on blue ring.

Amulets are also displayed in Wing V. This collection, involving virtually the entire collection of Palagi, has approximately 2,000 objects, organized into 120 types. The information indicates that the color green symbolizes vegetation and spring; blue, water and heavens; red, blood. One row contains forty-four Eyes of Horus in various colors of blue (most), green, and red; along with replicas of human eyes (lines made of circles/ eyes). In addition, there are three phallus amulets, one of which shows two eyes on the top of the amulet above a phallus; and one Bes amulet.

Petrie's classic discussion of amulets mentions several anti-Evil Eye amulets (1914:11, 16, 27, 28, 29), at least one of which he explicitly identifies as Egyptian (No. 111, p. 27: a Cardium edule shell, "prehistoric to VI dynasty of Egypt" (c. 2345–2181 BCE).

No. 13 (p. 11) a mano fica "a fist , thumb between first and second fingers"

No. 16 (p. 11) a phallus, solely Greco-Roman and not used by Egyptians

No. 104 (p. 26) a horn

No. 106 (p. 27) a coral

No. 107 (p. 27) a Cypraen shell against both the Evil Eye witchcraft

No. 114 (p. 27) a Pectunculus Violacesceus shell

No. 124 (p. 28) a bell

No. 128 (p. 28) a Medusa head (not, however, identified by Petrie as against the Evil Eye)

No. 130 (p. 29) a forehead pendant

310. Ogden 2002:46; see pp. 33–52 (Persia), 52–60 (Egypt); see also Pliny, *NH* 30 on the Persian magi.

Eye, so that traditional Egyptian motifs concerning the Evil Eye now receive a make-over in Greek and Roman dress.[311]

Numerous letters in Greek found in Roman Egypt begin or conclude with the apotropaic wish that "X (usually a family member and most often children) be kept safe from the Evil Eye (*abaskantos*)."[312] Appearances of the Greek term *abaskantos* in Egyptian papyri of the Ptolemaic and subsequent Roman period (332 BCE–) have been discussed by Danielle Bonneau (1982). *Abaskantos*, literally "not Evil-Eyed,"[313] is translated by Bonneau as "kept safe from malefactors" ("preserve des maléfices").[314] This word appears far more often in the papyri than the rare occurrences of other terms of the *bask-* family[315] as both an adjective and a proper name, both with apotropaic force. Christian authors continued the practice, as fourth-century personal letters reveal.[316] As a personal name, *Abaskantos* was used by Romans, Jews, and Christians throughout the Circum-Mediterranean world, especially in Greece and Anatolia (Asia Minor), its likely place of origin.[317] In the Nile valley, some thirty occurrences are found in papyri (19), ostraka (4) and one inscription, several (14) identifying slaves or ex-slaves and persons engaged in business.[318] An instance of the Latin equivalent, *Abascantus*, also functioning as the proper name of a slave, appears in an inscription from the coast of the Black Sea (CIL 3. 5122 = ILS 1679). As an adjective, *abaskantos* is attested from the first through the fourth centuries CE among Romans and Christians.[319] It appears in some seventy personal letters at either the opening or close, usually wishing protection for family

---

311. On the syncretism of this period in realm of occult wisdom and practice see Colpe 1976:615–626; Pinch 1994:161–173; for relevant texts from the first to fourth cents. CE see Ogden 2002:52–60, §§53–56.

312. On this term and the practice, see also Vol. 2.

313. The word consists of an alpha privative (*a-*) meaning "not" added to *baskantos* meaning "Evil-Eyed;" thus "not Evil-Eyed" = "not harmed by the Evil Eye."

314. Bonneau 1982:23.

315. So Bonneau 1982:24, who indicates one instance of *probaskania* (sixth cent. CE, BGU 954.9 [PGM 2: 217]; van Haelst, *Catalogue*, no. 720 (one instance of *baskanos*, sixth cent. CE), P.Rein. 82; cf. SB 10702 [SEG 24.1199, fourth cent. CE]); and one of *baskosynê* (sixth–seventh cent. CE, P.Turner 49.4).

316. Bonneau 1982:25.

317. Ibid., 26, 35–36.

318. Ibid., 26–29.

319. Ibid., 25.

members and especially children (c. 80% of the instances).[320] In two cases it even is used to provide protection for a horse.[321]

The Greek term, Bonneau notes, does not translate any Egyptian expression for Evil Eye.[322] It first appears in the Nile valley in the Roman period (30 BCE). Used in military contexts, it was probably introduced, she surmises, by elements of the Roman army, the cavalry in particular, and thereafter was employed in private correspondence as a formula of courtesy and good manners.[323] Bonneau's accumulation of data is useful, but deficient in its conclusion. Bonneau is aware of the relation of this term to the Evil Eye, as "apotropaic Abaskantos" in the article's title and other comments indicate.[324] But by describing it rather weakly as an expression of "good manners," she unjustifiably minimizes the significance of its use for repelling envy and the dreaded Evil Eye.

In an official complaint (dated May 22, 197 CE) registered by a certain Gemellus with Hierax, the strategos of the Arsinoite nome in Egypt, Gemellus accuses his neighbors Sotas and Sotas's brother, Julius, of using an Evil Eye device to frighten off Gemellus's tenant farmer and to aid in dispossessing Gemellus of his harvest.[325] Gemellus complains that his neighbor Sotas, and after Sotas' death, Sotas's brother Julius, had invaded his fields and stolen hay and olive shoots. Julius returned with accomplices, Zenas and his wife, and brought with them, he states, "a symbol of an Evil Eye (literally, a *brephos*—a replica of a "fetus" or "neonate," or a baby doll [?]) intending to enclose my tenant farmer with malicious envy (*pthônôi periklisai*)."[326] The frightened farmer fled from the field, with Julius and accomplices stealing the crop he had been harvesting. When Gemellus confronted Julius, "his [Julius's] party threw the Evil Eye symbol [*brephos*] at me intending to enclose me with malicious envy (*pthônôi periklisai*)" right in the presence of the village officials. Then, Gemellus continues, Julius took the Evil Eye symbol (*brephos*) and the remaining crops from the field and carried them off to

---

320. Ibid., 30 nn. 45–49.

321. Ibid., 30; see O.Amst. 18, 2; O.Florida 18, 5.

322. Ibid., 33–35.

323. Ibid., 23, 35–36.

324. Ibid., 23–25.

325. P.Mich. 6.423–424, edited by Youtie and Pearl and first published by them in 1944 among the Karanis papyri. For an English translation see Lewis 1983:78–79. For an analysis, see Bryen and Wypustek 2009; see also Frankfurter 2006.

326. I follow Lewis (1983:79) in taking *brephos* ("fetus" or "neonate") to be some "symbol of the Evil Eye" primarily because of the traditional concept of the Evil Eye as the mechanism by which envy is conveyed and because here this symbol is the specific means for working "malicious envy."

his own place. Gemellus's official complaint sought justice after this robbery and includes an accusation that he has been the victim of attack by an envious Evil Eye. While *phthonos* as "envy" would certainly fit the attitudes and actions of Sotas and Julius, it might also stand in here for *baskania* ("Evil Eye malice") with which it was so closely associated and which likewise had harmful effect.[327] Envy, then, it would have been claimed, motivated the hostility of Sotas and Julius, while it was their Evil Eye device that physically threatened Gemellus. The details of the incident are curious. Fetuses and neonates were, as a rule, the victims of, rather than the media for, for executing an Evil Eye attack. It is possible, however, that we have here an instance of thinking and action according to the principle of "sympathy," *similia similibus,* "like influences like." In this case, the *brephos* as a *means* of attack was in sympathy with the *brephos* as usual *object* of attack.[328] This case is also unusual in that the Evil Eye, which is customarily thought to be conveyed by a noxious glance, is here embodied in the noxious image of a neonate.[329]

Another Evil Eye accusation in similar circumstances possibly is part of an early second-century CE petition from Oxyrhynchus, Egypt. A woman is accused of embezzling proceeds from wine, but also of "casting an Evil Eye over us" (*hêmin katopteusasa,* line 29), possibly to hinder the victims from taking action.[330]

A papyrus document from Theadelphia, Egypt (280–281 CE) contains the minutes of a legal proceeding involving a widow, her two sons and another Evil Eye accusation.[331] A certain Syrion was charged in court by the widow Artemis and her two sons for having stolen animals left by the deceased father to the family. "Syrion," the advocate Isidorus charged, "cast an Evil Eye (*epophthalmiasas*) on the animals left by their father (who was a shepherd), and he seized them to the number of sixty." Syrion was ordered

---

327. As is noted below, *phthonos* and its paronyms occassionally were substituted for *baskania* and its family of terms to avoid the danger of even uttering these latter more potent words. Rakoczy describes this as the effect of a *Sprachtabu*; see Rakoczy 1996:41, 61–62, 83 n. 204, and Vol. 2.

328. This would be similar to the Greek masculine noun *baskanos* designating an Evil-Eyed aggressor and the related neuter noun *baskanon* (and the diminuative *baskanion*) designating an anti-Evil Eye protective.

329. Bryen and Wypustek (2009:551–52) propose, on the other hand, that Julius's throwing of the *brephos*/neonate image was a self-protective action on his part to ward off an Evil Eye of Gemellus.

330. P.Oxy. 22.2342. See Frankfurter 2006:38, n. 2. The compound verb *katopteusasa* represents another term belonging to the Evil Eye word field; compare *katabaskainô.* On the Greek terms for Evil Eye see, Vol. 2.

331. P. Thead. 15. Hunt and Edgar, *Select Papyri,* 1934 2:208–11.

by the authorities to return the sheep to the children but he resisted. So a new request for return of the stolen sheep was lodged. The relevant verb is *epophthalmiaô* ("cast an Evil Eye upon," or "eye enviiously"),[332] which action involved the theft of sixty animals. The disposition involved here is not so much envy (wishing the sheep destroyed) as greed (wanting the sheep for oneself).

Lucian, the second-century CE author and rhetorician, recounts a conversation concerning a certain Pancates, an Egyptian sacred scribe and performer of extraordinary acts (*Philopseudes* 33–36). A speaker, Eucrates, says in regard to Pancrates, "I was eager to acquire this power [of his], but I had no way of learning this from him." The explanatory clause that follows contains the standard Greek verb for "to Evil Eye" (*baskainen*), namely *ebaskaine*. Daniel Ogden's translation reads, "for he was jealous of it [*ebaskaine*], although openly generous with everything else."[333] This translation of the standard verb *baskainen* meaning "to Evil Eye" as "be jealous" is off the mark. The speaker's point is not that Pancrates feared being dispossessed of his power (= jealousy), but that Pancrates was *unwilling to share* his power with Eucrates; out of stinginess he *begrudged* lending it to anyone else. This sense of *baskainein* as *begrudging* a gift is associated with an the Evil Eye in the biblical text of Sir 14:8: "Evil (*ponêros*) is one who begrudges (*baskainôn*) with an [Evil] eye (*ophthalmô*); he turns away his face and disregards people."[334] Modern translators unfortunately often confuse or equate the terms "envy" and "jealousy," which in antiquity denoted related, but different, emotions and social dynamics.[335]

In the popular romance novel, the *Aethiopica*, by Heliodorus (*fl.* 220–250 CE), an Egyptian priest of Isis, Calasiris, clarifies for the protagonist, Theagenes, the true nature of Egyptian wisdom. One form is vulgar, earthly, and involved in illicit matters; the other facilitates contact with heaven and the gods and promotes everything good. Theagenes, a Thessalian noble, had sought the priest's aid in winning the affection of Chariclea, daughter of the queen of Ethiopia. The narrative contains an important scene in which the nature and working of the Evil Eye is discussed. The novel illustrates thinking on the nature and operation of the Evil Eye belief and practice in third-century CE Egypt.[336]

332. See also *epophthalmeô*, P. Thead. 19.9.

333. Ogden 2002:55.

334. For looking with an Evil Eye and begrudging a gift, see also Deut 15:7–11; 28:54, 57; Tob 4:7, 16.

335. On this point see Vols. 2 and 3.

336. This work will be discussed in Vol. 2.

In respect to Egyptian amulets, over fifteen hundred amulets have been found in Palestine at Ascelon and Acco showing Egyptian influence beyond its boundaries and the lively exchange of artifacts of popular culture.[337] Among these amulets are many designed to repel the Evil Eye (*wedjat* eyes, figures of Bes, figures with huge phalluses). Another type of anti-Evil Eye amulet is a small figurine (664–30 BCE) depicting a male sitting figure with bushy eyebrows and holding an overlarge phallus.[338]

Matthew W. Dickie speaks of "terminology, ideas, and images drawn from Egyptian religion [that] have been absorbed on the one hand into Greek magical texts and on the other into the iconography of magic amulets."[339] The Egyptian tradition of coping with illness and evil is evident in the *Greek Magical Papyri* found in Greco-Roman Egypt. This is a body of texts containing a variety of spells and formulae, hymns and rituals, mainly from the second to the fifth centuries CE.[340] These papyri are dramatic evidence of the syncretistic combination of Greek and Egyptian tradition in the Hellenistic period.[341] "Jewish material [contained in these papyri] appears to derive from hellenistic syncretistic Judaism," Hans Dieter Betz notes, "rather than from Jewish religion of the time of the Old Testament. The few 'Christian' elements are part of the hellenistic-Jewish syncretistic spells."[342] In these Greek Magical Papyri, however, the Evil Eye is rarely mentioned, though the prevalence of Evil Eye belief and practice is well documented by other sources.

Dellate and Derchain, writing on the Evil Eye in Egypt in the Hellenistic period, present a figure of a medallion to be worn as an amulet. On its reverse side is a representation of an envious Evil Eye (*phthoneros, kakos ophthalmos*) under attack.[343] The pictorial motif of the Evil Eye attacked by

---

337. See Herrmann 1994, 2002; Müller-Winkler 1987.

338. Herrmann 2002:141–42 and Cat. No. 117, p. 186, provenance not indicated; for parallels from Israel/Palestine see Herrmann 2002:142. On Egyptian amulets see Naville 1910; Petrie 1914:4–8 and passim; Lexa 1925; Bonner 1950; Delatte and Derchain 1964; Borghouts 1978; Budge 1978/1930:133–76; Pinch 1994:104–19.

339. Dickie 2001:203.

340. On the *Greek Magical Papyri*, see Preisendanz 1927, 1935, 1950, 1973–1974; Nock 1929; Nilsson 1947–1948; Vermaseren 1982; Betz 1986–1992, 1987.

341. Betz 1991:248–49.

342. Ibid., 249.

343. Delatte and Derchain 1964:72–73 and illustration. Text and description are given in Bernand 1991:102–3, who also comments on envy, the Evil Eye and apotropaics (85–105).

various enemies is a popular one in this period.[344] and is illustrated and discussed further in Volume Two and Volume Four, Chapter 2.

Nonnus of Panopolis, Egypt (fifth century CE), composed the work *Dionysiaca*, a story concerning the god Dionysus in forty-eight books. Here Megaera, the mythical figure notorious for her Evil Eye, played a role. Book 31 describes how the goddess Hera "swelling with envious passions" and directing envious anger against Perseus and Dionysus (vv. 24–25), persuaded Persephone to help her deceive Zeus. Persephone gave Hera a companion, Megaera, one of the Furies, so that with her Evil Eye she might aid Hera in her envious purpose (vv. 73–74).[345] Here we see in late Roman Egyptian antiquity the continued association of Megaera, envy, and the Evil Eye as found in earlier Greek and Roman sources.[346]

Illus. 2.12
Byzantine silver Seal of Solomon
medallion amulet, Evil Eye attacked
(from Seligmann 1910 2:443, fig. 230)

A marble block (now in the British Museum) has on its front depictions of the Egyptian deities Serapis and Isis-Tyche. On the back of the block is a scene in which various creatures are attacking an object which is difficult to decipher. A. Michaelis (1885) proposed a phallus, but Dunbabin and Dickie (1983:25–27) object that this would be unique and problematic because the phallus conventionally attacks an Evil Eye rather than being the object of an assault. They plausibly propose a figure of envy (*phthonos*). Serapis as protector against the Evil Eye appears repeatedly in the inscriptions; for example, "The one God Serapis—the Evil Eye is burst asunder"

344. For numerous examples see Vol. 2 on Greece and Rome. For a funery inscription of this Hellenistic period referring to the Evil Eye (*baskanie*) see Bernand 1969, nos. 64, 122b, reproduced in Bernand 199:100.

345. Walcot 1978: 89–90.

346. On Megaera, see Vol. 2.

(*eis Zeus Serapis baskanos lakêsetô*) and "Serapis conquers envy" (*nika ho Serapis ton phthonon*).[347]

A small apotropaic plaque of the Ptolemaic era shows a rider mounted on a horse (the so-called "cavalier" motif). The plaque once was affixed to the wall of a house. Paul Perdrizet (1922) discusses this motif on amulets and notes its similarity to a depiction of the Egyptian figure of Heron/Horus[348] on horseback spearing a serpent and called "very great God" (on a stele dated 67 BCE). It is also similar to amulets that depict Solomon as as a cavalier on horseback and spearing a serpent.[349] Mindful of the syncretism typical of this era, Perdrizet traced this apotropaic motif of the cavalier lancing a serpent (or some other object) to amulets, including Greco-Roman, Jewish, and Christian examples, ranging in date from the Ptolemaic period to late Roman antiquity. Later Egyptian Jewish and Christian (Syriac and Coptic) amulets with the same cavalier motif are associated with the wise and powerful King Solomon (cf. 2 Chr 1:14–17 for his cavalry), Saint Sisinnius (a double of St. Michael), and other Christian equestrian saints (Theodore, George, confessors, martyrs). The amulets were employed against the Evil Eye, the female infant-devouring demon Gyllou, one name for whom was *Baskosynê* ("Evil Eye"), and other evil forces. One amuletic medallion shows, on the obverse, Saint Sisinnius as cavalier with a lance piercing the goul Alabasdria, with an inscription mentioning the pursuit by both Sisinnius and Solomon. The reverse of the medallion shows a supine goul above which is an Evil Eye attacked by three daggers from above and, from the sides and below, two lions, an ibis, a serpent, and a scorpion. The inscription reads: *Phthonos* ("Envy/envious Evil Eye"), with the exergue expressing the appeal, "Seal of Solomon, drive away every evil from the bearer (of this amulet)" (*Sphragis Solomonis, apodioxon pan kakon apo tou porountos*).[350]

The depiction of an Evil Eye under attack is a common scene on amulets of this period.[351] Perdrizet mentions three related amulets. One is a black-white mosaic from a threshold of a store selling fine pearls (Co-

347. On this Xanthius marble see Michaelis 1885:287–318, and on the Woburn Marble, 313–18.

348. Perdrizet regards Greek *Hêrôn* as a Hellenized form of the name of the god Horus.

349. Perdrizet 1922:5–11, figs. 1–7.

350. Ibid., 27 and figs. 7–8.

351. For Syriac versions of this cavalier anti-Evil Eye image see Budge 1978/1930:272–82, facsimiles on 274, 275, 276, 278, 279 from the Syriac "The Little Book of Protection" edited and translated by Hermann Gollancz (1912); see also Ford 1998:213–216 on this concept of the Evil Eye as a demon, from Mesopotamian incantations onward. On the Greek Evil-Eye demon (*baskanos daimôn*), see Vol. 2.

elian Hill, Rome). It shows an Evil eye pierced by a lance and attacked by a hoard of beasts.[352] The second is a medallion with an owl on the obverse, and in the exergue the words, "the lion of the tribe of Judah, root of David, is victorious." On the reverse are words repelling *invidia invidiosa*, "envious Envy."[353] The third, a threshold mosaic discovered in Susa, Tunisia, North Africa, in the ruins of a Roman villa, shows an Evil Eye surrounded by two serpents and attacked from above by a phallus.[354] A fresco at Bawit, Egypt, shows a cavalier spearing from his horse a female figure. Above the head of this female demon is an Evil Eye pierced by three daggers from above and by an ibis, two serpents and a scorpion from below.[355] The Bawit fresco and the medallion function as apotropaics against the Evil Eye and show the prophylactic power attributed to the cavalier, St. Sisinnius, in antiquity.[356]

The numerous references to the Evil Eye in the biblical book of the Wisdom of Jesus Ben Sira, whose Greek version was composed in Alexandria Egypt (c. 190–180 BCE), attests the popularity of the belief among Egyptian Israelites of the Ptolemaic period.[357] The Israelite author and philosopher, Philo of Alexandria, Egypt, likewise knows and refers to the concept in the first century of the Common Era.[358] The third-century CE novel of Heliodorus, the *Aethiopica*, is set in Egypt, and includes an episode and a conversation about the Evil Eye. It illustrates the traditional identification of Egypt as the land of occult wisdom and practice, along with continued belief here in the Evil Eye.[359]

In his classic treatment of the Evil Eye, Seligmann makes brief mention of the Evil Eye in ancient Egyptian inscriptions and papyri and of the continuation of Evil Eye belief and practice in modern time among Nubians, Moors, the Kabyle, and Abyssians.[360] Ancient Abyssinia/Ethiopia was thoroughly "Egyptianized" by its neighbor to the north. Evil Eye belief

---

352. Perdrizet 1922:29, fig. 9.

353. Ibid., 30, fig. 10.

354. Ibid., 31, fig. 11; also in Jahn, plate III; also Daremberg-Saglio, fig. 2288, and Cagnat-Chapot, vol. 2 (1920), fig. 451.

355. Perdrizet 1922:13–15, 28 and fig. 6.

356. Ibid., 15. Naveh and Shaked (1987:120, fig. 20) reproduce the fresco but reject Perdrizet's identification of the cavalier Sisinnius as Parthian. On the apotropaic function of cavalier figures see the facsimiles from the Syriac *Book of Protection* (Gollancz 1912) of Solomon and others on horseback spearing a demoness representing an Evil Eye contained in Budge 1978/1930:274–76, 278–80. See also Vol. 4, chaps. 1 and 2.

357. On this text, see Vol. 3.

358. On Philo, see Vol. 3.

359. For a discussion of this novel, see Vol. 2.

360. Seligmann 1910 1:18.

and practice was one element of its absorption of Egyptian culture. Like the Egyptians, pagan Ethiopians also wore a wide variety of amulets to ward off the dangerous Evil Eye.[361] After their adoption of Christianity (fourth cent. CE) Christian Ethiopians continued the wearing of anti-Evil Eye amulets while also employing distinctively Christian written spells.[362] One Coptic spell took the form of a legend or short story that was written on many parchment amulets, the most common type of Ethiopian amulet. As summarized by Budge,[363] the story tells of Jesus and his disciples walking by the Sea of Tiberias and spotting

> a woman of most foul appearance and terrifying aspect sitting upon a seat of filth. Her eyes shot out rays of yellow light like the glitter of old, her hands and her feet seemed to be like wheels, or to move about like wheels, and flashes of fire sixty-eight cubits (i.e. over one hundred feet) came forth from her mouth.

The disciples asked, "what is this thing, O Lord" and Jesus replied,

> This is the Eye of Earth, evil and accursed. If a glance of it falls on a ship at sea, straightway that ship sinketh. If its glance followeth a horse, both horse and rider are cast down. If its glance falleth on a cow which is being milked, the milk goeth sour and is turned to blood. When this Eye looketh upon a woman with child, a miscarriage taketh place, and both child and mother are destroyed.

Jesus then spoke two words of power, *Asparaspes* and *Askoraskis*. The disciples, in turn, took (and slew, according to one version) the Eye of the Earth (alias *Aynat*, Ethiopian for "[evil] eye"), burned the old woman and scattered her ashes to the four winds. With this amulet its bearer was to be protected from the cursed Evil Eye.[364] The amulet illustrates how the Evil Eye was thought to threaten domestic animals, ruin milk, and cause miscarriages bringing about the deaths of mother and child.[365]

361. Budge 1978/1930:185.

362. Ibid., 178–99.

363. Ibid., 185–86, 361–62.

364. For a variant parallel see Winkler 1931:34; and Ford 1998:213.

365. Budge 1978/1930:180–97 depicts and discusses other Ethiopian amulets featuring saints like St. Sisinnius, the martyr and St. George of Lydda, both cavaliers on horseback. One parchment amulet in small book form, whose oldest parts are from the seventeenth cent. CE, consists of one strip of parchment 14 feet 4 inches long written on both sides in Ethiopic and includes an image of the Divine Face thought to avert the Evil Eye (Plates on pp. 188, 193). For Coptic amulets see Budge 1978/1930:126–132 and 361, although none of the amulets shown is identified as countering the the Evil Eye.

An Egyptian Christian apotropaic phylactery invokes Solomon and also the angel Gabriel or Michael to whom *baskania* is subordinated.[366] Another section of the same phylactery similarly invokes the archangel Michael, to whom the Evil Eye (*baskania*) and other evils are subordinated. It also charges the Evil Eye (*baskosynê*) to "fear the great name of God."[367] These sources, according to Richard Reitzenstein, show the close relation of "Glaube und Aberglaube"("faith and superstition") in Jewish and Christian as well as Greco-Roman societies.[368] The amulets portrayed and discussed by Campbell Bonner, his study's title indicates, are "chiefly Greco-Egyptian" in provenance.[369] The amulets defending specifically against the Evil Eye are mostly of Palestinian and Syrian provenance,[370] but share numerous motifs with other amulets in the collection. J. N. Ford's study of the Evil Eye in Mesopotamia, as discussed above,[371] shows several features that Egyptian Coptic Evil Eye lore has in common with the far older Mesopotamian anti-Evil Eye incantations.[372]

In modern Egypt, the belief is still widely held,[373] as it is in neighboring Ethiopia,[374] including the Amhara tribe,[375] and among the Gusii of Kenya.[376] The label "Gypsies" for the Romany people, who have preserved a strong Evil Eye belief, derives from the name "Egypt." It is a misnomer for an ethnic group that lives mostly in Europe and traces their origins not to Egypt but to the Indian subcontinent. The label illustrates, nevertheless, how in the popular mind the Romany have been associated with Egyptian soil and culture and Egypt's Evil Eye lore.

366. Reitzenstein 1904:295, referring to the Parisian manuscript ms *Parisinus graece*. 2316 (fifteenth cent. CE), 316, 1.2.

367. Ms. *Parisinus graece*. 2316, 318; Reitzenstein 1904:297–98.

368. Reitzenstein 1904:303; on Egyptian amulets, see ibid., 291–303.

369. Bonner 1950.

370. Ibid., 95–102, 208–28.

371. See above, in this chapter pp. 94–97.

372. See Ford 1998:213–14; see also the eighteenth cent. Ethiopian (Ge'ez) incantation, cited from Worell 1914/1915, and the seventeenth cent. Ethiopian (Ge'ez) incantation in Ford 1998:234, cited from Worrell 1910:93.

373. Lane 1895/1973; Gardiner 1916; Blackman 1927:71, 218; Griffiths 1938; Hocart 1938; Sainte Fare Garnot 1960 (personal names meant to ward off the Evil Eye); A. Fodor 1971; Spooner 1976a; Ghosh 1983; Dundes 1992:313; Inhorn 1994:205.

374. Budge 1978/1930:xxi–xxii, 177–99.

375. Reminick 1976; Ford 1998:252–53.

376. Matsuzono 1993.

EVIL EYE BELIEF AND PRACTICE
IN MESOPOTAMIA AND EGYPT—
SUMMARY AND CONCLUSION

The Physical, Social and Cultural Matrix
of Ancient Evil Eye Belief and Practice

The characteristics of societies in which Evil Eye belief has flourished have been described in chapter 1 above. The ethnological research on which this summarization of characteristics is based includes societies of ancient Mesopotamia and the Circum-Mediterranean regions. Historical and classical studies on the Evil Eye in antiquity tend to pass over this issue of physical, social, and cultural context. But since context always influences and shapes conceptualization and content, it seems appropriate at this early point in our study to recall the practical conditions that have been found to accompany and sustain belief in the Evil Eye.[377]

For the majority of people in these ancient civilizations, everyday existence was fraught with uncertainty and peril. Unfavorable conditions of soil, water and climate, limited technology, pestilence, plagues and war, meant unpredictable harvests, repeated famines and a tenuous existence for the Mesopotamian and Egyptian populations. Catastrophe and its causes was a constant concern. The rarity of large-scale population concentrations and the predominance of small-town agrarian settlements and villages allowing for regular face-to-face interactions were typical. Mixed economies of agriculture and herding resulted in competition and conflict between mobile herding and settled farming communities. Populations were unequally divided into the relatively few "haves" and the predominant "have nots" living on the edge of subsistence. Survival of the latter regularly depended upon the beneficence and generosity of the former. Economic disparity and steep social stratification resulted from and intensified the conflict between herders and farmers, thereby creating "agonistic" cultures and mentalities. Limited availability of goods and resources supported the impression that life was a zero-sum game in which one group's gain came only at another's loss. Envy among rivals, fueled by this sense of limited good, was ubiquitous

---

377. On the worldviews, perceptions and values of Ancient Mediterranean and Near East societies vs. modern Western societies see, among others, Romein 1958 (the "common human pattern" of conceptualizing the world and experience [nature, life, thought, time, authority, work] and how it diverges from the modern Western pattern); Sjoberg 1960; Wolf 1966; Carney 1975; Scott 1977; Rohrbaugh 1978, 1991, 1996; Hofstede 1991, 2001; Malina 1989, 1992, 2001 (esp. Table 2, pp. 76–78); Malina and Neyrey 1988:145–51; Oakman 1991; Lenski et al., 1995; Domeris 2007 passim.

and constant. These were "collectivist" societies which located identity in the group rather than in the individual. Their priority was the welfare of the group over that of the individual, with strong group control over attitudes, norms, and behavior, and focus on exterior appearance and group opinion, with little if any concern for individualistic self-inspection or self-realization.

Harsh and generally unfriendly forces of nature made daily existence and survival uncertain. Unsanitary living conditions, infected water, and limited availability of food stuffs led to malnutrition, rampant illness and death, especially of the very young. Health and illness inevitably were major concerns. Residence near mosquito-infested swamps and marshes, unsanitary conditions in the towns, villages, and especially the cities with their overcrowding, stifling heat and stinking streets filled with human waste, infected water, repeated outbreaks of infectious disease—all contributed to a high rate of sickness and death. Contagious eye diseases (ophthalmia) were especially common. In these traditional cultures, the sickness and death resulting from these deplorable physical and social conditions were ascribed not to germs, bacteria, and viruses (of which there was no knowledge) but to *personal agencies*—punishing gods, marauding demons and spirits, malevolent human neighbors and enemies with their noxious Evil Eyes. In cases of illness and death, witches are often suspected. According to the ethnographer George Murdock, this involves

> the ascription of the impairment of health to the suspected voluntary or involuntary aggressive action of a member of a special class of human beings believed to be endowed with a special power and propensity for evil.[378]

"When witchcraft [and the evil eye] is suspected," he notes,

> attention is likely to be directed to any category of powerful or privileged persons, including the wellborn, the wealthy, and those with political authority. Since these are usually secure, it tends to be deflected or displaced to other noticeable but unpopular types of people—foreigners, hunchbacks, senile women, or individuals with piercing stare.[379]

Belief in the existence of spirits, demons and witches with extraordinary powers and dread of persons with a harmful Evil Eye were part of the "mental furniture" of the age. Human as well as transcendent beings (deities, spirits, demons) were imagined to threaten human life, health, and

378. Murdock 1980:21.
379. Ibid., 67.

well being at every turn. Murdock included ancient Babylonia, Egypt, and the Hebrews in a cross-cultural analysis of 139 societies from past to present in regard to their concepts of illness and its causes. Witchcraft and the Evil Eye were considered causes in fifty-four of these societies. "It is practically universal in the Circum-Mediterranean region but surprisingly rare elsewhere in the world," he noted.[380] He found correlations of witchcraft and Evil Eye belief with advanced agriculture and intensive techniques of cultivation; pastoralism; socially complex, stratified societies with complex political organization; money as medium of exchange; patrilinity, payment of bride price, polygamy, writing, belief in high gods involved in human affairs; theories of spirit aggression; and intensive concern about envy.[381] A sense of vulnerability to the forces (human, divine, and demonic) dangerous to one's life and livelihood contributed to a constant feeling of insecurity and dread. Evil Eye belief and practice was an expression of, and reaction to, this insecurity and dread.

Affliction from an Evil Eye was one of the presumed causes of sickness and death in Mesopotamia and Egypt, as throughout the ancient world. Jewish sages of the post-biblical period were still declaring that, "Out of one hundred persons, ninety-nine die of an Evil Eye" (*b. Baba Metzi'a* 107b). Assistance in the struggle for survival was sought not only from human patrons but also from witches and sorcerers for protecting oneself and harming enemies. Protection against all hostile powers, including the Evil Eye demon and humans with an Evil Eye, was sought in power-laden words, expressions, incantations, gestures, actions, and amulets. The numerous practices and devices devised to ward off the Evil Eye were designed to keep evil and misfortune at bay and thus to provide some sense of solace in an unpredictable and dangerous world.

SUMMARY AND CONCLUSION

The four millennia and more history of Evil Eye belief and practice has its roots in the ancient civilizations of Mesopotamia and Egypt. Intense and ongoing infatuation with eyes, eye designs and symbols, eye beads, eye divinities, manufactured eye idols, and mythologies concerning eyes of heaven and lost and restored eyes was accompanied by a widespread belief in an Evil Eye and practices designed to thwart it and drive it off. The minority view of Louise Thomsen that the Evil Eye was a relatively rare and harmless notion in Mesopotamian history runs counter to the extant evidence and

380. Ibid., 21; see also 40, 49, 58, and Table 3, pp. 50–51.
381. Ibid., 57–85; for similar correlations see Roberts 1976.

has attracted few followers. The meticulous and comprehensive study of J. F. Ford identifies numerous features of an Evil Eye belief complex found in Sumerian, Sumero-Akkadian, Akkadian, and Ugaritic incantations that appear also in ancient texts from later centuries (Hebrew, Aramaic, Syriac, Coptic, and Mandaic). Greek and Roman parallels (not discussed by Ford), along with biblical texts (not discussed by Ford), are further important components of this picture. This points to an extensive diffusion of Evil Eye lore around the Circum-Mediterranean and ancient Near East with strikingly common and stable features.

Attention to the Evil Eye was rather a serious matter since this malicious Eye was thought capable of wreaking serious damage, destruction, and death. Possessors of the Evil Eye, whether humans (males and females) or demons, could harm humans, households, livestock (oxen, sheep) and fields; ruin milk production; cause drought; destroy harvests and bring about starvation, illness, and death. The Mesopotamian evidence of the Evil Eye (Sumerian: *igi ḫul;* Akkadian: *īni limuttum*), predominantly incantations, shows how the eye was regarded as an active organ whose glance was capable of inflicting great harm and destruction. Its possessors (humans, animals, demons), we also learn, were thought to roam about and invade homes, bringing suffering to its residents and damaging the property. Witches with an "evil glare" were said to rob young men of their manliness and young women of their beauty. Among the range of victims, infants were especially vulnerable to the Evil Eye and the Evil Eyed demoness Lamashtu. Damage included the ruin of a potter's kiln, jars, a weaver's loom, a shrine, a boat; harm to oxen, donkey, horse, livestock; and discord among brothers.

The purpose of anti-Evil Eye incantations was to curse, inveigh against, ward off, and drive away the noxious Evil Eye. Jewelry and pendants served as amulets and the colors of blue and red were thought to have apotropaic power. Counter-attacks included driving the Evil-Eyed demon away, binding its feet, slapping its face, filling its eyes with salt and its mouth with ashes. Remedies and rituals for removing the Evil Eye's effect were attempted: animal sacrifice, beer libation, and the offering of bread, incense and prayer.

Ford's excellent study[382] is rich in texts and linguistic analysis that show salient features of Mesopotamian Evil Eye belief and practice and the continuation of these features in texts of other cultures and periods.[383] An appendix[384] lists and textually documents four motifs indicating "thematic

---

382. Ford 1998; see also Ford 2000.

383. Ford's desire to distinguish between "magical" and "non-magical" senses of the Evil Eye, however, is given no compelling support and fails to convince.

384. Ford 1998:256–68.

continuity" in anti-Evil Eye incantations from third/second millennium BCE Sumero-Akkadian incantations to third-century CE Mandaic texts, both of a Mesopotamian provenance: (1) repeated reference to the menacing roaming of the Evil Eye; (2) the pernicious effects of the Evil Eye [breaking the yoke, discord among family members; disruption of weaving; destruction of food-bearing plants] (3) the Evil Eye as a net that ensnares; (4) the Evil Eye as a sick, defective, dimmed, or bloodshot eye. Later sources displaying parallels to the Mesopotamian texts will be discussed in Vol. 4, chap. 1 on postbiblical Israel.[385]

The danger posed by a child-killing female demon, possessed of, or linked with, an Evil Eye, is another concept of Mesopotamian lore that has spanned the centuries. Alexey Lyavdansky traces this concept, so widely disseminated in the Circum-Mediterranean and Ancient Near East, back to ancient Mesopotamia, not later than the Old Babylonian period (1800–1600 BCE). It was borrowed by adjacent Aramaic-speaking people in Syria, as attested by the text from Arslan Tash (c. seventh cent. BCE), and by the creators of Aramaic magic bowls in Sassanian Mesopotamia (fifth–seventh cents. CE). The "strangling female demon" was inherited by the tradition of Syriac charms from the language of Aramaic magic bowls together with many other figures, motifs and formulas, common to these two traditions.[386]

As another illustration of the centuries-long continuity of Mesopotamian Evil Eye lore into modern time, Ford cites in his conclusion part of an ethnographical description of the Evil Eye belief of the Amhara people of modern Ethiopia (central highlands of the Shoa province). Bold font in the citation identifies ancient Mesopotamian Evil Eye motifs appearing in this modern report.

> The real threat of the *buda* people [a separate category of the population of different ethnic origin believed to congenitally possess an evil eye—JN Ford] to the *rega* people [Amhara of 'pure' lineage—JN Ford] is the ever-present possibility of attack. Most people are **fearful of even mentioning the *buda***, especially at night, because if they are overheard by a *buda* he will become angry and may 'eat' one of the family, thereby **causing sickness or death** . . . The peasant who is especially **good looking** or whose **child is considered beautiful**, or someone who does **something extraordinary**, may fear the attack of the evil

385. For later incantations against the Evil Eye in various dialects of Aramaic (Ford 1999:202 n. 1) see Hazard 1893:284–86; Gollancz 1912: Codex A §23, §39; cf. §54; Codex B §9; Codex C §19, cf. §1; Drower 1937, 1938; 1943:152, 170; Neveh and Shaked 1985:133; cf. 40–45, 172–75; 1993: 99–101, 120–22.

386. Lyavdansky 2001.

eye because of the envy believed to be kindled in the *buda* . . .
When a person is **'eaten'** he may know immediately that he has
been attacked, for the consequences may occur at the same time
as the strike. But the symptoms can just as easily be delayed for
a few hours, a day, or a week . . . The process of attack may occur in one of several different manners. Because of the power
of the evil eye, *buda* people can change into hyenas and **roam
the countryside** at night . . . Once transformed into a hyena,
**he then searches for a victim, and on finding one, fixes the
unfortunate person with an evil gaze**, returns home, rolls in
the ashes to turn back into human form, and waits for the victim
to die . . . A *rega* who sleeps with a *buda* will **grow thinner and
thinner** because **the eye of the *buda* will such out the blood
out of the victim**, causing the victim to lose his or her appetite
and to become weak and helpless . . . The warm, affectionate relationship can be maintained without serious danger [sic!], but
when there is a quarrel, the *rega*, already weakened by the blood
given up to the *buda*, will be **'eaten' and become seriously ill**.[387]

We shall see in the following volumes that several more features of the Evil
Eye in Mesopotamian texts appear as well in ancient Greek and Roman,
Jewish and Christian sources.

This impression of the wide extent and notable stability of Evil Eye
belief and features over time and across cultures is strengthened by the
Egyptian evidence. Egyptian mythology tells of Egyptian deities and their
association with the celestial luminaries of sun and moon considered as
the eyes of heaven, and of Horus, his titanic battle with brother Seth, his
wounding and his restored eye (*wedjat*, alias *udjat*). The former provided
models for imagining the active power of the eye and its casting of rays, like
those of the sun. The latter provided the conceptual basis for one of the most
widespread anti-Evil Eye amulets of the ancient world, the falcon-winged
and potent Eye of Horus.

From Egypt also comes evidence of several aspects of Evil Eye belief
and practice, supplementing, and in many cases overlapping, the evidence
from Mesopotamian sources: the notion of the vulnerability of mothers and
newborns to Evil Eye attack and the employment of incantations, prayers,
spells, and amulets to protect them; preoccupation with the eye (*irt*) in general and the use of representations of an eye as a protective amulet, especially the falcon-winged Eye of Horus; the belief, as in Mesopotamia, that the
Evil Eye could be thwarted and repelled; the practice of protecting persons,

387. Ford 1998:252–53, citing the study of Reminick 1976:88–90, and marking the
parallel features with boldface type.

homes, temple, tombs, and boats with an eye or the *wedjat* Eye of Horus; the additional use of the Eye of Horus to heal (since his eye itself was healed and restored by Thoth or Isis); the use of eyes of other deities to protect and heal (e.g., Sakmet, Bastet, Hathor); the appeal to particular deities for protection (Thoth, Horus etc.); the protection expected from the deformed dwarf deity Bes, inspiring later use of replicas of dwarfs and grotesques against the Evil Eye; the practice of assigning to persons an apotropaic name to neutralize the Evil Eye, a custom likely originating in Egypt and then adopted in Greece and Rome;[388] and the continued prominence of the colors blue/turquoise and red as protective colors and as the colors of countless amuletic eyes of Horus.[389] The chief distinctive feature of Egyptian Evil Eye belief is the Egyptian linking of this belief to the sky-god Horus[390] and the myth(s) of the conflict between Seth and Horus (compare the Mesopotamian parallel of the struggle between Evil-Eyed Tiamat and Marduk), the destruction of Horus's eye by his brother Seth and then its restoration by Thoth as the sound eye (*udjat/wedjat*), which is then regarded as replete with apotropaic power. This conviction concerning the power of the Eye of Horus is consistent with the production and use of the vast number of amuletic eyes of Horus that circulated throughout the ancient world.

Amulets of Ptolemaic and later time with their images of cavaliers lancing an Evil Eye provided prototypes for similar Jewish and Christian amulets with Solomon and St. Sisinnius as cavaliers, as we shall see in Vol. 4, chaps. 1 and 2. This evidence of Egyptian Evil Eye belief and practice also includes accusations of possessing and injuring with an envious Evil Eye that were leveled at neighbors deemed to be dangerous or malevolent. We will meet similar accusations in Greco-Roman and Christian sources in the following volumes. The gradual syncretistic melding of Mesopotamian, Egyptian, Greek, Roman and then Egyptian Jewish and Christian cultures in general is reflected, in particular, in the growth and variation of Egyptian tradition concerning the Evil Eye and its aversion. Evil Eye belief and practice among Greeks and Romans, and among Israelites and Christians, as we shall see, show a remarkable similarity and overlap with the concepts and practices of Mesopotamian and Egyptian Evil Eye lore.

---

388. So Sauneron 1966:51, 63 and nn. 77–78; Bernand 1991:103.

389. It is likely that the color blue continues Mesopotamian practice where it was also prominent. On blue as apotropaic in Egypt see Abd el-Azim el-Adly 1994. Blue and red were employed as apotropaic colors by the Israelites as well; see Vol. 3. [**X-ref**]

390. Egyptians also associated other deities with the Evil Eye and its aversion, but Horus and his eye were by far the most prominent.

BIBLIOGRAPHY
· FOR CHAPTER 1:
INTRODUCTION

1. PRIMARY SOURCES

Alexander of Aphrodisias. 1841. *Problemata Physica*. In I. L.Ideler, *Physici et Medici Graeci minores*. 2 vols. Berlin: Reimer, 1841–1842. Vol. 1 (1841) 3–80. Reprinted, Amsterdam 1963.

The Babylonian Talmud. Translated and edited by Rabbi Dr. I. Epstein. 34 vols. in 6 parts. London: Soncino, 1935–1960.

Basil of Caesarea. *Peri phthonou/De invidia/Concerning Envy* (Homily 11). PG 31:372–85.

Carmichael, Alexander. 1900. *The Carmina Gadelica*. 2 vols. Edinburgh: T. & S. Constable.

Hunt, A. S., and C. C. Edgar. 1932–1934. *Select Papyri*. 2 vols. LCL. New York: Putnam.

Mackenzie, William. 1895. *Gaelic Incantations, Charms and Blessings of the Hebrides*. Inverness: Northern Counties Newspaper and Printing and Publishing.

Kramer, Heinrich, and James Sprenger. *Malleus Maleficarum*. Cologne, 1487. English translation: *The Malleus Maleficarum of Heinrich Kramer and James Sprenger*, by Montague Summers. London: Rodker, 1928. Reprinted, New York: Dover, 1988.

Mackay, Christopher S., ed. and trans. *Malleus Maleficarum*. 2 vols. Cambridge: Cambridge University Press, 2006.

Midrash Rabbah. Vilna, Lithuania: Romm, 1884–1887. Reprinted, Jerusalem 1961. ET: *The Midrash Rabba*. Translated by H. Freedman and Maurice Simon. 5 vols. Reprint, London, 1977.

Midrash Bereshit Rabbah. Edited by J. Theodor and H. Albeck. 1812–1931. Reprinted 2nd ed., Jerusalem, 1962.

Otsar Midrashim: A Library of Two Hundred Minor Midrashim. 2 vols. Edited by J. D. Eisenstein. New York: Eisenstein, 1915. Reprinted, 1969.

Papyri Osloenses. Fasc. 1. *Magical Papyri*. Edited by Samson E. Eitrem. Oslo: Dybwad, 1925.

Papyri Osloenses. Edited by S. Eitrem and L. Amundsen. 3 vols. Oslo: Dybwad, 1925–36. (P. Oslo)

Pesiqta Rabbati. Edited by M. Friedmann. Vienna: self-published, 1880.

Pesiqta de-Rav Kahana. Edited by Solomon Buber. Lyck, 1868. Edited by Bernard Mandelbaum. New York: Bet ha-midrash le-rabanim sheba-'Amerikah, 1962.

Philostratus. *Philostratus: The Life of Apollonius of Tyana.* 2 vols. Translated by F. C. Conybeare. LCL. Cambridge: Harvard University Press, 1912, 1948.

Pliny the Elder. *Pliny Natural History.* Translated by H. Rackham et al. 10 vols. LCL. Cambridge: Harvard University Press, 1938–1963.

Plutarch. *Plutarch: Moralia.* Translated by F. C. Babbitt et al. 16 vols. LCL. Cambridge: Harvard University Press, 1927–1969.

The Qur'an: A New Translation. Translated by Tarif Khalidi. New York: Penguin Classics, 2008.

2. SECONDARY STUDIES, REFERENCE WORKS

Abbott, G. F. 1903. *Macedonian Folklore.* Cambridge: Cambridge University Press.

Abeghian, Manuk. 1899. *Der armenische Volksglaube.* Leipzig: Drugulin.

Abu-Rabia, Aref. 2005. "The Evil Eye and Cultural Beliefs among the Bedouin Tribes of the Negev, Middle East." *Folklore* 116:241–54.

Abusch, Tzvi, and Karel van der Toorn, eds. 1999. *Mesopotamian Magic: Textual, Historical, and Interpretive Perspectives.* Studies in Ancient Magic and Divination 1. Groningen: Styx.

Achté, Kalle, and Taina Schakir. 1982. "Psychiatric Aspects of Fear of the Evil Eye." *Psychiatria Fennica* 11–20.

Acocella, Joan. 2000. "The Neapolitan Finger." *The New York Review of Books* 47/20 (12/21/2000) 48–55. Review of Andrea De Jorio, *Gestures in Naples and Gesture in Classical Antiquity.* Translated and edited by Adam Kendon. Advances in Semiotics Series. Bloomington: Indiana University Press, 2000 (1832).

Adalsteinsson, Jón Hnefill. 1993. "The Evil Eye: A Casebook [Review of Alan Dundes 1992a]." *Asian Folklore Studies* 52:397–99.

Adamson, Joseph. 1997. *Melville, Shame, and the Evil Eye: A Psychoanalytic Reading.* SUNY Series in Psychoanalysis and Culture. Albany: State University of New York Press.

Al-Khalili, Jim. 2011. *The House of Wisdom. How Arabic Science Saved Ancient Knowledge and Gave Us the Renaissance.* New York: Penguin.

Allison, Dale C. Jr. 1987. "The Eye is the Lamp of the Body (Matthew 6.22–23=Luke 11.34–36)." *New Testament Studies* 33:61–83.

———. 1997. "The Eye as a Lamp: Finding the Sense." In *The Jesus Tradition in Q,* 133–67. Harrisburg, PA: Trinity.

Almagro, Francisco, and José Fernández Carpintero. 1977. *Heurística a Villena y los tres tratados.* Madrid: Editora Nacional.

Alsarius, Vincentius. 1595. *De invidia et fascino veterum libellus.* Lucae.

Alvar Nuño, Antón. 2006–2008. "Falsas consideraciones en los estudios sobre el mal de ojo en el mundo clásico." *Antigüedad, Religiones y Sociedades* 7:101–14.

———. 2009–2010. "Nocturnae aves: su simbolismo religioso y function mágica en el mundo romano. Nocturnae Aves: Their Religious Symbolism and Magical Function in the Roman World." *Antigüedad, Religiones y Sociedades* 8:187–202.

————. 2012a. *Envidia y fascinación: el mal de ojo en el occidente romano.* Antigüedad, Religiones y Sociedades Supplements 3. Huelva: Universidad de Huelva.

————. 2012b. "Ocular Pathologies and the Evil Eye in the Early Roman Principate." *Numen* 59:295–321.

Alvarez Chanca, Diego. 2001. *Libro del ojo* (1499). Edited by J. Sanz Hermida. Salamanca.

Andrée, Richard. 1878. *Ethnographische Parallelen und Vergleiche.* Stuttgart: Maier.

Andreesco-Miereanu, Iona. 1987. "Magic in Eastern Europe." In *Encyclopedia of Religion* 9:101–4.

————. 1989. "Magic in Eastern Europe." In *Hidden Truths*, edited by L. E. Sulllivan, 116–21. New York: Macmillan.

Anonymous. 1887. "Jettatura e Malocchio." *The Celtic Magazine* 415–18.

Anonymous. 1907–1930. "Mal de ojo." In *Enciclopedia universal ilustrada. Europeo-Americana*, 32:408–12. Barcelona: Esposa.

Anonymous. 1911. "Evil Eye." In *Encyclopaedia Brittanica*, 10:21–22. 11th ed. Chicago: Encyclopaedia Britannica.

Anonymous. 1929. "Evil Eye." In *Encyclopaedia Britannica*, 8:915. 14th ed. New York: Encyclopaedia Britannica.

Anonymous. 1983. "Eye." In *Man, Myth, and Magic: The Illustrated Encyclopedia of Mythology, Religion and the Unknown.* 21 vols. Edited by Richard Cavendish et al., 4:885–94. New edition edited and complied by Yvonne Deutsch. New York: Cavendish.

Anonymous. 1997. "Nazar Boncuk, the Little Magic Stone that Protects One from the 'Evil Eye.'" *Holiday News from Turkey* (Istanbul) 9/1:6.

Anonymous. 2001. "Fascination." In *Encyclopedia of Occultism & Parapsychology.* Edited by J. Gordon Melton and Leslie A. Shepard, 1:547–48. 5th ed. Detroit: Gale Research, 1984.

Apostolides, Anastasia. 2008. "Western Ethnocentrism: A Comparison between African Witchcraft and the Greek Evil Eye from a Sociology of Religion Perspective." M.A. thesis, Faculty of Theology, University of Pretoria, South Africa.

Apostolides, Anastasia, and Yolanda Dreyer. 2008. "The Greek Evil Eye, African Witchcraft, and Western Ethnocentrism." *HTS Teologiese Studies* 64:1021–42.

Appel, Willa. 1975. "The Evil Eye and Peasant Identity in Southern Italy." Ph.D. diss., Cornell University.

————. 1976. "The Myth of the Jettatura." In *The Evil Eye*, edited by Clarence Maloney, 16–27. New York: Columbia University Press.

————. 1977. "Idioms of Power in Southern Italy." *Dialectical Anthropology* 2:74–80.

Aquaro, Robert A. 2001. "Vaskania: Envy and the Evil Eye in the Bible." M.A. thesis, St. Vladimir's Seminary.

————. 2004. *Death by Envy: The Evil Eye and Envy in the Christian Tradition.* New York: iUniverse.

Arditi, Michele. 1825. *Il fascino e l'amuleto contro del fascino: Illustrazione di un antico basso-rilievo rinvenuto in un forno della città di Pompei.* Naples: Stampieria Reale.

Argyle, Michael, and Mark Cook. 1976. *Gaze and Mutual Gaze.* Cambridge: Cambridge University Press.

Arieli, A. 1970. "Certain Magical Beliefs in Mental Diseases." *The Israel Annals of Psychiatry and Related Disciplines* 8:173–85.

Aschkenazi, S. 1984. "The Belief in the 'Evil Eye' as Reflected in Jewish Folklore." *Yes'a Am* 22:100–111. [Hebrew]

Aune, David E. 1980. "Magic in Early Christianity." In *Aufstieg und Niedergang der römischen Welt*, edited by Hildegard Temporini and Wolfgang Haase, II.23.2, 1507–57. Berlin: de Gruyter.

———. 1986. "Magic; Magician." In *ISBE* 3:213–19.

———. 2007. "Magic in Early Christianity and Its Ancient Mediterranean Context: A Survey of Some Recent Scholarship." *Annali di storia dell'esegesi* 24:229–94.

Ayers, Mary. 2004. *Mother-infant Attachment and Psychoanalysis: The Eyes of Shame.* New York: Brunner Routledge.

Azuela, Mariano. 2008 (1915). *The Underdogs: A Novel of the Mexican Revolution.* Reprinted, New York: Penguin.

Bacon, Francis. 1890. "Of Envy." In *The Essays of Counsels, Civil and Moral.* Edited by S. H. Reynolds. Oxford: Clarendon.

———. 2000. *A Critical Edition of the Major Works.* Edited by Brian Vickers. Oxford: Oxford University Press.

———. 2002. *Francis Bacon. The Major Works.* Edited by Brian Vickers. Oxford World's Classics. Oxford: Oxford University Press.

Ball, R. A. 1967. "The Evil Eye in Cristabel." *Journal of the Ohio Folklore Society* 2:47–71.

Barb, A. A. 1963. "The Survival of Magic Arts." In *Paganism and Christianity in the Fourth Century*, edited by A. Momigliano, 100–125. Wartburg Studies 1. Oxford: Clarendon.

Barnard, Alan, and Jonathan Spencer, eds. 2002. *Encyclopedia of Social and Cultural Anthropology.* New York: Routledge.

Barth, Frederick. 1956. *Nomads of South Persia.* London: Allen & Unwin.

Beare, John I. 1996 (1906). *Greek Theories of Elementary Cognition from Alcaeon to Aristotle.* 1906. Reprinted, Oxford: Oxford University Press.

Bearman, P. J. et al., eds. 1960–2005. *Encyclopedia of Islam.* 2nd ed. 12 vols. Leiden: Brill.

Bendersky, Borekh. 2003. "An Evil Eye" (short story). In *Yiddish South of the Border: An Anthology of Latin American Yiddish Writing.* Edited by Alan Astro. Albuquerque: University of New Mexico Press.

Benvenuto, Sergio, and Marguerite Pozzoli. 2008. "Une superstition des Lumières à Naples: le jettatore." *La pensée de midi* 23/1:163–74.

Berger, Arthur Asa. 1978. *Li'l Abner: A Study in American Satire.* New York: Twayne.

Berke, Joseph H. 1988. "The Evil Eye." In *The Tyrrany of Malice: Exploring the Dark Side of Character and Culture*, 35–56, 294–306. New York: Simon & Schuster.

Berry, Veronica. 1968. "Neopolitan Charms Against the Evil-Eye." *Folkore* 79:250–56.

Bertrand-Rousseau, Pierette. 1976. "Contribution à l'etude de mauvais oeil en Corse." *Ethnopsychologie: revue de psychologie des peuples* 31:5–18.

———. 1978. *Ile de Corse et magie blanche.* Paris: Publications de la Sorbonne.

Betz, Hans Dieter. 1979 (1992). "Matthew vi.22f. and Ancient Greek Theories of Vision." In *Text and Interpretation: Studies in the New Testament Presented to Mattthew Black*, edited by E. Best and R. McL. Wilson, 43–56. Cambridge: Cambridge University Press. Reprinted in Betz, *Synoptische Studien*, 140–52. Tübingen: Mohr/Siebeck, 1992.

————. 1995. *The Sermon on the Mount: A Commentary on the Sermon on the Mount, Including the Sermon on the Plain (Matthew 5:3—7:27 and Luke 6:20-49)*. Hermeneia. Minneapolis: Fortress.

Bille, Mikkel. 2010. "Seeking Providence through Things: The Word of God versus Black Cumin." In *An Anthropology of Absence: Materializations of Transcendence and Loss*, edited by Mikkel Bille et al., 167-84. New York: Springer.

Binsbergen, Wim van, and Frans Wiggermann. 1999. "Magic in History: A Theoretical Perspective and Its Application to Ancient Mesopotamia. In *Mesopotamian Magic: Textual, Historical, and Interpretive Perspectives*, edited by Tzvi Abusch and Karel van der Toorn, 3-34. Studies in Ancient Magic and Divination, 1. Groningen: Styx.

Blackman, Winifried S. 1927. *The Fellahin of Upper Egypt: Their Religious, Social and Industrial Life To-day with Special Reference to Survivals from Ancient Times*. London: Harrup.

Blum, Richard, and Eva Blum. 1965. *Health and Healing in Rural Greece: A Study of Three Communities*. Stanford: Stanford University Press.

————. 1970. *The Dangerous Hour: The Lore and Culture of Crisis and Mystery in Rural Greece*. London: Chatto & Windus.

Boehm, Armin. 2009. *Der böse Blick*. Cologne: Snoeck. (= *Armin Boehm: The Evil Eye. Exhibition*: Kunstverein Braunschweig, 6/27-8/30/2009. Exhibition catalogue edited by Hilke Wagner; texts [German/English] by Martin Engler, Gregor Jansen, Veit Loers, and Gabriele Sand, and an interview with Armin Boehm by Sarah Frost).

Bohigian, George M. 1997. "The History of the Evil Eye and Its Influence on Ophthalmology, Medicine and Social Customs." *Documenta Ophthalmologica* 94:91-100.

————. 1998. "The Evil Eye and Its Influence on Medicine and Social Customs." *Skeptic* 6/1:43-47.

Boileau, Pierre, and Thomas Narcejac. 1959. *The Evil Eye*. London: Hutchinson.

Bourguignon, Erika. 1983. "Evil Eye." In *Encyclopedia Americana*, 10:733. Danbury, CT: Grolier.

Bowen, Donna Lee, and Evelyn A. Early, eds. 1993. *Everyday Life in the Muslim Middle East*. Bloomington: Indiana University Press.

Bowie, Fiona. 2006. "Witchcraft and the Evil Eye." In *The Anthropology of Religion: An Introduction*, 200-236. 2nd ed. Oxford: Wiley-Blackwell.

Brav, Aaron. 1992 (1908). "The Evil Eye among the Hebrews." In *The Evil Eye: A Casebook,* edited by Alan Dundes, 44-54. 2nd ed. Madison: University of Wisconsin Press. *Ophthalmology* 5 (1908) 427-35.

Bremmer, Jan N. 1999. "The Birth of the Term 'Magic.'" *Zeitschrift für Papyrologie und Epigraphik* 126:1-12.

Bremmer, Jan and Roodenburg, Herman, eds. 1991. *A Cultural History of Gesture*. Ithaca: Cornell University Press.

Brenk, Frederick E. 1998. "Caesar and the Evil Eye or What Do You Do with *kai su, teknon*." In *Qui Miscuit Utile Dulci: Festschrift Essays for Paul Lachlan MacKendrick*, edited by Gareth Schmeling and Jon D. Mikalson, 31-49. Wauconda, IL: Bolchazy-Carducci.

Brögger, Jan. 1968. "The Evil Eye in a Calabrese Village." *Folk: Dansk etnografisk tidsskrift* 10:13-24.

Bronzini, Giovanni Battista. 1981. "Malocchio, Invidia, Diagnosi e Terapia Magica nella Cultura Contadina Lucana degli Anni Venti." *Lares* 47:265–90.

Brown, H. R. 1909–10. "The Evil Eye." *Quarterly Journal of the Mythic Society* 1:57–77.

Brown, Penelope, and Stephen Levinson. 1978. "Universals in Language: Politeness Phenomena." In *Questions and Politeness*, edited by Easter N. Goody, 56–311. Cambridge: Cambridge University Press.

Brugnatelli, Vermondo. 1985–86 "Aspetti linguistici delle credenze sul malocchio in Cabilia." *Atti Sodalizio Glottologico Milanese* 27:82–95.

Bruzza, L. 1975. "Intorno ad un campanello d'oro trovato sull' esquilino ed all'uso del suono per respingere il fascino." *Annali dell'Istituto* 47:50–68.

Buonanno, Michael. 1989 (1984). "Becoming White: Notes on an Italian-American Explan-ation of Evil Eye." In *Magic, Witchcraft, and Religion: An Anthropological Study of the Supernatural*, edited by Arthur C. Lehmann and James E. Meyers, 239–46. 2nd ed. Mountain View, CA: Mayfield, 1989. Reprinted from *New York Folklore* 10/1–2 (1984) 39–53.

Burleigh, E., C. Dardano, and J. R. Cruz. 1990. "Colors, Humors and Evil Eye: Indigenous Classification and Treatment of Childhood Diarrhea in Highland Guatemala." *Medical Anthropology* 12:419–41.

Caillois, R. 1960. "Der Komplex Medusa." *Antaios* 1:527–55.

Caisson, Max. 1998. "La science du mauvais oeil (malocchio). Structuration du sujet dans la 'pensée folklorique.'" *Terrain (Revue d'ethnologie de l'Europe)* 30:35–48. Online: http://terrain.revues.org/3304.

Calder, W. III, H. Cancik, and B. Kytzler, eds. 1991. *Otto Jahn: Eine Geisteswissenschaftler zwischen Kassizismus und Historismus*. Stuttgart: Steiner.

Callisen, S. A. 1937. "The Evil Eye in Italian Art." *Art Bulletin* 19:450–62.

Campbell, Åke. 1933. "Det onda ögat och besläktade föreställningar i svensk folk-tradition." *Folkminnen ock folktankar* 20:121–46.

Campbell, J. G. 1900. *Superstitions of the Highlands and Islands of Scotland*. Glasgow: Macklehose.

Campbell, John. K. 1964. *Honour, Family and Patronage: A Study of Institutions and Moral Values in a Greek Mountain Community*. Oxford: Clarendon.

Campo, Juan E. 2009a. *Encyclopedia of Islam*. Encyclopedia of World Religions. New York: Facts on Files, 2009.

———. 2009b. "Evil Eye." In *Encyclopedia of Islam*, 220–21. Encyclopedia of World Religions. New York: Facts on Files, 2009.

Canaan, Tewfik. 1914. *Aberglaube und Volkmedizin in Lande der Bibel*. Abhandlungen des Hamburgischen Kolonialinstituts 20.Volkerkunde, Kulturgeschichte und Sprachen 12. Hamburg: Friederichsen, 1914.

Capp, Al. 1953. *The World of Li'l Abner*. New York: Ballentine.

———. 1964. *From Dogpatch to Slobbovia: The—Gasp!!—World of Li'l Abner*. Boston: Beacon.

———. 1978. *The Best of Li'l Abner*. New York: Holt, Rinehart & Winston. ·

Capelle, Wilhelm. "Baskanos daimon." *Rheinisches Museum für Philologie* 96 (1953) 378.

Carleton, William. 1882. "The Evil Eye; or, The Black Spectre." In *The Works of William Carleton*, 1:613–775. New York: Collier.

Carroll, Michael. 1984. "On the Psychological Origins of the Evil Eye: A Kleinian View." *Journal of Psychoanalytic Anthropology* 7:171–87.

Casey, Conerly, and Robert B. Edgerton, eds. 2005. *A Companion to Psychological Anthropology: Modernity and Psychocultural Change*. Oxford: Blackwell.

Cátedra Tomás, M. 1976 "Notas sobre la 'envidia': los 'ojos malos' entre los vaqueiros de Alzada." In *Temas de Antropología española*, edited by C. Lisón, 9–48. Madrid: Akal.

Cavendish, Richard, and Yvonne Deutsch, eds. 1983. *Man, Myth and Magic: The Illustrated Encyclopedia of Mythology, Religion, and the Unknown*. 12 vols. New York: Cavendish.

Centini, Massimo. 2002. *Malocchio e iettatura: Conoscerli e sconfiggerli*. Rome: Mediterranee.

Chiardona, Michael, and James T. Vance. 2011. *Malocchio: The Evil Eye Murders*. Evil Eye Murder Series 1. Charlottesville, VA: PathBinder.

Chryssanthropoulos, Vassiliki. 2008. "The Evil Eye among the Greeks of Australia: Identity, Continuity, Modernization." In *Greek Magic: Ancient Medieval and Modern*, edited by J. C. B. Petropoulos, 106–18. Routledge Monographs in Classical Studies. London/New York: Routledge.

Classen, Constance. 1993. *Worlds of Sense: Exploring the Senses in History and across Cultures*. London: Routledge.

Cohen, Leonard. 1994. *Stranger Music: Selected Poems and Songs*. New York: Random House–Vintage.

Cohen, Maria Manzari. 1995. "The Mediterranean Evil Eye Charms." *Faces* 12/4:10.

Collins, Derek. 2000. "The Trial of Theoris of Lemnos: A 4th Century Witch or Folk Healer?" *Western Folklore* 59:251–78.

Cooke, W. 1926. *Religion and Folklore of Northern India*. 2 vols. London: Oxford University Press.

Coote Lake, Evelyn. F. 1933. "Some Notes on the Evil Eye Round the Mediterranean Basin." *Folklore* 44:93–98.

Coppola, Nunzio. 1971. "La jettatura e i meriti di un grande archeologo." *L'osservatore Politico Letterario* 12 December, 3–23.

Corso, Rose. 1959. "The Evil Eye." *Polish Folklore* 4:6.

Cosminsky, Sheila. 1976. "The Evil Eye in a Quiché Community." In *The Evil Eye*, edited by Clarence Maloney, 163–74. New York: Columbia University Press.

Coss, Richard G. 1992 (1974). "Reflections on the Evil Eye." In *The Evil Eye: A Casebook*, edited by Alan Dundes, 181–91. 2nd ed. Madison: University of Wisconsin Press. Reprinted from *Human Behavior* 3 (1974) 16–21.

Crenshaw, Nadine. 1996. *Celtic Tales. Balor of the Evil Eye. A Novel*. New York: Prima.

Croce, Benedetto. 1945. "La 'Ciccalata' di Nicola Valletta." *Quaderni di Critica* 1/3:20–24.

Crooke, William. 1896 (1968). *An Introduction to the Popular Religion and Folklore of Northern India*. 2 vols. 1896. Reprinted, Dehli: Munshiram Monoharlal, 1968.

Crooke, W. 1913. "Simulated Change of Sex to Baffle the Evil Eye." *Folk-Lore* 24/3:385.

Crooke, William, and R. E. Enthoven. 1972. *Religion & Folklore of Northern India*. New Dehli: Chand.

Cunningham, Graham. 1999. *Religion and Magic: Approaches and Theories*. Edinburgh: Edinburgh University Press.

Dante Alighieri. 1982. *The Divine Comedy of Dante Alighieri. Inferno. A Verse Translation* by Allen Mandelbaum. New York: Bantam.

Davidson, Thomas. 1949. *Rowan Tree and Red Thread: A Scottish Witchcraft Miscellany of Tales, Legends and Ballads; Together with a Description of the Witches' Rites and Ceremonies.* Edinburgh: Oliver & Boyd.

———. 1992 (1950). "Scoring Aboon the Breath: Defeating the Evil Eye." In *The Evil Eye: A Casebook,* edited by Alan Dundes, 143–49. 2nd ed. Madison: University of Wisconsin Press, 1992. Reprinted from *Chamber's Journal* (1950) 308–11.

Davidson, William L. 1923. "Envy and Emulation." In *HERE* 5:322–23.

Davies, James A. 1856. "On the Evil Eye." *Transactions of the Royal Society of Literature of the United Kingdom,* 2nd ser. 5, 187–211.

Debray, Régis. 1992. *Vie et mort de l'image: Une histoire du regard en Occident.* Paris: Gallimard.

De Ceglia, Francesco Paolo. 2011. "'It's not true, but I believe it:' Discussions on *jettatura* in Naples between the End of the Eighteenth and Beginning of the Nineteenth Centuries." *Journal of the History of Ideas* 72:75–97.

De Cunha, John. 1886–89a. "On the Evil Eye among the Bunnias." *Journal of the Anthropological Society of Bombay* 1:128–32.

———. 1886–89b. "On the Belief in the Evil Eye among the Modern Persians." *Journal of the Anthropological Society of Bombay* 1:149–53.

DeForest, Mary. 1993. "Clytemnestra's Breast and the Evil Eye." In *Woman's Power, Man's Game: Essays on Classical Antiquity in Honor of Joy K. King,* edited by Mary Deforest, 129–48. Wauconda, IL: Bolchazy-Carducci.

De Jorio, Andrea. 1832. *La mimica degli antichi investigata nel gestire napolitano.* Naples: Fibreno.

———. 2000. *Gestures in Naples and Gesture in Classical Antiquity.* Translated and edited by Adam Kendon. Advances in Semiotics Series. Bloomington, IN: Indiana University Press.

de la Mora, Gonzalo Fernàndez. 1987. *Egalitarian Envy: The Political Foundations of Social Justice.* Translated by Antonia T. de Nicholàs. New York: Paragon.

Del Rio, Martinus Antonius. 1599–1600/1603. *Disquisitionum magicarum, libri sex in tres tomos partiti.* Louvain: Albinum.

———. 2000. *Martín Del Rio: Investigations into Magic.* Translated and edited by P. G. Maxwell-Stuart. Manchester: Manchester University Press.

De Martino, Ernesto. 2004. *Sud e magia.* Milan: Feltrinelli.

Devish, René. 2005. "Witchcraft and Sorcery." In *A Companion to Psychological Anthropology: Modernity and Psychocultural Change,* 389–416. Oxford: Blackwell.

Dewar, Stephen. 1970. *Witchcraft and the Evil Eye in Guernsey.* 2nd ed. Guernsey: Toucan.

Diamond, Ann. 1994. *Evil Eye.* Montreal: Vehicle.

Díaz Ojeda, M.A. 1982. "La creencia en el mal de ojo: psicoterapia popular." *I Jornades d'Antropologia de la Medicina: Arxiu d'Etnografia de Catalunya* (Tarragona) 2:235–53.

Díaz Ojeda, M. A., and J. L Sevilla. 1980. "Patología popular y mal de ojo." In *La Antropología Médica en España,* 209–23. Barcelona: Anagrama.

Dickie, Matthew W. 1991. "Heliodorus and Plutarch on the Evil Eye." *Classical Philology* 86:17–29.

———. 1995. "The Fathers of the Church and the Evil Eye." In *Byzantine Magic: Papers from Dumbarton Oaks Colloquium,* edited by H. Maguire, 9–34. Washington, DC: Dumbarton Oaks Research Library and Collection.

———. 2001. *Magic and Magicians in the Greco-Roman World*. New York: Routledge.

Dictionnaire de la Bible. 1895–1912. 5 vols. Edited by F. Vigouroux. Paris: Letouzeyet.

Diego Cuscoy, Luis. 1969. "Mal de Ojo, Amuletos, Ensalmos y Santiguadores en la Isla de Teneriffe." In *Etologia y Tradiciones Populares*, 499–520. Zaragoza: Institucion "Fernando El Catolico."

Di Grigoli, Veronica. 2008. *Evil Eye*. YouWriterOn.

Djéribi, Muriel. 1988. "Le Mauvais oeil et la lait." *L'Homme* 28:35–47.

Dionisopoulos-Mass, Regina. 1976. "The Evil Eye and Bewitchment in a Peasant Village." In *The Evil Eye*, edited by Clarence Maloney, 42–62. New York: Columbia University Press.

Djordjevic, Tihomir. 1934. "Zle oci verovanju muslimana u Ohridu." *Glasnik Etnografski Muzej* 9:1–30.

———. 1938. "Zle oci verovanju juznih Slovena." *Srpski etnografski zbornik* 53:1–347.

DiStasi, Lawrence. 1981. *Mal Occhio: The Underside of Vision*. San Francisco: North Point.

Di Tota, Mia Funrud. 1982a. "Magi og religion." In *Sør-Italia: En europeisk koloni*, 86–120. Oslo: University of Oslo Press.

———. 1982b. "Magi—overtro eller virkelighet? En analyse foretillingen om det onde oyet i Syd-Italia." *Tidsskrift for Samfunnsforskning* 23:323–42.

Dodwell, Edward. 1819. *A Classical and Topographical Tour through Greece, during the Years 1801, 1805, and 1806*. 2 vols. London: Rodwell & Martin.

Donaldson, Bess Allen. 1992 (1938). *The Wild Rue: A Study of Muhammadan Magic and Folklore in Iran*. London: Luzac, 1938. Reprinted as "The Evil Eye in Iran," in *The Evil Eye: A Casebook*, edited by Alan Dundes, 66–77. 2nd ed. Madison: University of Wisconsin Press, 1992.

Domash, Leanne. 1983. "Self and Object Representations and the 'Evil Eye.'" *Bulletin of the Menninger Clinic* 47:217–224.

Dossey, Larry. 1997. "The Evil Eye." In *Be Careful What You Pray For . . . You Just Might Get It: What We Can Do about the Unintentional Effects of Our Thoughts, Prayers, and Wishes*. San Francisco: HarperSanFrancisco.

———. 1998. "The Evil Eye." *Alternative Therapies* 4:9–18.

Douglas, Mary. 1966. *Purity and Danger: An Analysis of Concepts of Pollution and Taboo*. New York: Praeger.

Doutté, Edmond. 1909. *Magie et Religion dans l'Afrique du Nord*. Algiers: Jourdan.

Downing, F. Gerald. 2003. "Magic and Scepticism in and around the First Christian Century." In *Magic in the Biblical World: From the Rod of Aaron to the Ring of Solomon*, edited by Todd Klutz, 86–99. JSNTSup 245. Sheffield: Sheffield Academic.

Dregni, Michael. 2004. *Django: The Life and Music of a Gypsy Legend*. Oxford: Oxford University Press.

Dundes, Alan, ed. 1965. *The Study of Folklore*. Englewood Cliffs, NJ: Prentice-Hall.

———, ed. 1992a *The Evil Eye: A Casebook*. 2nd ed. Madison: University of Wisconsin Press. (1st ed.: *The Evil Eye: A Folklore Casebook*, New York: Garland, 1981).

———. 1992b. "Wet and Dry, the Evil Eye: An Essay in Indo-European and Semitic Worldview." In *The Evil Eye: A Casebook*, edited by Alan Dundes, 257–312. 2nd ed. Madison: University of Wisconsin Press.

Durand, Vincent Mark and David H. Barlow. 2002. *Essentials of Abnormal Psychology*. Belmont, CA: Thomson Wadsworth.

Eco, Umberto. 2002. *Baudolino*. Translated by William Weaver. New York: Harcourt.

Edwards, Dennis. 1971. "The 'Evil Eye' and Middle Eastern Culture." *Folklore Annual* (Austin, Texas) 3:33–40.

Ehly, Ehren. 1989. *Evil Eye.* New York: Leisure.

Eisen, M. J. 1927. "Kuri silm." *Eesti Kirjandus* 21:34–43, 153–60.

Einszler, Lydia. 1899. "Das böse Auge." *Zeitschrift des deutschen Palästinavereins* 12: 200–222.

Elliott, John H. 1988. "The Fear of the Leer. The Evil Eye from the Bible to Li'l Abner." *Forum* 4/4:42–71.

———. 1990. "Paul, Galatians, and the Evil Eye." *Currents in Theology and Mission* 17:262–73.

———. 1991. "The Evil Eye in the First Testament: The Ecology and Culture of a Pervasive Belief." In *The Bible and the Politics of Exegesis. Essays in Honor of Norman K. Gottwald on His Sixty-Fifth Birthday*, edited by David Jobling et al., 147–59. Cleveland, OH: Pilgrim.

———. 1992. "Matthew 20:1–15: A Parable of Invidious Comparison and Evil Eye Accusation." *Biblical Theology Bulletin* 22:52–65.

———. 1993. *What Is Social-Scientific Criticism?* Guides to Biblical Scholarship. Minneapolis: Fortress.

———. 1994. "The Evil Eye and the Sermon on the Mount: Contours of a Pervasive Belief in Social Scientific Perspective." *Biblical Interpretation* 2:51–84.

———. 2004. "Look it Up: It's in BDAG." In *Biblical Greek Language and Lexicography. Essays in Honor of Frederick W. Danker.* Edited by Bernard A. Taylor et al., 48–52. Grand Rapids: Eerdmans.

———. 2005a. "Jesus, Mark, and the Evil Eye." *Lutheran Theological Journal* (Festschrift in honour of Victor C. Pfitzner) 39/2–3:157–68.

———. 2005b. "Lecture socioscientifique: Illustration par l'accusation du Mauvais Oeil en Galatie." In *Guide des nouvelles lectures de la Bible*, edited by André Lacocque, 141–67. Translated by Jean-Pierre Prévost. Paris: Bayard.

———. 2007a. "Envy and the Evil Eye: More on Mark 7:22 and Mark's 'Anatomy of Envy.'" In *In Other Words: Essays on Social Science Methods and New Testament in Honor of Jerome H. Neyrey*, edited by Anselm Hagedorn et al., 87–105. Social World of Biblical Antiquity 2/1. Sheffield: Sheffield Phoenix.

———. 2007b. "Envy, Jealousy and Zeal in the Bible: Sorting Out the Social Differences and Theological Implications—No Envy for YHWH." In *To Break Every Yoke: Essays in Honor of Marvin C. Chaney*, edited by Robert Coote and Norman K. Gottwald, 344–63. Social World of Biblical Antiquity 2/3. Sheffield: Sheffield Phoenix.

———. 2008. "God—Zealous or Jealous but never Envious: The Theological Consequences of Linguistic and Social Distinctions." *The Social Sciences and Biblical Translation*, edited by Dietmar Neufeld, 79–96. SBL Symposium Series 41. Atlanta: Society of Biblical Literature.

———. 2011. "Social-scientific Criticism: Perspective, Process, Payoff. Evil Eye Accusation at Galatia as Illustration of the Method." *Hervormde Teologies Studies* 67/1: 114–23.

———. 2015. "Jesus, Paulus und der Böse Blick: Was die modernen Bibelversionen und Kommentare uns nicht sagen." In *Alte Texte in neuen Kontexten: Wo steht die sozialwissenschaftliche Bibelexegese?*, edited by Wolfgang Stegemann and Richard E. DeMaris, 85–104. Stuttgart: Kohlhammer.

————. 2016a. "Envy." In *The Ancient Mediterranean Social World: A Sourcebook.* Edited by Zeba Cook. Grand Rapids: Eerdmans (forthcoming).

————. 2016b. "Evil Eye." In *Social Scientific Sourcebook.* Edited by Zeba Crook. Grand Rapids: Eedrmans (forthcoming).

Elsie, Robert. 2001. "Evil Eye." In *A Dictionary of Albanian Religion, Mythology and Folk Culture,* 86–87. New York: New York University Press.

Elworthy, Frederick Thomas. 1895 (1958). *The Evil Eye: An Account of This Ancient and Widespread Superstition.* London: Murray. Reprinted with an Introduction by Louis S. Barron. New York: Julian.

Elworthy, Frederick Thomas. 1912. "The Evil Eye." In *HERE* 5:608–15.

Encyclopedia Americana. 1983. 30 vols. Danbury, CT: Grolier.

Encyclopedia Britannica. 1910–11. 29 Vols. 11th ed. Chicago: Encyclopaedia Britannica.

Enciclopedia dell'arte medioevale. 1991–2002. 12 vols. Rome: Istituto della Enciclopedia italiana.

Engelbert of Admont. *Tractatus de fascinatione* (c. 1331).

Epstein, Joseph. *Envy.* The Seven Deadly Sins Series. New York: Oxford University Press, 2003.

Erkoreka, Anton. 1984. *El mal de ojo en Euskal Herria.* Salamanca-Bilbao, Instituto de Historia de la Medicina—Euskal Medikuntzaren Historia-Mintegia.

————. 1995. *Begizkoa: El Mal de Ojo entre los Vascos.* Bilbao: Ekain.

————. 2002. *Análisis de la medicina popular vasca.* Barcelona: Bibliotex.

————. 2005. "Mal de ojo: una creencia supersticiosa remota, compleja y aún viva. The evil eye: a remote superstitious belief, which is complex and still present." *Munibe* (Antropologia-Arkeologia) 57 Homenaje a Jesús Altuna. San Sebastián: Sociedad de Ciencias Aranzadi. Pp. 391–400.

Esler, Philip F. 1994. *The First Christians in Their Social Worlds: Socio-scientific Approaches to New Testament Interpretation.* London: Routledge.

Espinosa, Aurelio M. 1985. *The Folklore of Spain in the American Southwest: Traditional Spanish Folk Literature in Northern New Mexico and Southern Colorado,* edited by J. Manuel Espinosa, 75–76. Norman: University of Oklahoma Press.

Euthoven, R. C. 1924. *Folklore of Bombay.* Oxford: Clarendon.

Evans, H. C. 1925. "The Evil Eye." *Psyche* 6:101–6.

Evans, William N. 1975. "The Eye of Jealousy and Envy." *Psychoanalytic Review* 62:481–92.

Fariña, M.A. 1982. "Introducción al estudio del 'mal de ojo' en las isles Canarias." *I Jornades d'Antropologia de la Medicina. Arxiu d'Etnografia de Catalunya* (Tarragona) 2/2:287–310.

Feilberg, H. F. 1901. "Der böse Blick in nordischer Überlieferung." *Zeitschrift für Volkskunde* 11:304–30, 420–30.

Ferenczi, Sandor. 1913. "Zur Augensymbolik." *Internationale Zeitschrift für ärtzliche Psychoanalyse* 1:161–64.

————. 1956. "On Eye Symbolism." In *Sex and Psycho-Analysis,* 228–33. New York: Dover.

Ficino, Marcilio. 1576. *Opera omnia.* Basel: Henricpetri.

Fiensy, David A. 1999. "The Importance of New Testament Background Studies in Biblical Research: The 'Evil Eye' in Luke 11:34 as a Case Study." *Stone-Campbell Journal* 2/1:75–88.

————. 2007. *Jesus the Galilean: Soundings in a First Century Life*. Piscataway, NJ: Gorgias.

Finneran, Niall. 2003. "Ethiopian Evil Eye Belief and the Magical Symbolism of Iron Working." *Folklore* 114:427–32.

Flores-Meiser, Enya. 1976. "The Hot Mouth and Evil Eye." In *The Evil Eye*, edited by Clarence Maloney, 149–62. New York: Columbia University Press.

Fodor, Alexander. 1971. "The Evil Eye in Today's Egypt." *Folia Orientalia* (Krackow) 13:51–66.

Foskolou, Vassiliki. 2005. "The Virgin, the Christ-child and the Evil Eye." In *Images of the Mother of God: Perceptions of the Theotokos in Byzantium*, edited by Maria Vassilaki, 251–62, with 7 plates. Adelshot, UK: Ashgate.

Foster, George M. 1965. "Peasant Society and the Image of Limited Good." *American Anthropologist* 67:293–315.

————. 1972. "The Anatomy of Envy: A Study in Symbolic Behavior." *Current Anthropology* 13:165–202.

————. 1976. "Disease Etiologies in Non-Western Medical Systems." *American Anthropologist* 78:773–82.

Foulks, Edward, Daniel M. A Freeman, Florence Kaslow, and Leo Madow. 1977. "The Italian Evil Eye: Mal Occhio." *Journal of Operational Psychiatry* 8:28–34.

Fowler, G. B. 1970. "Engelberti Admontensis Tractatus de fascinatione." *Recherches de théologie ancienne et médiévale* 37:187–231.

Fracastorius, Hieronymus. 1555. *De Sympathia et Antipathia Rerum*. In *Opera Omnia*. Venice: Giunta.

Frachtenberg, Leo J. 1918. "Allusions to Witchcraft and Other Primitive Beliefs in Zoroastrian Literature." In *The Dastur Hoshang Memorial Volume*, 419–24. Bombay: Fort Printing Press.

Franzen, Jonathan. 2000. *The Corrections*. New York: Farrer, Straus & Giroux.

Frazer, James George. 1890. *The Golden Bough: A Study in Comparative Religion*. 2 vols. London: Macmillan.

————. 1906–1915. *The Golden Bough: A Study in Magic and Religion*. 12 vols. 3rd enlarged ed. London: Macmillan.

————. 1911. Vol. 2. *The Magic Art and the Evolution of Kings*. 3rd ed. London: Macmillan.

Fredrick, David, ed. 2002. *The Roman Gaze: Vision, Power and the Body*. Baltimore: Johns Hopkins University Press.

Freedman, David Noel, ed. 1992. *The Anchor Bible Dictionary*. 6 vols. New York: Doubleday.

Frenschkowski, Marco. 2010. "Magie." In *RAC* 23:cols. 857–957.

Freud, Sigmund. 1919. "Das Unheimliche." *Imago: Zeitschrift für Anwendung der Psychoanalyse auf die Geisteswissenschaften* (1919) 297–324. Reprinted in *Gesammelte Werke*, 12:227–68. ET: "The Uncanny." In *Standard Edition*, 17:218–52.

————. 1940–1952 (1999). *Gesammelte Werke: Chronologisch geordnet*. 17 vols. Edited by Anna Freud et al. Reprinted, Frankfurt: Fischer Taschenbuch.

————. 1953–1974. *The Standard Edition of the Complete Psychological Works of Sigmund Freud*. 24 vols. Translated and edited by James Strachey, with Anna Freud. London: Hogarth and the Institute of Psycho-Analysis.

————. "Das Medusenhaupt." In *Gesammelte Werke*, vol. 17:45–48. ET: "Medusa's Head." In *Standard edition*, 18:272–74.

Frey, Dagobert. 1953. *Dämonie des Blicks*. Akademie der Wissenschaften und der Literatur. Abhandlungen der Geistes- und Sozialwissenschaftlichen Klasse. Jahrgang 1952, Nr. 6. Wiesbaden: Steiner.

Frisch, Mechthild. 1995. "Gegen den bösen Blick." [Contemporary art]. Online: http://www.staedtische-galerie-delmenhorst.de/fs-publikationen.html.

Frommann, Johannes Christian. 1675. *Tractatus de fascinatione novus et singularis*. Nürnberg: Endter.

Gaborieau, Marc et al., eds. 2007–14. *Encyclopedia of Islam*. 3rd edition. Leiden: Brill.

Gaidoz, Henri. 1912. "Jules Tuchmann." In *Mélusine* 11:148–51. Paris: Viaut.

Gallina, Anna Maria, ed. 1978. *Enrique de Villena, Tratado de aojamiento*. Bari: Adriatica.

Gallini, Clara. 1973. *Dono e Malocchio*. Palermo: Flaccovio.

Galt, Anthony H. 1982. "The Evil Eye as Synthetic Image and Its Meanings on the Island of Pantelleria, Italy." *American Ethnologist* 9:664–81. Discussion: *American Ethnologist* 12 (1985) 778–80.

Gamache, Henri. 1946 (1969). *Terrors of the Evil Eye Exposed*. New York: Raymond. Reprinted as *Protection Against Evil*. New York: Raymond.

Gardiner, Alan H. 1916. "A Shawahti-Figure with Interesting Names: The Evil Eye in Egypt." *Proceedings of the Society of Biblical Archaeology* 38:129–30.

Garnett, Lucy M. J. 1890. *The Women of Turkey and Their Folk-Lore: The Christian Women*. London: Nutt.

———. 1891. *The Women of Turkey and Their Folk-Lore: The Jewish and Moslem Women*. London: Nutt.

Garrison, Vivian, and Conrad M. Arensburg. 1976. "The Evil Eye: Envy or Risk of Seizure? Paranoia or Patronal Dependency?" In *The Evil Eye*, edited by Clarence Maloney, 287–328. New York: Columbia University Press.

Gautier, Theophile. 1863. "Jettatura." In *Romans et Contes*. Paris: Charpentier, 1863; Reprinted in Gautier, *Racconti fantastici*. Milan: Garzanti, 1993, 2006. See also Gauter, *Jettatura*. Paris: C. Marpon & E. Flammarion, 1887. ET: *Jettatura*. Edited by A. Schinz, with Introduction and Notes. Boston: Heath, 1900.

Gennep, Arnold van. 1992 (1967). "The Research Topic: Or, Folklore without End." In *The Evil Eye. A Casebook*, edited by Alan Dundes, 3–8. 2nd ed. Madison: University of Wisconsin Press. Reprinted from *The Semi-Scholars*, 32–36. London: Routledge & Kegan Paul, 1967.

Gershman, Boris. 2011a. "The Two Sides of Envy." Brown University, October 2011. Online: http://www.thearda.com/asrec/archive/papers/Gershman%20%20Two%20Sides%20of%20Envy.pdf.

———. 2011b "The Economic Origins of the Evil Eye Belief." Working Paper, Brown University. Brown University, October. Online: http://www.american.edu/cas/economics/research/upload/2013-14.pdf.

Georges, Robert A. 1962. "Matiasma: Living Folk Belief." *Midwest Folklore* 12:69–74.

Ghosh, Amitar. 1983. "The Relations of Envy in an Egyptian Village." *Ethnology* 22:211–23.

Giancristofaro, Emiliano. 1970. "Viaggio nel Mondo Magico Abruzzese: Il malocchio." *Rivista Abruzzese* 23:180–93.

Gibb, H. A. R., and J. H. Kramers, eds. 1953. *Shorter Encyclopädia of Islam*. Leiden: Brill. [Extracted from *Encyclopädia of Islam*, 1st ed., 1913–1938.]

Gifford, Edward S. 1957. "The Evil Eye in Medical History." *American Journal of Ophthalmology* 44:237–43.

———. 1958. *The Evil Eye: Studies in the Folklore of Vision*. New York: Macmillan.

———. 1960. "The Evil Eye in Pennsylvania Medical History." *Keystone Folklore Quarterly* 5:3.

———. 1971. "The Evil Eye in Philadelphia." *Pennsylvania Folklife* 20:58–59.

Gilmore, David D. 1982. "Anthropology of the Mediterannean Area." *Annual Review of Anthropology* 11:175–205.

———. 1987a. "Evil Eyes and Hard Looks." In *Aggression and Community: Paradoxes of Andalusian Culture*. New Haven: Yale University Press.

———, ed. 1987b. *Honor and Shame and the Unity of the Mediterranean*. American Anthropological Association Special Publication 22. Washington, DC: American Anthropological Association.

Glucklich, Ariel. 1997. *The End of Magic*. New York: Oxford University Press.

Goldin, Judah. 1976. "The Magic of Magic and Superstition." In *Aspects of Religious Propaganda in Judaism and Early Christianity*, edited by Elisabeth Schüssler Fiorenza, 113–47. Notre Dame: University of Notre Dame Press. Reprinted in *Studies in Midrash and Related Literature*, edited by Barry L. Eichler and Jeffrey H. Tigay, 353–57. JPS Scholar of Distinction Series. Philadelphia: Jewish Publication Society, 1988.

Gombrich, Richard F. 1978. "The Buddha's Eye, the Evil Eye, and Dr. Ruelius." In *Buddhism in Ceylon and Studies on Religious Syncretism in Buddhist Countries*, edited by Heinz Bechert, 335–38. Göttingen: Vandenhoeck & Ruprecht.

Gonda, J. 1969. *Eye and Gaze in the Veda*. Verhandelingen der koniklijke Nederlandse Akademie van Westenschappen, Afd. Letterkunde 75.1. Amsterdam: North-Holland.

Gonzalez Palencia, Angel. 1932. "La Doncella Que Se Saco Los Ojos." *Revista de la Biblioteca, Archivo y Museo* 9:272–94.

Goodwin, Jason. 2011. *An Evil Eye: A Novel*. New York: Macmillan/Picador.

Gordon, Benjamin Lee. 1937. "Oculus fascinus (Fascination, Evil Eye)." *Archives of Ophthalmology* 17:290–319. Reprinted as "The Evil Eye." *Hebrew Medical Journal* 34 (1961) 261–91.

Gorski, Eric. 2009. "Americans Mix, Match Religions." *Chicago Sun-Times*, 10 December.

Graevius, J. G. 1694–99. *Thesaurus Antiquitatum Romanarum*. Leiden: Halma & van der Aa.

Grandqvist, H. 1950. *Child Problems among the Arabs*. Helsinki: Söderström.

Grant, Meg. 2012. "Fighting for Love." *AARP The Magazine*, September, 48–51, 84.

Gravel, Pierre Bettez. 1995. *The Malevolent Eye: An Essay on the Evil Eye, Fertility and the Concept of Mana*. American University Studies, Series 11. Anthropology and Sociology 64. New York: Lang.

Greenacre, Phyllis. 1925–26. "The Eye Motif in Delusion and Fantasy." *American Journal of Psychiatry* 82:553–79.

Gregory, Isabella Augusta. 1920. *Visions and Beliefs in the West of Ireland*. First Series Vol. 1. New York: Putnam.

Gregory, James R. 1975. "Image of Limited Good, or Expectation of Reciprocity?" *Current Anthropology* 16:73–92.

Griffiths, J. Gwynn. 1938. "A Protection against the Evil Eye in Lower Nubia and Upper Egypt." *Man* 38:68–70.

Gross, Charles G. 1999. "The Fire That Comes from the Eye." *The Neuroscientist* 5/4:58–64.

Grossi, Vincenzo. 1886. *Il fascino e la jettatura nell' Antico Oriente*. Milan-Torino: Fratelli Dumolard.

Gregory, James R. 1975. "Image of Limited Good, or Expectation of Reciprocity?" *Current Anthropology* 16:73–92.

Gubbins, J. K. 1946. "Some Observations on the Evil Eye in Modern Greece." *Folk-Lore* 57:195–97.

Gülerman, Piraye. 1993. "'Beware the Evil Eye' 'Nazar Degmesin! . . .'" *Skylife Ocak* (January) 58–61.

Gutierrez, Johannes Lazarus. 1653. *Opusculum de fascino*. Lyons: Borde et al.

Hahm, David E. 1978. "Early Hellenistic Theories of Vision and the Perception of Color." In *Studies in Perception: Interrelations in the History of Philosophy and Science*, edited by Peter K. Machamer and Robert G. Turnbill, 60–95. Colombus: Ohio State University Press.

Haimowitz, Morris L. and Natalie Reader Haimowitz. 1966. "The Evil Eye: Fear of Success." In *Human Development: Selected Readings*, edited by Morris L. Haimowitz and Natalie Reader Haimowitz, 677–85. 2nd ed. New York: Crowell.

Hanchuk, Rena Jeanne. 1999. *The Word and Wax: A Medical Folk Ritual Among Ukrainians in Alberta*. Canadian Series in Ukranian Ethnology 2. Alberta: Canadian Institute of Ukrainian Studies Press.

Hand, Wayland D. 1976 (1992). "The Evil Eye in Its Folk Medical Aspects: A Survey of North America." In *The Evil Eye: A Casebook,* edited by Alan Dundes, 169–80. 2nd ed. Madison: University of Wisconsin Press, 1992. Reprinted from In *Actas del XLI Congreso Internacional de Americanistas, Mexico, 2–7 de Septiembre 1974,* 3:183–89. Mexico City, 1976. Also reprinted in Hand, *Magical Medicine: The Folkoric Component of Medicine in the Folk Belief, Custom, and Ritual of the Peoples of Europe and America. Selected Essays of Wayland D. Hand,* 239–49. Berkeley: University of California Press, 1980.

Handwörterbuch des deutschen Aberglaubens. 1927–1942. 10 vols. Edited by Hanns Bächtold-Stäubli and E. Hoffmann-Krayer. Berlin: de Gruyter. Reprinted, Berlin, 1987. "Auge," 1:685–90; "berufen, beschreien," 2:1096–102; "Gebärde," 3.328–37; "loben," 5:1311–16.

Hardie, Margaret M. [Mrs. F. W. Hasluck]. 1992 (1923). "The Evil Eye in Some Greek Villages of the Upper Haliakmon Valley in West Macedonia." In *The Evil Eye: A Casebook,* edited by Alan Dundes, 107–23. 2nd ed. Madison: University of Wisconsin Press, 1992. Reprinted from *Journal of the Royal Anthropological Institute* 53 (1923) 160–72.

Harfouche, Jamal Karam. 1992 (1965). "The Evil Eye and Infant Health in Lebanon." In *The Evil Eye: A Casebook,* edited by Alan Dundes, 86–106. 2nd ed. Madison: University of Wisconsin Press, 1992. Reprinted from *Infant Health in Lebanon: Customs and Taboos*. Beirut: Khayats, 1965.

Harris, Marvin. 1976. "History and Significance of the Emic-Etic Distinction." *Annual Review of Anthropology* 5 (1976) 329–50.

Hart, Henry Harper. "The Eye in Symbol and Symptom." *The Psychoanalytic Review* 36 (1949) 1–21.

Hartman, Peter, and Karyl McIntosh. "Evil Eye Beliefs Collected in Utica, New York." *New York Folklore* 4 (1978) 60–69.

Hastings, James A. et al., eds. 1908–26. *Encyclopaedia of Religion and Ethics.* 13 vols. Edinburgh: Scribner, 1908–1927. [Vol. 1 (1908); vols 2–4 (1910; vol 5 (1912); 6 (1914; 7 (1915); 8 (1916); 9 (1917); 10 (1918); 11 (1919); 12 (1922); Index (1926).

Hauschild, Thomas. 1979a. *Der Böse Blick: Ideengeschichtliche und Sozialpsychologische Untersuchungen.* Beiträge zur Ethnomedizin, Ethnobotanik und Ethnozoologie VII. Hamburg: Arbeitskreis Ethnomedizin, 1979. 2nd ed. Berlin: Mensch & Leben, 1982.

————. 1979b. "Sind Heilrituale dasselbe wie Psychotherapien? Kritik einer ethnomedizischen Denkgewohnheit am Beispiel des süditalienischen Heilrituals gegen den bösen Blick." *Curare* 2:241–56.

Headland, Thomas; Kenneth Pike, and Marvin Harris, eds. 1990. *Emics and Etics: The Insider/Outsider Debate.* Frontiers of Anthropology 7. New York: Sage.

Hedayot, Kamyar N., M.D. and Roya Pirzadeh, M.D. 2001. "Issues in Islamic Biomedical Ethics: A Primer for the Pediatrician." *Pediatrics* 108:965–71.

Hemmer, Ragnar. 1912/13. "Det onda ögat i skandinavisk folktro." *Brage Årsskrift* 7:52–75.

Henderson, George. 1911. *Survivals in Belief Among the Celts.* Glasgow: Maclehose.

Herber, J. 1927. "Le Main de Fathima." *Hesperis* 7:209–19.

Hermann, Antal. 1888. "Rumänische Besprechungsformel gegen den bösen Blick." *Ethnologische Mitteilungen aus Ungarn* 1:175–76.

Herzfeld, Michael. 1981. "Meaning and Morality: A Semiotic Approach to Evil Eye Accusations in a Greek Village." *American Ethnologist* 8:560–74.

————. 1984. "The Horns of the Mediterranean dilemmma." *American Ethnologist* 11:439–54; Discussion: 12 (1985) 369–371.

————. 1986. "Closure as Cure: Tropes in the Exploration of Bodily and Social Disorder." *Current Anthropology* 27:107–20.

Hess, Eckhard H. 1975. *The Tell-Tale Eye. How Your Eyes Reveal Hidden Thoughts and Emotions.* New York: Van Nostrand Reinhold.

Hirschberg, Julius. 1982. *The History of Ophthalmology.* Vol. 1, *Antiquity.* Bonn: Wayenborgh. [German ed., 1899.]

Hocart, A. M. 1938. "The Mechanism of the Evil Eye." *Folklore* 49:156–57.

Hoffman, Susannah M. 1972. *Kypseli: Women and Men Apart, A Divided Reality.* A documentary film on the village of Kypseli, on the Aegian Island of Thera/Santorini by anthropologist Susannah Hoffmann, of the Sociology Department, University of San Francisco, San Francisco, CA.

————. 1976. "Discussion of the Film "Kypseli: Women and Men Apart, A Divided Reality." *Greek Students Annals of the New York Academy of Sciences* 268:382–84.

————. "1988. The Controversy about Kypseli." In *Anthropological Filmmaking: Anthropological Perspectives on the Production of Film and Video for General Public Audiences,* edited by Jack R. Rollwagen, 161–69. London: Harwood Academic.

Hoorn, W., van. 1972. *As Images Unwind: Ancient and Modern Theories of Visual Perception.* Amsterdam: University Press of Amsterdam.

Houtsma, M. T. et al., eds. 1913–38. *The Encyclopædia of Islam: A Dictionary of the Geography, Ethnography and Biography of the Muhammadan Peoples.* 4 vols. and Supplement. Leiden: Brill.

Hughes, C. 1985. "Glossary of 'Culture-Bound' or Folk Psychiatric Syndromes." In *The Culture-Bound Syndromes: Folk Illnesses of Psychiatric and Anthropological Interest,* edited by R. C. Simons and C. C. Hughes, 469–505. Dordrecht: Reidel.

Huxley, Francis. 1990. *The Eye, the Seer and the Seen.* New York: Thames & Hudson.

Ibn Khaldun. 1858–. *Al-muqaddimah.* Edited by M. Quatremère. Paris.

———. 1967. *The Muqaddimah: An Introduction to History.* Translated by Franz Rosenthal and edited by N. J. Dawood. 2nd ed. 3 vols. Princeton: Princeton University Press.

Ibrahim, Abdullahi Ali. 1991. "Sahir and Muslim Moral Space." *International Journal of Middle East Studies* 23:387–99.

———. 1994. *Assaulting with Words: Popular Discourse and the Bridle of Shariah.* Evanston: Northwestern University Press.

Illich, Ivan. 1994. *Guarding the Eye in the Age of Show.* Issue 4 of Science, Technology and Society Working Papers. University Park: Pennsylvania State University.

Inhorn, Marcia C. 1994. *Quest for Conception: Gender, Infertility, and Egyptian Medical Traditions.* Philadephia: University of Pennsylvania Press.

Irimia, M. P., and J. A. Fernandez de Rota. 1976. "Envidia y mal de ojo en la cultura gallega: sus implicaciones sociales." *Ethnica* 12:25–40.

Issroff, Judith. 1999. *Pilot Study of a Multi-ethnic Investigation of Traditional and Current Beliefs, Practices, and Customs in Relation to Respiratory Distress in Israel.* Online: http://www.priory.com/psych/asthma.htm.

Izzi, Giuseppe, ed. 1980. *Scrittori della Jettatura, con una premessa di Giorgio Manganelli e una nota antropologica di Luigi Lombardi Satriani.* Rome: Salerno.

Jaeger, Wolfgang. 1979. *Augenmotive: Votivgaben, Votivbilder, Amulette.* Sigmaringen: Thorbecke.

Jahn, Otto. 1855. *Über den Aberglauben des bösen Blickes bei den Alten.* Berichte der Sächsischen Gesellschaft der Wissenschaften zu Leipzig. Philologisch-Historische Classe. Leipzig: Hirzel.

Jarass, Heidrun and Leon Wurmser. 2008. "'Evil Eye and 'Searing Look' in the Magic Gaze." In *Jealousy and Envy: New Views About Two Powerful Feelings.* Edited by Leon Wurmser and Heidrun Jarass, 149–78. New York: Analytic Press.

Jaussen, J.-A. 1924. "Le mauvais oeil." *RB* 33:396–407.

Jay, Martin. 1986. "In the Empire of the Gaze: Foucault and the Denigration of Vision in Twentieth-Century French Thought." In *Foucault: A Critical Reader,* edited by David C. Hay, 175–204. Oxford: Basil Blackwell.

———. 1993. *Downcast Eyes: The Denigration of Vision in Twentieth Century French Thought.* Berkeley: University of California Press.

Jay, Richard. 2010. *Stalking the Evil Eye.* Bloomington, IN: Xlibris.

Jeffers, Ann. 1996. *Magic and Divination in Ancient Palestine and Syria.* Studies in the History and Culture of the Ancient Near East 8. Leiden: Brill.

"Jettare, jettatore, jettatura." 1957. In *Dizionario Enciclopedico Italiano,* 6:24. Rome: Enciclopedia Italiana.

Johner, Lutz. 1977. "Kinder jagten die Frau mit dem bösen Blick." *Hamburger Abendblatt,* no. 36:3.

Johnson, Clarence Richard. 1924–25. "The Evil Eye and Other Superstitions in Turkey." *Journal of Applied Sociology* 9:259–68.

Jonas, Wayne B. 2005. *Mosby's Dictionary of Complementary and Alternative Medicine.* Amsterdam: Elsevier.

Jones, Louis C. 1992 (1951). "The Evil Eye among European-Americans." In *The Evil Eye: A Casebook,* edited by A. Dundes, 150–68. 2nd ed. Madison: University of Wisconsin Press. Reprinted from *Western Folklore* 10:11–25.

Joshi, Purushottan Balkrishma. 1886–89. "On the Evil Eye in the Konkan." *Journal of the Anthropological Society of Bombay* 1:120–28.

Kahl, Thede. 2006. "Der Böse Blick. Ein gemeinsames Element im Volksglauben von Christen und Muslimen." In *Religion und Magie in Ostmitteleuropa: Spielräume theologischer Normierungsprozesse in Spätmittelalter und Früher Neuzeit*, edited by Thomas Wünsch, 321–36. Religions- und Kulturgeschichte in Ostmittel- und Südosteuropa 8. Münster: Lit-Verlag.

Kanafani, Aida S. 1993. "Rites of Hospitality and Aesthetics." In *Everyday Life in the Muslim Middle East*, edited by Donna Lee Bowen and Evelyn A. Early, 128–35. Bloomington: Indiana University Press.

Kearney, Michael. 1976. "A World-View Explanation of the Evil Eye." In *The Evil Eye*, edited by Clarence Maloney, 175–92. New York: Columbia University Press.

———. 1984. *World View*. Novato, CA: Chandler & Sharp.

Keeley, Brian L. 2002. "Eye Gaze Information-Processing Theory: A Case Study in Primate Cognitive Neuroethology." In *The Cognitive Animal*, edited by M. Berkoff et al., 443–50. MIT Press.

Kilborne, Benjamin. 2008. "The Evil Eye, Envy, and Shame. On Emotions and Explanations." In *Jealousy and Envy: New Views About Two Powerful Feelings*. Edited by Leon Wurmser and Heidrun Jarass, 129–48. New York: Analytic Press.

Klatzkin, Jacob et al., eds. 1928–34. *Encyclopaedia Judaica*. 10 vols. Berlin: Eschkol.

Klein, Melanie. 1957. *Envy and Gratitude: A Study of Unconscious Sources*. New York: Basic Books.

———. 1975. *Envy and Gratitude, and Other Works, 1946–1963*. London: Hogarth.

Kluckhohn, Clyde. 1944. *Navaho Witchcraft*. Boston: Beacon.

Klutz, Todd, ed. 2003a. *Magic in the Biblical World: From the Rod of Aaron to the Ring of Solomon*. JSNTSup 245. Sheffield: Sheffield Academic.

———. 2003b "Reinterpreting 'Magic' in the World of Jewish and Christian Scripture: An Introduction." In *Magic in the Biblical World: From the Rod of Aaron to the Ring of Solomon*, edited by Todd Klutz, 1–9. JSNTSup 245. Sheffield: Sheffield Academic.

Knecht, S. 1968. "Matiasma—der böse Blick." *Medizinische Welt* 44:2455–61.

Knortz, Karl. 1899. "Der böse Blick." *Folkloristische Streifzüge*, 280–91. Leipzig: Maske.

Koebert, R. 1948. "Zur Lehre des Tafsir über den bösen Blick." *Islam* 28:111–121.

Koenig, Otto. 1975. *Urmotiv Auge. Neuentdeckte Grundzüge menschlichen Verhaltens*. Munich: Piper.

Koerper, Henry C., and Nancy Whitney-Desautels. 1999. "A Cowry Shell Artifact from Bolsa Chica: An Example of Prehistoric Exchange." *PCAS Quarterly* 35/2–3:81–95.

Kottis, Michaeline. 1999. "Le mauvais oeil en Grèce: le champ de l'emotion et de parenté." *Ethnologie Française* 29/4:653–64.

Kotzé, Zak. 2006. "Laban's Evil Eye: a cognitive linguistic interpretation of ynd) yny(b rxy l) ('el yiher b'ene 'adoni) in Gn 31:35." *Old Testament Essays* 19:1215–24.

———. 2007. "The Evil Eye as Witchcraft Technique in the Hebrew Bible." *Journal for Semitics* 16:141–49.

———. 2008. "The Evil Eye of YHWH." *Journal for Semitics* 17:207–18.

Koukoules, Phaidon. 1948–1957. *Byzantinôn bios kai politismos / Vie et civilisation byzantine*. 6 vols. Athens: Institut francais d'Athenes. Vol. 1.1: 244–48.

Koyen, Jeff. 2002. "The Evil Eye." *Fortean Times*. Online: http://www.forteantimes.com/features/articles/241/the_evil_eye.html.

Kramer, Heinrich, and James Sprenger. 1928 *Malleus Maleficarum*. Rome, c. 1486, with many subsequent editions. ET: *The Malleus Maleficarum of Heinrich Kramer and James Sprenger,* translated with Introductions, Bibliography and Notes by Montague Summers. London: John Rodker, 1928. Reprinted, New York: Dover, 1971 (1928, 1948).

Krappe, Alexander Haggerty. 1927. *Balor with the Evil Eye: Studies in Celtic and French Literature.* Institut des études français. New York: Columbia University Institut des Études Français.

Kriss, Rudolf and Hubert Kriss-Heinrich. 1962. *Volksglaube im Bereich des Islam.* Vol. 2. *Amulette, Zauberformen und Beschwörungen.* Wiesbaden: Harrassowitz.

Küçükerman, Önder. 1988. *Glass Beads: Anatolian glass bead making, the final traces of three millennia of glass making in the Mediterranean region.* Translated by Maggie Quigley Pinar. Istanbul: Turkish Touring and Automobile Association.

Kunesh, T. P. 1998. "The Eye in the Hand. A Visual Study of an Historic Multi-cultural Icon." Online: http://www.darkfiber.com/eyeinhand/

Kuriks, O. 1930. "Kuri silm ja tema pilgu maagiline moju. " *Eesti Arst* 9:265–75.

Landtman, Gunnar. 1939. "Tron pa det onda ögat i svenska Finland." *Bodkavlen* 18:34–42.

Lane, Edward William. 1973 (1895). *An Account of the Manners and Customs of the Modern Egyptians.* London: Gardner. 5th ed. New York: Dover.

Lauer, H. H. 1983. "Böser Blick." In *Lexikon des Mittelalters* 2:470–72.

Lawson, John Cuthbert. 1910. *Modern Greek Folklore and Ancient Greek Religion.* Cambridge: Cambridge University Press.

Leach, Edmund. 1982. *Social Anthropology.* London: Fontana.

Lexikon der byzantinischen Gräzitität, besonders des 9.-12. Jahrhunderts. Edited by E. Trapp et al. Vienna: Austrian Akademy of Science, 2001–2007.

Lexikon des Mittelalters. 9 vols. Edited by Bruno Mariacher. Munich: Artemis & Winkler (vols. 1–6); Munich: LexMA-Verlag (vols. 7–9), 1980–1998. Munich: dtv-Verlag, 2002.

Liddell, H. G., R. Scott, and H. S. Jones. 1968. *A Greek–English Lexicon.* Oxford: Clarendon, 1968.

Lindberg, David C. 1976. *Theories of Vision from Al-kindi to Kepler.* University of Chicago History of Science and Medicine. Chicago: University of Chicago Press.

Lindquist, Edna. 1936. "Rue and the Evil Eye in Persia." *The Moslim World* 26:170–75.

Löwinger, Adolf. 1926. "Der Böse Blick nach jüdischen Quellen." *Menorah* 4:551–69.

Lopsaic, Alexander. 1978. "Animal Lore and the Evil-eye in Shepherd Sardinia." In *Animals in Folklore,* edited by J. R. Porter and W. M. S. Russell, 59–69. Totowa, NJ: Rowman & Littlefield.

Lykiaropoulos, Amica. 1981. "The Evil Eye: Towards an Exhaustive Study." *Folklore* 92:221–30.

MacCorkill, Nancy. 2002. "The Evil Eye. Folklore of the Irish and Highland and Island Scots." Online: http://www.reocities.com/Athens/Parthenon/2897/evileye3.html

Machovec, Frank J. 1976. "The Evil Eye: Superstition or Hypnotic Phenomenon?" *American Journal of Clinical Hypnosis* 19:74–79.

Mack, John. 1988. *Ethnic Jewelry.* New York: Abrams.

Mack, R. 2002. "Facing Down Medusa (An Aetiology of the Gaze)." *Art History* 25:571–604.

Maclagan, Robert Craig. 1902. *Evil Eye in the Western Highlands.* London: Nutt.

Magnani, Franca. 1977. "Der böse Blick." In "Römische Skizzen," Bayerische Rundfunk, ARD 11/13/1977, 17.45 PM.

Malina, Bruce J. 2001. "Envy—The Most Grievous of All Evils." In *The New Testament World: Insights from Cultural Anthropology*, 108–33. 3rd ed. Louisville: Westminster John Knox.

"Mal ojo." 1908–1930. *Enciclopedia universal ilustrada europeo-americana*. 72 vols. Madrid: Espas Calpe, 1908–1930, plus an appended ten-volumes (1930–1933), plus 33 supplemental volumes (1935–2003), plus an index, appendix, and atlas, for a grand total of 118 vols. Vol. 32: 408–412.

Maloney, Clarence. 1976. "Don't Say 'Pretty Baby' Lest You Zap It with Your Eye—The Evil Eye in South Asia." In *The Evil Eye*, edited by Clarence Maloney, 102–48. New York: Columbia University Press.

Maloney, Clarence, ed. 1976. *The Evil Eye*. New York: Columbia University Press.

Malpezzi, Frances M., and William M. Clements. 1992. *Italian-American Folklore*. Little Rock, AR: August House.

Mancini, Anthony. 1977. *Minnie Santangelo and the Evil Eye*. New York: Fawcett Crest.

Mandelbaum, Allen. 1982. *The Divine Comedy of Dante Aligheri. A Verse Translation*. 3 vols. *I. Inferno, II. Purgatorio, III Paradiso*. New York: Bantam Classic.

Maple, Eric. 1983. "The Evil Eye." In *Man, Myth and Magic. The Illustrated Encyclopedia of Mythology, Religion, and the Unknown*. Edited by Richard Cavendish and Yvonne Deutsch, 4:888–94. New York: Marshall Cavendish.

Marçais, Philippe H. 1960. "Ayn and the Evil Eye." In *Encyclopedia of Islam*, edited by H. A. R. Gibb et al., 1:784–86. 2nd ed. Leiden: Brill.

Martin, Dale B. 1997. "Hellenistic Superstition: The Problems of Defining a Vice." In *Conventional Values of the Hellenistic Greeks*, edited by Per Bilde, 128–58. Studies in Hellenistic Civilization 8. Aarhus: Aarhus University Press.

———. 2004. *Inventing Superstition: From the Hippocratics to the Christians*. Cambridge: Harvard University Press.

De Martino, Ernesto. 1959. *Sud e magia*. Milan: Feltrinelli.

Marugi, Giovanni Leonardo. 1815. *Capricci sulla jettatura*. Naples: Nobile.

Mather, Frank Jewett. 1910. "The Evil Eye." *Century Magazine* 80:42–47.

Matsuzono, M. 1993. "Rubbing Off the Dirt: Evil-Eye Belief among the Gusii." *Nilo-Ethiopian Studies* 1:1–13.

McDaniel, Walton Brooks. 1918 (1971). "The Pupula Duplex and Other Tokens of an 'Evil Eye' in the Light of Ophthalmology." *Classical Philology* 13:335–46. Reprinted in *Perspectives in Biology and Medicine* 15/1:72–79.

McKenzie, Dan. 1927. *The Infancy of Medicine: An Enquiry into the Influence of Folklore upon the Evolution of Scientific Medicine*. London: Macmillan.

Meerloo, Joost Abraham Maurits. 1971. *Intuition and the Evil Eye: The Natural History of a Superstition*. Wassenaar, Netherlands: Servire.

Meltzl de Lomnitz, Hugo. 1884. "Le mauvais oeil chez les Arabes." *Archivio per lo Studio delle Tradizioni Popolari* 3:133–34.

Meslin, M. 1987. "Eye." In *Encyclopedia of Religion*, edited by Mircea Eliade, 5:236–39. New York: Macmillan.

Mesmer, F. Anton. 1814. *Mesmerismus*. Edited by K. C. Wolfart. Berlin: Nikolaische, 1814.

Mesner, Douglas. 2010. "Letter to the Editor: A Dialogue Regarding Colin Ross' article 'The Electrophysiological Basis of Evil Eye Belief.'" *Anthropology of Consciousness* 21/2:103–5.

Migliore, Sam. 1983. "Evil Eye or Delusions: On the 'Consistency' of Folk Models." *Medical Anthropology Quarterly* 14:4–9.

———. 1990. "Etiology, Distress, and Classification: The Development of a Tri–Axial Model." *Western Canadian Anthropologist* 7:3–35.

———. 1997. *Mal'uocchiu: Ambiguity, Evil Eye, and the Language of Distress.* Anthropological Horizons 10. Toronto: University of Toronto Press.

Migne, J. P., ed. 1857–1866. *Patrologiae Cursus Completus.* Series Graeca. 161 vols. Paris: Garnier Freres.

Modi, Jivanji Jamshedji. 1924. "A Few Notes From and On Recent Anthropological Literature." *Journal of the Anthropological Society of Bombay* 13:113–31.

Moretti, Pietrina. 1955. "Contra il Malocchio del Bestiame in Sardegna." *La Lapa* 3:105.

Morris, Desmond. 1977. *Manwatching. A Field Guide to Human Behavior.* New York: Harry N. Abrams.

———. 1985. *Bodywatching: A Field Guide to the Human Species.* New York: Crown, 1985.

Morris, Desmond, P. Collett, P. Marsh, and M. O'Shaughnessy, eds. *Gestures: Their Origins and Distribution.* New York: Stein & Day, 1977, 1979, 1985.

Moss, Leonard W., and Stephen C. Cappannari. 1976. "Mal'occhio, Ayin ha ra, Oculus Fascinus, Judenblick: The Evil Eye Hovers Above." In *The Evil Eye*, edited by Clarence Maloney, 1–15. New York: Columbia University Press.

Mundt, Theodor. 1870. "Der Blick ist der Mensch." *Europa* 10:298–306.

Murdock, George Peter. 1962–1980. *The Ethnographic Atlas* (published in 29 successive installments in the journal *Ethnology*).

———. 1967. "Ethnographic Atlas: A Summary." *Ethnology* 6/2 (1967) 109–236.

———. 1980a. *Atlas of World Cultures.* Pittsburgh: University of Pittsburgh Press.

———. 1980b. *Theories of Illness: A World Survey.* Pittsburgh: University of Pittsburgh Press.

Murdock, George P. and D. R. White. 1969. "Standard Cross-Cultural Sample." *Ethnology* 8:329–69.

Murgoci, A. 1992 (1923). "The Evil Eye in Roumania, and Its Antidotes." In *The Evil Eye. A Casebook*, edited by Alan Dundes, 124–29. 2nd ed. Madison: University of Wisconsin Press. Reprinted from *Folk-Lore* 34:357–362.

Muthu Cidambaram, S. 1980. "The Evil Eye: Its Prevention and Expulsion." In *A Festschrift for Prof. M. Shanmugam Pillai*, edited by M. Israel et al., 1:321–28. Madurai: Muthu Patippakam.

Nádaská, Katarína and Martina Sekulová. 2005. "Elements of Magical—Medicinal Practice. The Position of the Witch and Wizard in Slovakia." In *The Role of Magic in the Past: Learned and Popular Magic, Popular Beliefs and Diversity of Attitudes.* Edited by Blanka Szeghyova, 137–50. Bratislava: Pro Historia. [Pp. 144–47 on the Evil Eye in Slavonic culture].

Nador, George, ed. 1975. *An Incantation against the Evil Eye.* Academia Maimonideana. Documenta inedita 2. Middlesex, UK: Bina.

Naff, Alixa. 1965. "Belief in the Evil Eye among the Christian Syrian-Lebanese in America." *Journal of American Folklore* 78:46–51.

Nagarajan, Vijaya. 1993. "Hosting the Divine. The Kôlam in Tamil Nadu." In *Mud, Mirror and Thread: Folk Traditions of Rural India*, edited by Nora Fisher, 192–204. Santa Fe: Museum of New Mexico.

Nanos, Mark. D. 2002. *The Irony of Galatians. Paul's Letter in First-Century Context*. Minneapolis: Fortress.

Napier, James. 1879. *Folk-Lore or Superstitious Beliefs in the West of Scotland within This Century*. Paisely: Gardner.

Neusner, Jacob, Ernest S. Frerichs and Paul V. M. Flesher, eds. 1989. *Religion, Science and Magic in Concert and in Conflict*. New York: Oxford University Press.

New Catholic Encyclopedia. 1967. 15 vols. New York: McGraw-Hill.

Neyrey, Jerome H. 1988. "Bewitched in Galatia: Paul and Cultural Anthropology." *Catholic Biblical Quarterly* 50:72–100. Revised form in Neyrey 1990.

———. 1990. "Bewitched in Galatia: Paul's Accusations of Witchcraft." In Neyrey, *Paul, In Other Words: A Cultural Reading of His Letters*, 181–206. Louisville: Westminster John Knox.

Nicholson, Mervyn. 1999. *Male Envy: The Logic of Malice in Literature and Culture*. Lanham, MD: Lexington.

Nichter, M. 1981. "Idioms of Distress: Alternatives in the Expression of Psycho-Social Distress: A Case Study from South India." *Culture, Medicine, and Psychiatry* 5:379–408.

Oates, Joyce Carol. 2013. *Evil Eye: Four Novellas of Love Gone Wrong*. New York: Mysterious Press/Grove Atlantic.

O'Neil, Bernard. 1908. "The Evil Eye." *The Occult Review* 8:5–18.

Oyler, D. S. 1992 (1919). "The Shilluk's Belief in the Evil Eye: The Evil Medicine Man." In *The Evil Eye: A Casebook*, edited by Alan Dundes, 78–85. 2nd ed. Madison: University of Wisconsin Press. Reprinted from *Sudan Notes and Records* 2:122–128.

Papanikolas, H. 2002. *An Amulet of Greek Earth. Generations of Immigrant Folk Culture*. Athens: Ohio University Press.

Park, David. 1998. *The Fire within the Eye. A Historical Essay on the Nature and Meaning of Light*. Princeton: Princeton University Press.

Park, Roswell, M.D. 1912. "The Evil Eye." In *The Evil Eye, Thanatology, and Other Essays*, 9–31. Boston: Badger.

Parsons, C. D. F. 1984. "Idioms of Distress: Kinship and Sickness among the People of the Kingdom of Tonga." *Culture, Medicine, and Psychiatry* 8:71–93.

Parsons, C. D. F. and P. Wakeley. 1991. "Idioms of Distress: Somatic Responses to Distress in Everyday Life." *Culture, Medicine, and Psychiatry* 15:111–32.

Pasquale, E. A. 1984. The Evil Eye Phenomenon: Its Implications in Community Health Nursing. *Home Healthcare Nurse* 2/3:32–35.

Patai, Raphael. 1983. *The Arab Mind*. Rev. ed. New York: Scribner.

Pauli, L. 1975. *Keltischer Volksglaube: Amulette u. Sonderbestattungen am Dürrnberg bei Hallein und im eisenzeitlichen Mitteleuropa*. Mùnich: Beck.

Pauly, A. F. 1839–1852. *Paulys Real-encyclopädie der classischen Altertumswissenschaft*. Vols. 1–6. New Edition begun by G. Wissowa et al. 70+ vols. Stuttgart: J. B. Metzlersche Verlagsbuchhandlung, 1892–1980. (*Pauly-Wissowa* or *PW* or *RE*)

Pavese, Cesare. 1966. "The Evil Eye" (*Jettatura*). In *Summer Storm and Other Stories*. Translated and with an Introduction by A. E. Murch. London: Owen.

Pavesi, Lucia. 1995. *Malocchio, Possessioni, Esorcismi. come proteggersi dalle influenze negativa*. Milan: de Vecchi.

Pazzini, A. 1948. *La medicina popolare in Italia.* Storia, tradizioni, leggende. Trieste: Zigiotti.

Peake, Richard Brinsley. 1831. *The Evil Eye, A Legend of the Levant: A Romantic Musical Drama in Two Acts.* London. Lacy.

Pelligrino, Luciano. 1966. "Together with the Saints, Or Taken by the Eye: Person, Community and Magico-Religious Expressions in a Southern Italian Town." M.A. thesis, Hunter College, New York.

Penner, Hans H. 1989. "Rationality, Ritual, and Science." In *Religion, Science and Magic in Concert and in Conflict,* edited by Jacob Neusner et al., 11–24. New York: Oxford University Press.

Perdiguero Gil, E. 1986. "El mal de ojo: de la literatura antisuperticiosa a la Antropología Médica." *Asclepio* 38:47–66.

Peringer, Gustaf. 1685. *De amuletis Hebraeorum dissertatio.* Uppsala University. Holmiæ: Eberdt.

Perkmann, Adelgard. 1927. "Berufen, beschreien." In *Handwörterbuch des deutschen Aberglaubens,* edited by Hanns Bächtold-Stäubli, 1:1096–102. Berlin: de Gruyter.

Peter of Limoges. 2012. *The Moral Treatise on the Eye* (*Tractatus moralis de oculo,* c. 1274/75–1289). Translated and with an introduction by Richard Newhauser. Medieval Sources in Translation 51. Toronto: Pontifical Institute of Medieval Studies.

Peterson-Bidoshi, Kristin. 2006. "The *Dordolec*: Albanian House Dolls and the Evil Eye." *Journal of American Folklore* 119 (473) 337–55.

Phillips, Jonas B., and George Jones. 1831. *The Evil Eye: A Melo-drama, in Two Acts.* New York: Clayton & Neal.

Pilch, John J. 1996. "Actions Speak Louder Than Words." *The Bible Today* 34:172–76.

———. 2000a. *Healing in the New Testament: Insights from Medical and Mediterranean Anthropology.* Minneapolis: Fortress.

———. 2000b. "Improving Bible Translations: The Examples of Sickness and Healing." *Biblical Theology Bulletin* 30:129–34

———. 2002. *Cultural Tools for Interpreting the Good News.* Collegeville: Liturgical.

———. 2004. "A Window into the Biblical World: The Evil Eye." *The Bible Today* 42/1:49–53.

———. 2012. "The Evil Eye." In *A Cultural Handbook to the Bible,* 176–81. Grand Rapids: Eerdmans.

Pilch, John J. and Bruce J. Malina, eds. 1998. *Handbook of Biblical Social Values.* 2nd ed. Peabody, MA: Hendrickson.

Pinch, Geraldine. 1994. *Magic in Ancient Egypt.* Austin: University of Texas Press.

Pirandello, Luigi. 1964. "The License" (*La Patente,* 1919). In *Pirandello's One-Act Plays,* 119–38. Garden City, NY: Doubleday.

Pitrè, Giuseppe. 1884. "*La jettatura e il malocchio in Sicilia.*" *Acta Comparationis Litterarum Universarum/Journal of Comparative Literature* n.s. 11/1–2:4–8.

———. 1992 (1889). "The Jettatura and the Evil Eye." In *The Evil Eye: A Casebook,* edited by Alan Dundes, 130–42. 2nd ed. Madison: University of Wisconsin Press. Translated from "La Jettatura ed il Malocchio." *Biblioteca delle Tradizioni Populari Siciliane,* 17:235–49. Palermo: Lauriel, 1889.

———. 1913. "Jettatura e Malocchio. Scongiuri, Antidoti ed Amuleti." *Biblioteca delle Tradizioni Populari Siciliane,* 25:193–211. Palermo: Reber.

Pitt-Rivers, Julian A. 1971. *The People of the Sierra*. 2nd ed. Chicago: University of Chicago Press.

Pocock, D. F. 1992. "The Evil Eye—Envy and Greed among the Patidar of Central Gujerat." In *The Evil Eye: A Casebook*, edited by Alan Dundes, 201–10. 2nd ed. Madison: University of Wisconsin Press, 1992.

Pocock, P. 1991. "The Evil Eye." In *Religion in India*, edited by T. N. Madan, 50–62. New Dehli: Oxford University Press.

Poe, Edgar Allan. 1969. "Lenore." In *The Collected Works of Edgar Allan Poe*, edited by Thomas Ollive Mabbott (and E. A. Poe), vol. 1, *Poems*, 330–39. Cambridge, MA: Belknap.

Potts, Albert M. 1982. *The World's Eye*. Lexington: University of Kentucky Press.

Potts, William John. 1890. "The Evil Eye." *Journal of American Folklore* 3:70.

Press, Irwin. 1973. "Bureaucracy Versus Folk Medicine: Implications from Seville, Spain." *Urban Anthropology* 2:232–47. Online: http://www.jstor.org/stable/40552650.

Price, David. 2001. *The Evil Eye*. Calne, Wiltshire, UK: BJM Press/Rainfall Books.

Radin, Dean. 1997. *The Conscious Universe. The Scientific Truth of Psychic Phenomena*. New York: HarperCollins.

Rājamōkan, [tokuppu]. 1987. *Tiruṣṭikalum parikārankalum*. Cennai: Yamunā Piracuram.

Rakoczy, Thomas. 1996. *Böser Blick, Macht des Auges und Neid der Götter: Eine Untersuchung zur Kraft des Blickes in der griechischen Literatur*. Classica Monacensia 13. Tübingen: Narr.

Ranke, K. 1911. "Böser Blick." *Reallexikon der Germanischen Altertumskunde*. Vol 3:323–24.

Reallexikon für Antike und Christentum. 26+ vols. Edited by Theodore Klauser et al. Stuttgart: A. Hiersemann, 1950–.

Reallexikon der Germanischen Altertumskunde. 4 vols. Edited by Johannes Hoops, Strassburg: K. J. Trübner, 1911–1919. 2nd edition, 35 vols. Edited by Herbert Jankuhn, Heinrich Beck et al. Berlin: de Gruyter, 1968/1973–2007.

Rebhun, Linda-Anne. 1995. "Contemporary Evil Eye in Northeast Brazil." In *Folklore Interpreted: Essays in Honor of Alan Dundes*, edited by Regina Bendix and Rosemary Lévy Zumwalt, 213–33. New York: Garland.

Reitler, Rudolf. 1913. "Zur Augensymbolik." *Internationale Zeitschrift für Ärtzliche Psychoanalyse* 1:159–61.

Reminick, Ronald A. 1974 (1976). "The Evil Eye Belief among the Amhara of Ethiopia." *Ethnology* 13:279–91. Reprinted in *The Evil Eye*, edited by Clarence Maloney, 85–101. New York: Columbia University Press.

Reminick, Ronald A. 1975. "The structure and function of religious belief among the Amhara of Ethiopia." In *United States Conferences on Ethiopian Studies*, 25–42. 1st Proceedings, Michigan State University, 1973. East Lansing: Michigan State Universitry Press.

Rheubottom, David. 1985. "The Seed of Evil Within." In *The Anthropology of Evil*, edited by D. Parkin, 79–91. Oxford: Blackwell.

Ribichini, Sergio. 1999. "Nel mondo dei miti. Lo sguardo che ucccide." *Archeo* 15/1: 102–4.

Rivera, G. Jr. and J. J. Wanderer. 1986. "Curanderismo and Childhood Illnesses." *The Social Science Journal* 23:361–72.

Robbins, Rossell Hope. 1959. "Fascination." In *The Encyclopedia of Witchcraft and Demonology*, 193–94. New York: Crown.

Roberts, John M. 1976. "Belief in the Evil Eye in World Perspective." In *The Evil Eye*, edited by Clarence Maloney, 223–78. New York: Columbia University Press.

Roheim, Géza. 1992 (1952). "The Evil Eye." In *The Evil Eye: A Casebook*, edited by A. Dundes, 211–22. 2nd ed. Madison: University of Wisconsin Press. Reprinted from *American Imago* 9 (1952) 351–63.

Rohrbaugh, Richard L. 2007. *The New Testament in Cross-Cultural Perspective*. Matrix. Eugene, OR: Cascade Books.

Rolfe, Eustace Neville, and Holcombe Ingleby. 1888 *Naples in 1888*. London: Trübner.

Rolleston, J. D. 1942. "Ophthalmic Folk-Lore." *The British Journal of Ophthalmology* 26:481–502.

Ronchi, Vasco. 1970. *The Nature of Light. An Historical Survey*. Cambridge, MA: Harvard University Press.

Roodenburg, Herman. 1991. "The 'Hand of Friendship': Shaking Hands and Other Gestures in the Dutch Republic." In *A Cultural History of Gesture*, edited by Jan Bremmer and Herman Roodenburg, 152–89. Ithaca, NY: Cornell University Press.

Rosenbaum, Brenda Z. 1985. *How to Avoid the Evil Eye*. Illustrated by Stuart Copans. New York: St. Martin's.

Rosner, V. 1958. "Some Observations on the Soul Concept and the Evil Eye among the Adivasis of Chota Nagpur." *Anthropos* 53:608–10.

Ross, Colin Andrew. 2010. "Hypothesis: The Electrophysiological Basis of Evil Eye Belief." *Anthropology of Consciousness* 21:47–57.

Roth, Cecil, and Geoffrey Wigoder, eds. 1972. *Encyclopedia Judaica*. 14 vols. Jerusalem: Keter.

Roussou, Eugenia. 2014. "Believing in the Supernatural through the 'Evil Eye': Perception and Science in the Modern Greek Cosmos." *Journal of Contemporary Religion* 29/3:425–38.

Rousseau, Pierette Bertrand. 1976. "Contribution à l'etude de mauvais oeil en Corse." *Ethnopsychologie* 31:5–18.

Rush, John A. 1974. *Witchcraft and Sorcery. An Anthropological Perspective on the Occult*. Springfield, IL: Thomas.

Rypka, Jan. 1965. "Der böse Blick bei Nizmi." *Ural-Altaische Jahrbücher* 36:397–401.

Sachs, Lisbeth. 1983. *Evil Eye or Bacteria: Turkish Migrant Women and Swedish Health Care*. Studies in Social Anthropology 12. Stockholm: University of Stockholm.

Salillas, Raphael. 1905 (2005). *La fascinación en España. Brujas, brujerías, amuletos*. Madrid: Arias.

Salmon, F., and M. Cabre. 1998. "Fascinating Women: The Evil Eye in Medieval Scholasticism." In *Medicine from the Black Death to the French Disease*, edited by R. French et al., 53–84. Aldershot, UK: Ashgate.

Salomone-Marino, Salvatore. 1882. "Rimedii e Fòrmole contro la Jettatura." *Archivio per lo Studio delle Tradizioni Popolari* 1:132–34.

Sanders, Ed. 2014. *Envy and Jealousy in Classical Athens: A Socio-Psychological Approach*. Emotions of the Past. Oxford: Oxford University Press.

Sanders, G. M. 1967. "Evil Eye." In *New Catholic Encyclopedia* 5:671.

Sanfo, Valerio. 1987. *Mal de Ojo y Hechizos*. Barcelona: Editorial de Vecchi.

Sanz Hermida, J. 2001. *Cuatro tratados médicos renacentistas sobre el mal de ojo*. Salamanca: Junta de Castilla y León.

Satriani, Raffaele Lombardi. 1951. *Credenze populari Calabrese.* Naples: De Simone.

Sault, N. L. 1990. "The Evil Eye, Both Hot and Dry: Gender and Generation among the Zapotec of Mexico." *Journal of Latin American Lore* 16:69–89.

Sastriar, E. N. Mahadeva. 1899. "The Evil Eye and the Scaring of Ghosts." *Journal of the Asiatic Society of Bengal* 68:56–60.

Sheikh-Dilthey, H. 1990. "Der Böse Blick: Vom Schutz des Lebensgehemnisses und der Abwehr schadenbringender Kräfte in Zentralarabien." *Der Islam* 67:140–49.

Schimizu, Y. 1983. "Trends in the Anthropological Study of the Evil Eye—An Annotated Review of Recent Works." [In Japanese] *Minzoku Gaku Kenkyu [Japanese Journal of Ethnology]* 48:91–100.

Schioppa, Antonino. 1830. *Antidoto al Fascino detto volgarmente Jettatura per servire d'appendice alla Cicalata di Niccola Valletta.* Naples: del Pierro.

Schlesier, R. 1991. "Mythenwahrheit versus Aberglaube: Otto Jahn und der böse Blick." In *Otto Jahn (1813–1868): Ein Geisteswissenschaftler zwischen Klassizismus und Historismus,* edited by William M. Calder III, Hubert Cancik, and Bernhard Kytzler, 234–67. Stuttgart: Steiner.

Schmid, Daniela. 2012. "Jüdische Amulette aus Osteuropa—Phänomene, Rituale, Formensprache." PhD dissertation, University of Vienna.

Schmidt, Bernhard. 1913. "Der böse Blick und ähnlicher Zauber im neugreichischen Volksglauben." *Neue Jahrbücher für das klassische Altertums Geschichte und Deutsche Literatur* 31:574–613.

Schoeck, Helmut. 1992 (1955). "The Evil Eye: Forms and Dynamics of a Universal Superstition." In *The Evil Eye: A Casebook,* edited by A. Dundes, 192–200. 2nd ed. Madison: University of Wisconsin Press. Reprinted from *Emory University Quarterly* 11:153–61.

Scurlock, Jo Ann. 1992. "Magic: Ancient Near East." In *ABD* 4:464–68.

Segal, Alan F. 1981 (1987). "Hellenistic Magic. Some Questions of Definition." In *Studies in Gnosticism and Hellenistic Religions,* edited by R. van den Broek and M. Vermaseren, 349–75. EPRO 91. Leiden: Brill. Reprinted in Alan F. Segal, *The Other Judaisms of Late Antiquity,* 79–108. Brown Judaic Studies 127. Atlanta: Scholars.

Segal, Alan F. 1995. "On the Nature of Magic: Report on a Dialogue between a Historian and a Sociologist." In *The Social World of the First Christians,* edited by L. Michael White and O. Larry Yarbrough, 275–92. Minneapolis: Fortress.

Seligmann, Siegfried, M.D. 1910 (1985). *Der Böse Blick und Verwandtes. Ein Beitrag zur Geschichte des Aberglaubens aller Zeiten und Völker.* 2 vols. Berlin: Barsdorf, 1910. Reprinted, Hildesheim: Olms.

———. 1912–1913. "Antike Malocchio-Darstellungen." *Archiv für die Geschichte der Medizin* 6:94–119.

———. 1914a. "Die Angst vor dem bösen Blick." *Zeitschrift für Augenheilkunde* 3:341–47, 513–19.

———. 1914b. "Die Angst vor dem bösen Blick und ihre Bekämpfung." *Klinisch-Therapeutische Wochenschrift* 21.38/41:980–83.

———. 1922 (1980). *Die Zauberkraft des Auges und das Berufen: Ein Kapitel aus der Geschichte des Aberglaubens.* Hamburg: Friederichsen. Reprinted, Den Haag: Couvreur.

———. 1927a *Die magischen Heil- und Schutzmittel aus der unbelebten Natur, mit besonderer Berücksichtigung der Mittel gegen den Bösen Blick. Eine Geschichte des Amulett-wesens.* Stuttgart: Strecker & Schroeder, 1927. Reprinted, 3 vols. (Vol.

1, das Planzenreich; Vol. 2, das Tierreich; Vol. 3, der Mensch). Edited by Jürgen Zwernemann. Berlin: Reimer Verlag, 1996–.

———. 1927b. "Auge." In *Handwörterbuch des deutschen Aberglaubens*, edited by Hanns Bächtold-Stäubli, 1:679–701. Berlin: de Gruyter.

Seymour-Smith, Charlotte. 1986a. "Folklore." In *Macmillan Dictionary of Anthropology*, edited by Charlotte Seymour-Smith, 120. London: Macmillan Reference Books.

———, 1986b. "Limited Good." In *Macmillan Dictionary of Anthropology*, edited by Charlotte Seymour-Smith, 168–69. London: Macmillan Reference Books.

———, ed. 1986c. *Macmillan Dictionary of Anthropology*. London: Macmillan Reference Books.

Servadio, Emilio. 1936. "Die Angst vor dem bösem Blick." *Imago* 22:396–408.

Shapiro, Gary. 2003. "The Evil Eye and Its Radiant Other." In *Archaeologies of Vision: Foucault and Nietzsche on Seeing and Saying*, 163–70. Chicago: University of Chicago Press.

Shakespeare, William. 1900. *The Complete Works of William Shakespeare. Thirty-seven Volumes in One*. New York: Black.

Sheikh-Dilthey, H. 1990. "Der Böse Blick: Vom Schutz des Lebensgeheimnisses und der Abwehr schadenbringender Kräfte in Zentalarabien." *Der Islam* 67:140–49

Sheldrake, Rupert. 2003. *The Sense of Being Starred at and Other Unexplained Powers of the Human Mind*. New York: Crown.

Shimizu, Y. 1983. "Trends in the Anthropological Study of the Evil Eye—An Annotated Review of Recent Works." [in Japanese]. *Minzo-kugaku kenkyu* [Japanese Journal of Ethnology] 48:91–100.

Shrut, Samuel. 1960. "Coping with the 'Evil Eye' or Early Rabbinical Attempts at Psychotherapy." *American Imago* 17:201–13.

Siebers, Tobin. 1983. *The Mirror of Medusa*. Berkeley: University of California Press, 1983.

Simeon, G. 1973. "The Evil Eye in a Guatemalan Village." *Ethnomedizin* 2:437–41.

Simon, G. 1988. *Le regard, l'être et l'apparence dans l'optique de l'Antiquité*. Paris: Seuil.

———. 1992. *Der Blick, das Sein und die Erscheinung in der antiken Optik*. Munich.

Singer, Isaac Bashevis. 1967. *The Manor*. New York: Farrar, Straus & Giroux.

Skolnik, Fred, ed. 2006. *Encyclopedia Judaica*. 2nd ed. 22 vols. New York: Thomson Gale.

Slade, Michael. 1997. *Evil Eye*. New York: Penguin, 1997.

Smedley, Edward et al. 1855. *The Occult Sciences: Sketches of the Traditions and Superstitions of Past Times, and the Marvels of the Present Day*. London: Griffin.

Soderlund, O. and H. Soderlund. 2013. "The Evil Eye in Cultural and Church History." Online: http://aslansplace.com/wp-content/uploads/2013/07/The_Evil_Eye_In_Cultural_and_Church_History-Soderlund.pdf.

Spence, Lewis. 2006. "Fascination." *Encyclopaedia of Occultism*, 156–58. New Hyde Park, NY: University Books.

Spooner, Brian. 1976 [1970]. "The Evil Eye in the Middle East." In *The Evil Eye*, edited by Clarence Maloney, 76–84. New York: Columbia University Press. Reprinted from *Witchcraft Confessions and Accusation*, edited by Mary Douglas, 311–19. Association of Social Anthropologists Monograph 9. London: Tavistock, 1970.

———. 1976b. "Anthropology and the Evil Eye." In *The Evil Eye*, edited by Clarence Maloney, 279–85. New York: Columbia University Press.

St. Clair, David. 1971. *Drum & Candle: First-hand Experiences and Accounts of Brazilian Voodoo and Spiritism.* Garden City, NY: Doubleday.

Staude, Wilhelm. 1934. "Le mauvais oeil dans la peinture chrétienne d'Abyssinie." *Journal Asiatique* 225:231–57.

Staude, Wilhelm. 1954. "Die Profilregeln in der christlichen Malerei Äthiopiens und die Furcht von dem 'Bösen Blick.'" *Archiv für Völkerkunde* 9:116–61.

Stein, Gordon, ed. 1996. *Encyclopedia of the Paranormal.* Amherst, New York: Prometheus.

Stein, Howard F. 1974 (1992). "Envy and the Evil Eye among Slovak-Americans: An Essay in the Psychological Ontology of Belief and Ritual." *Ethos* 2:15–46. Reprinted with minor sylistic changes in *The Evil Eye*, edited by Clarence Maloney, 193–222. New York: Columbia University Press, 1976. Also reprinted in *The Evil Eye: A Casebook*, edited by Alan Dundes, 223–56. 2nd ed. Madison: University of Wisconsin Press, 1992.

Steinbach, Ulrich. 1973. "Anstarren bei 'rot': Der böse Blick wird in einem simplen Versuch gemessen." *Frankfurter Rundschau* 5/4:103.

Stephenson, Peter H. 1979. "Hutterite Belief in Evil Eye: Beyond Paranoia and towards a General Theory of Invidia." *Culture, Medicine and Psychiatry* 3:247–65.

Stevens, Phillips Jr. 1996. "Evil Eye." In *The Encyclopedia of the Paranormal*, edited by Gordon Stein, 235–41. Amherst, NY: Prometheus.

Stillmann, Yedida. 1970. "The Evil Eye in Morocco." In *Folklore Research Center Studies*. Vol. 1. Edited by Dov Noy and Issachar Ben Ami, 81–94. Jerusalem: Magnes.

Stocchetti, Sara. 1941. "Interpretazione Storico-critica di una Diffusa Superstitione Populare." *Lares* 12:6–22.

Storace, Patricia. 1997. *Dinner with Persephone.* New York: Vintage.

Story, William Wetmore. 1860. "Roba di Roma: The Evil Eye and Other Superstitions." *Atlantic Monthly* 5:694–704.

Story, William Wetmore. 1877. *Castle St. Angelo and the Evil Eye Being Additional Chapters to "Roba di Roma."* London: Chapman & Hall.

Stratton, Kimberly B. 2007. *Naming the Witch: Magic, Ideology, and Stereotype in the Ancient World. Gender, Theory, and Religion.* New York: Columbia University Press.

Swiderski, Richard. 1976. "From Folk to Popular: Plastic Evil Eye Charms." In *The Evil Eye*, edited by Clarence Maloney, 28–42. New York: Columbia University Press, 1976.

Synnott, Anthony. "The Eye and I: A Sociology of Sight." *International Journal of Politics, Culture, and Society* 5 (1992) 617–36.

Szeghyova, Blanka, ed. 2005. *The Role of Magic in the Past: Learned and Popular Magic, Popular Beliefs and Diversity of Attitudes.* Bratislava: Pro Historia.

Tamborino, J. *De antiquorum daemonismo.* Religionsgeschichtliche Versuche und Vorarbeiten 7.3. Giessen: Topelmann, 1909.

Taylor, Mark P. 1933. "Evil Eye." *Folk-Lore* 44:308–9.

Teiltelbaum, Joel M. 1976. "The Leer and the Loom—Social Controls on Handloom Weavers." In *The Evil Eye*, edited by Clarence Maloney, 63–75. New York: Columbia University Press.

Theroux, Paul. 2013. "The Furies." *The New Yorker* 2/25/2013, pp. 66–73.

Thurston, Edgar. 1912. *Omens and Superstitions of Southern India.* London: Unwin. [Evil Eye, pp. 109–20].

Touhami, Slimane. 2007. "Contrer l'œil envieux. Croire et faire autour de l'*aïn* dans le Maghreb de France. " Doctoral dissertation, l'Université de Toulouse.

Touhami, Slimane. 2010. *La Part de l'oeil: Une ethnologie du Maghreb de France.* Paris: Editions du Comité des travaux historiques et scientifiques.

Tourney, Garfield, and Dean J. Plazak. 1954. "Evil Eye in Myth and Schizophrenia." *Psychiatric Quarterly* 28:478–95.

Trede, T. 1909. *Bilder aus dem religiösen und sittlichen Volksleben Süditaliens.* Gotha: Berthes.

Tuchmann, Jules [1830–1901]. "La fascination." *Mélusine. Recueil de mythologie, litterature populaire, traditions et usages.* Edited by Henri Gaidoz and Eugène Rolland. Paris: Librairie Viaut, 1878–1912. Vols 2 to 11 (1884–1912). 90 segments of study on the Evil Eye and the occult. On Tuchman see Gaidoz 1912; van Gennep 1967/1992.

Unschuld, Paul U. 1988. "Culture and Pharmaceutics: Some Epistemological Observations on Pharmacological Systems in Ancient Europe and Medieval China." In *The Context of Medicines in Developing Countries: Studies in Pharmaceutical Anthropology,* edited by Sjaak van de Geest and Susan Reynolds White, 179–97. Dordrecht: Kluwer Academic.

Vailland, Roger. 1958. *The Law.* Translated by Peter Wiles. New York: Knopf.

Vairus, Leonardus [1540–1603]. *De fascino. libri tres. In quibus omnes fascini species et causae optima methodo describuntur, et ex philosophorum ac theologorum sententiis scitè et eleganter explicantur: nec non contra praestigias, imposturas, illusionesque daemonum, cautiones et amuleta praescribuntur: ac denique nugae, quae de iisdem narrari solent, dilucidè confutantur.* Paris: Nicolas Chesneau, 1583; Venice: Aldo Manuzio the Younger, 1589.

Valla, Filippo. 1894. "La Jettatura (Ocru malu) in Sardegna (Barbagia)." *Archivio per lo Studio delle Tradizioni Populari* 13:419–32.

Valletta, Nicola. [1750–1814]. *Cicalata sul fascino volgarmente detto jettatura.* Naples: Morelli, 1777 (many editions: 1777/1787/1794; 2. ed. 1818/1820). Most recently, N. Valletta, *Cicalata sul fascino volgarmente detto jettatura* edited by Umberto Attardi, with a Hypothesis by Renato de Falco. Naples: Colonnese, 1988. Cf. Croce, Benedetto. "La 'Ciccalata' di Niccola Valletta." *Quaderni di Critica* 1/3 (1945) 20–24.

Vanel, Alvar. 2004. *Mal de ojo y envidia: amuletos hechizos infallibles.* Buenos Aires: Amigo.

Vecchiato, N. 1994. "Evil Eye, Health Beliefs and Social Tensions among the Sidama." In *New Trends in Ethiopian Studies. Proceedings of the 12th International Conference of Ethiopian Studies,* edited by H. Marcus, 1033–43. Asmara, NJ: Red Sea.

Vega, Juan José Hurtado. 1968. "'El Ojo': Creencias y Practicas Médicas Populares en Guatemala." *Tradiciones de Guatemala* 1:13–25.

Veikou, Christina. 1998. *Kako mati: hē koinōnikē kataskeuē tēs optikēs epikoinōnias.* Athens: Hellēnika Grammata.

———. 2008. "Ritual World and Symbolic Movement in Spells against the Evil Eye." In *Greek Magic: Ancient Medieval and Modern,* edited by J. C. B. Petropoulos, 95–105. Routledge Monographs in Classical Studies. London: Routledge.

Ven, N. van de, M. Zeelenberg, and R. Pieters. 2010. "Warding off the Evil Eye: When the Fear of Being Envied Increases Prosocial Behavior." *Psychological Science* 21: 1671–77.

Vereecken, J. L. 1968. "A propos du mauvais oeil." *L'hygiène mentale* 57:25–38.

Vigouroux, F. 1899. "Fascination." In *Dictionnaire de la Bible* 2:2180–81.

Vijaya-Tunga, J. 1935. "The Evil Eye." *The Spectator* 154:1011–12.

Villena, Enrique de Aragon, Marqués de [1384–1434.]. *Tratado de aojamiento o fascinología* (1411, 1422, 1425). New editions: F. Almagro and José Fernández Carpintero, eds., *Heurística a Villena Y Los Tres Tratados.* Madrid: Editora Nacional, 1977; Anna Maria Gallina, ed., *Enrique de Villena, Tratado de aojamiento.* Bari: Adriatica, 1978.

Vuorela, Turvo. 1967. *Der böse Blick in Lichte der finnischen Überlieferung.* Folklore Fellows Communication 201. Helsinki: Academia Scientiarum Fennica.

Wagner, Max Leopaldo. 1913. "Il Malocchio e credenze affini in Sardegna." *Lares* 2:129–50.

Waterman, Philip F. 1929. "The Evil Eye." In *The Story of Superstition.* New York: Knopf.

Wazana, Nili. 2007. "A Case of the Evil Eye: Qohelet 4:4–8." *Journal of Biblical Literature* 126:685–702.

Webster's New Collegiate Dictionary. 1977. Springfield, MA: Merrian.

Weller, Susan C., Roberta D. Baer, Javier Garcia de Alba Garcia, Mark Glazer, Robert Trotter II, Ana L. Salcedo Rocha, Robert E. Klein, and Lee M. Pachter. 2015. "Variation and Persistence in Latin American Beliefs About Evil Eye." *Cross-Cultural Research* 49/2: 174–203.

West, John O. 1974. "Mal Ojo." In *The Folklore of Texas Cultures*, edited by Francis Edward Abernethy, 82–84. Publications of the Texas Folklore Society 23. Austin: Encino.

Westermarck, Edvard Alexander. 1926 (1968). *Ritual and Belief in Morocco.* 2 vols. London: Macmillan. Reprinted, New York: University Books, 1968.

Wewerka, Franz. 1965. "Abergläubische Gebräuche gegen den 'bösen Blick' in Kärnten." *Die Kärntner Landmannschaft* 10:19–20.

Winer, Gerald A., and Jane E. Cottrell. 1996. "Does Anything Leave the Eye When We See? Extramission Beliefs of Children and Adults." *Current Directions in Psychological Science* 5:137–42.

Winer, Gerald A. et al. 2002. "Fundamentally Misunderstanding Visual Perception: Adults' Belief in Visual Emission." *American Psychologist* 57:417–24.

———. 2003. "Do Adults Believe in Visual Emissions?" *American Psychologist* 58:495–96.

Winkelmann, Michael. 1982. "Magic: A Theoretical Reassessment." *Current Anthropology* 23:37–66.

Wolf, E. 1955. "Types of Latin American Peasantry: A Preliminary Discussion." *American Anthropologist* 57:452–71.

Woodburne, A. Stewart. 1992 (1935). "The Evil Eye in South Indian Folklore." In *The Evil Eye: A Casebook*, edited by Alan Dundes, 55–65. 2nd ed. Madison: University of Wisconsin Press, 1992. Reprinted from *International Review of Missions* 24:237–47.

Yale, Charles H. and Sidney R Ellis. 1898. *The Evil Eye and the Many Merry Mishaps of Nid and the Weird, Wonderful Wandering of Nod: A Fantastical Spectacular Trick Comedy in Three Acts.* Washington, DC: Grossmann & Strafford.

Zammit-Maempel, G. 1968. "The Evil Eye and Protective Cattle Horns in Malta." *Folklore* 79:1–16.

Zinvovieff, Sofka. 1991. "Inside Out and Outside In: Gossip, Hospitality and the Greek Character." *Journal of Mediterranean Studies* 1:120–34.

Zumwalt, Rosemary Lévy. 1996. "'Let it go to the garlic': Evil Eye and the Fertility of Women among the Sephardim." *Western Folklore* 55:261–80.

BIBLIOGRAPHY
FOR CHAPTER 2:
MESOPOTAMIA AND EGYPT

1. PRIMARY TEXTS/SOURCES

1.1. Mesopotamian Texts

Cunningham, Graham. 1997. 'Deliver Me From Evil': Mesopotamian Incantations 2500–1500 BC. Studia Pohl Series Maior 17. Rome: Pontifical Biblical Institute.

Dijk, J. van. 1967. "VAT 8382. Ein zweisprachiges Königsritual." In Heidelberger Studien zum Alten Orient: Adam Falkenstein zum 17. September 1966, edited by Dietz Otto Edzard, 233–68. Wiesbaden: Harrassowitz, 1967.

Farber, W. 1981. "Zur älteren akkadischen Beschwörungsliteratur." ZA 71:51–72.

Foster, Benjamin R. 2005. Before the Muses: An Anthology of Akkadian Literature. Bethesda, MD: CDL Press, 1993; 2nd edition, 2 vols., 1996; 3rd. ed., one vol., 2005.

Gaster, T. H. 1973. "A Hang-up for Hang-ups: The Second Amuletic Plaque from Arslan Tash." BASOR 209:18–26.

Geller, Markham J. 2003. "Paranoia, the Evil Eye, and the Face of Evil." In Literatur, Politik und Recht in Mesopotamien, edited by W. Sallaberger, 115–34. Wiesbaden: Harrassowitz.

———. 2004. "Akkadian Evil Eye Incantations from Assur." Zeitschrift für Assyriologie und vorderasiatische Archäologie 94:52–58.

———. 2007. Evil Demons: Canonical Utukkū Lemnūtu Incantations. State Archives of Assyria Cuneiform Texts, 5. Helsinki: Neo-Assyrian Text Corpus Project University of Helsinki.

Genouillac, Henri de. 1930. Textes religieux sumériens du Louvre. 2 vols. Textes Cunéiform, Musée de Louvre, vols. 15 and 16. Paris: Geuthner. Vol. 2 (ML 16), Plates 82–173 =TCL 16.

Langdon, Stephen. 1913. Babylonian Liturgies. Paris: Geuthner.

———. 1919. Sumerian Liturgies and Psalms. Publications of the Babylonian Section vol. 10 no. 4. Philadelphia: University of Pennsylvania Museum.

————. 1992 [1913]. "An Incantation in the 'House of Light' against the Evil Eye." In *The Evil Eye: A Casebook*, edited by Alan Dundes, 39–40. 2nd ed. Madison: University of Wisconsin Press, 1992. Reprinted from Langdon, *Babylonian Liturgies*, 11–12.

Meissner, Bruno, ed. 1917. *Altorientalische Texte und Untersuchungen*. 2 vols. Leiden: Brill.

Montgomery, James A. 1913. *Aramaic Incantation Texts from Nippur*. University of Pennsylvania, The Museum, Publications of the Babylonian Section, vol. 3. Philadelphia: University Museum.

Thompson, R. Campbell. 1903–4. *The Devils and Evil Spirits of Babylonia: Being Babylonian and Assyrian Incantations Against the Demons, Ghouls, Vampires, Hobgoblins, Ghosts, and Kindred Evil Spirits, Which Attack Mankind*. 2 vols. London: Luzac.

Veldhuis, Niek. 1992. "Comments on *Igi-hul.*" *Nouvelles Assyriologiques Brèves et Utilitaires* 43/2:33–34.

1.2. Ugaritic Texts

Cunchillos, J.-L. et al. 2003. *Texts of the Ugaritic Data Bank*. Translated by A. Lacadena and A. Castro. Piscataway, NJ: Gorgias.

Moor, J. C. de. 1987. *An Anthology of Religious Texts from Ugarit*. NISABA 16. Leiden: Brill.

Parker, Simon B., ed. 1997. *Ugaritic Narrative Poetry*. Writings from the Ancient World. Atlanta: Scholars.

Wyatt, Nick. 2002. "KTU 1.96: A Spell against the Evil Eye." In *Religious Texts from Ugarit*, 375–77. 2nd ed. Biblical Seminar 53. London: Sheffield Academic.

1.3. Egyptian Texts/Sources

Ägyptische Urkunden aus den Staatlichen Museen zu Berlin: Griechische Urkunden. Vols. 1–4. Berlin: Weidmann, 1895–1912.

Ancient Egyptian Book of the Dead: Journey through the Afterlife. Edited by John H. Taylor. London: British Museum Press, 2010.

The Ancient Egyptian Coffin Texts. Translated by Raymond O. Faulkner. 3 vols. in 1. Warminster: Aris & Philipps, 2004.

The Ancient Egyptian Pyramid Texts. Translated by James P. Allen. Atlanta: Society of Biblical Literature, 2005.

The Ancient Egyptian Pyramid Texts. Translated by R. O. Faulkner. 2 vols. Oxford: Clarendon, 1969.

Bagnell, R. S., ed. 1976. *The Florida Ostraka: Documents from the Roman Army in Upper Egypt*. Durham, NC, 1976. (Abbrev.: O.Flor.)

Bagnall, R. S., P. J. Sijpesteijn, and K. A. Worp, eds. 1976. *Ostraka in Amsterdam Collections (O. Amst.)*. Studia Amstelodamensia ad epigraphicam, ius antiquum et papyrologicam pertinentia 9. Zutphen: Terra.

Bernand, Étienne. 1969. *Inscriptions métriques de l'Égypte gréco-romaine. Recherches sur la poésie épigrammatique des Grecs en Égypte*. Annales littéraires de l'Université de Besançon 98. Paris: Belles lettres.

———. 1982. *Inscriptions grecques d'Égypte et de Nubie: Répertoire bibliographique des OGIS*. Annales littéraires de l'Université de Besançon 272. Centre de Recherche d'Histoire Ancienne 45; Paris: Belles lettres.

Betz, Hans Dieter et al., eds. 1992. *The Greek Magical Papyri in Translation Including the Demotic Spells*. 2 vols. 2nd ed. Chicago: University of Chicago Press.

Borghouts, J. F., trans. 1978. *Ancient Egyptian Magical Texts*. Nisaba 9. Leiden: Brill.

Bouquet, A. C. 1954. *A Companion Source-Book to Comparitive Religion*. Baltimore: Penguin.

Buck, Adriaan de, and A. H. Gardiner, eds. 1936–1963. *The Egyptian Coffin Texts*. 7 vols. Oriental Institute Publications 34, 49, 64, 67, 73, 81, 87. Chicago: University of Chicago Press.

Lichtheim, Miriam. 1973. *Ancient Egyptian Literature*. Vol. 1, *The Old and Middle Kingdoms*. Berkeley: University of California Press.

Piankoff, Alexandre. 1964. *The Litany of Re*. Egyptian Religious Texts and Representations 4. Princeton: Princeton University Press.

Priesigke, Friedrich et al., eds. 1915 [2013]. *Sammelbuch griechischer Urkunden aus Ägypten*. Reprinted, Strassburg: Trübner.

Rossiter, Evelyn, ed. *The Book of the Dead: Papyri of Ani, Hunefer, Anhaï, with Commentaries*. Fribourg: Liber, 1979.

Sethe, Kurt, ed. 1904–16. *Hieroglyphische Urkunden der griechisch-römischen Zeit*. Leipzig: Hinrichs.

1.4. Aramaic Sources

Isbell, Charles D., ed. 1975. *Corpus of Aramaic Incantation Bowls*. SBLDS 17. Missoula, MT: Scholars.

Naveh, Joseph, and Shaul Shaked. 2009 [1985]. *Amulets and Magic Bowls. Aramaic Incantations of Late Antiquity*. 2nd ed. Reprinted, Varda, 2009.

———. 1993. *Magic Spells and Formulae: Aramaic Incantations of Late Antiquity*. Jerusalem: Magnes.

1.5. Mandaean Sources

Drower, E. S. 1937. "Shafta d Pishra d Ainia: A Mandaean Magical Text." *JRAS* 69:589–611. [*Šapta d-Pišra d-Ainia* ("Scroll for the Exorcism of (Evil) Eyes")]. Syriac Mandaic.

———. 1938. "Shafta d Pishra d Ainia: A Mandaean Magical Text.." *JRAS* 70:1–20. [*Šapta d-Pišra d-Ainia* ("Scroll for the Exorcism of (Evil) Eyes")]. Syriac Mandaic.

———. 1943. "A Mandaean Book of Black Magic." *JRAS* 75:149–81.

Yamauchi, E. M., ed. 1967. *Mandaic Incantation Texts*. American Oriental Series, 49. New Haven: Yale University Press.

1.6. Syriac Sources

Gollancz, Hermann. 2012 [1912]. *The Book of Protection, being a Collection of Charms Now Edited for the First Time from Syriac MSS with Translation, Introduction and Notes, with 27 Illustrations.* Piscataway, NJ: Gorgias, 2012.

1.7. Greek and Roman Writings

Catullus. 1913. *Poems.* Translated by F. W. Cornish. LCL. Cambridge: Harvard University Press.

Heliodorus. 1961. *Ethiopian Story.* Translated by W. Lamb. Everyman's Library 276. London: Dent.

Heliodorus. 1935–43. *Héliodore: Les Éthiopiques. Téagène et Chariclé.* Edited by R. M. Rattenbury and T. W. Lamb. Translated by J. Maillon. 3 vols. Paris: "Les Belles Lettres."

Lucian of Samosata. 1913–67. *Lucian.* 8 vols. Translated by A. M. Harmon et al. LCL. Cambridge: Harvard University Press; London: Heinemann.

Nonnus of Panopolis. 1940. *Nonnus, Dionysiaca* (48 Books). 3 vols. Translated by W H D. Rouse. LCL. Cambridge: Harvard University Press.

Pliny the Elder. *Pliny: Natural History.* 10 vols. Translated by H. Rackham et al. LCL. Cambridge: Harvard University Press, 1938–63.

Plutarch. *Plutarch: Moralia.* Translated by F. C. Babbitt et al. 16 vols. LCL. Cambridge: Harvard University Press, 1927–69.

Porphyry of Tyre. 1987. *The Life of Pythagoras.* In *The Pythagorean Sourcebook and Library: An Anthology of Ancient Writings Which Relate to Pythagoras and Pythagorean Philosophy.* Compiled and translated by Kenneth Sylvan Guthrie. Edited by David R. Fiedler. Newburyport, MA: Red Wheel Weiser Conari/Phanes Press.

Pseudo-Lucian. 1967. *Affairs of the Heart.* Translated by M. D. Macleod. LCL. Cambridge: Harvard University Press.

Virgil. 1916. *Eclogues, Georgics, Aeneid.* Translated by H. R. Fairclough. LCL. Cambridge: Harvard University Press.

2. SECONDARY LITERATURE

Abd el-Azim el-Adly, S. 1994. "Der böse Blick und der blaue Stein." *Göttinger Miszellen* 138:7–10.

Abusch, I. Tzvi. 1987. *Babylonian Witchcraft Literature: Case Studies.* Brown Judaic Studies 132. Atlanta: Scholars.

———. 1989. "The Demonic Image of the Witch in Standard Babylonian Literature: The Reworking of Popular Conceptions by Learned Exorcists." In *Religion, Science, and Magic in Concert and in Conflict,* edited by Jacob Neusner et al., 27–58. New York: Oxford University Press.

———. 2002. *Mesopotamian Witchcraft: Toward a History and Understanding of Babylonian Witchcraft Beliefs and Literature.* Ancient Magic and Divination, 5. Leiden: Styx-Brill.

————. 2008. *Omina, Orakel, Rituale und Beschwörungen*. Texte aus der Umwelt des Alten Testament 4. Gütersloh: Gütersloher.

Abusch, Tzvi, and David Schwemer. 2011. *Corpus of Mesopotamian Anti-Witchcraft Rituals*. Ancient Magic and Divination 8/1. Leiden: Brill.

Abusch, Tzvi, and Karel van der Toorn, eds. 1999. *Mesopotamian Magic: Textual, Historical, and Interpretive Perspectives*. Studies in Ancient Magic and Divination 1. Groningen: Styx.

Andrews, Carol A. R. 1988. *Jewelry 1: From the Earliest Times to the Seventeenth Dynasty*. Catalogue of Egyptian Antiquities in the British Museum 6. London: British Museum.

————. 1994. *Amulets of Ancient Egypt*. London: British Museum, 1994.

————. 1997 [1990]. *Ancient Egyptian Jewelry*. Reprinted, New York: Abrams.

————. 2001. "Amulets." *Oxford Encyclopedia of Ancient Egypt*, 1:75–82. 3 vols. New York: Oxford University Press.

Anthes, Rudolf. 1961. "Das *Sonnenauge* in den Pyramidentexten." *ZÄS* 86:1–21.

Arnaud, Louis. 1912. "*La baskania* ou le mauvais oeil chez les Grecs modernes." *Échos d'Orient* 15:385–94, 510–24.

Astour, M. C. 1988. "Remarks on KTU 1.96." *SEL* 5:13–24.

Aune, David. E. 1986. "Magic; Magician." In *ISBE* 3:213–19.

Ball, Philip. 2001. *Bright Earth: Art and the Invention of Color*. Chicago: University of Chicago Press. "The Problem of Blue," Pp. 231–49.

Barba de Piña Chán, Beatriz. 1989. "Spells." Translated by Erica Meltzer. In *Hidden Truths: Magic, Alchemy, and the Occult*, edited by Lawrence E. Sullivan, 217–23. New York: Macmillan.

Barjamovic, Gojko, and Mogens Trolle Larsen. 2008. "An Old Assyrian Incantation against the Evil Eye." *Altorientalische Forschungen* 38/1:144–55.

Bernand, André. 1991. *Sorciers grecs*. Paris: Fayard.

Black, Jeremy et al. 1992. *Gods, Demons and Symbols of Ancient Mesopotamia: An Illustrated Dictionary*. London: British Museum Press.

Blackman, Winifried S. 1927. *The Fellahin of Upper Egypt.Their Religious, Social and Industrial Life To-day with Special Reference to Survivals from Ancient Times*. London: Harrup.

Blum, Richard, and Eva Blum. 1970. *The Dangerous Hour: The Lore and Culture of Crisis and Mystery in Rural Greece*. London: Chatto & Windus.

Bonneau, D. 1982. "L'apotropaïque 'Abáskantos' en Égypte." *Revue de l'historie des religions* 99/1:23–36.

Bonner, Campbell. 1950. *Studies in Magical Amulets Chiefly Graeco-Egyptian*. Ann Arbor: University of Michigan Press.

————. 1951. "Amulets Chiefly in the British Museum: A Supplementary Article." *Hesperia* 20:301–45 (plates 96–100).

Bonnet, Hans, ed. 1971. *Reallexikon der ägyptischen Religionsgeschichte*. 2nd ed. Berlin: de Gruyter.

————. 2000. "Böser Blick." In *Lexikon der ägyptischen Religionsgeschichte*, 122. Hamburg: Nikol.

Borg, Alexander, ed. 1999. *The Language of Color in the Mediterranean: An Anthropology of Linguistic and Ethnographic Color Terms*. Stockholm: Almqvist & Wiksell.

Bouquet, A. C. 1954. *A Companion Source-Book to Comparative Religion*. Baltimore: Penguin.

Bo[u]rghouts, J. F. 1973. "The Evil Eye of Apopis." *Journal of Egyptian Archaeology* 59:114–50.

Bowie, Fiona. 2006. "Witchcraft and the Evil Eye." In *The Anthropology of Religion*, 200–236. 2nd ed. Oxford: Wiley-Blackwell.

Brandon, S. G. F. 1983. "The Eye Goddess." In *Man, Myth, and Magic: The Illustrated Encyclopedia of Mythology, Religion and the Unknown*, edited by Richard Cavendish, 4:888. New edition edited and compiled by Yvonne Deutsch. New York: Cavenidish.

Brashear, William. 1994. "Horos." In *RAC* 16:574–97.

Braudel, Fernand. 2001. *Memory and the Mediterranean*. Translated by A. Reynolds. New York: Knopf.

Braun-Holzinger, Eva A. 1999. "Apotropaic Figures at Mesopotamian Temples in the Third and Second Millennia." In *Mesopotamian Magic: Textual, Historical, and Interpretative Perspectives*, edited by Tzvi Abusch and Karel van der Toorn, 149–72. Studies in Ancient Magic and Divination 1. Groningen: Styx.

Brenk, Frederick E. 1998. "Caesar and the Evil Eye or What Do You Do with *kai su, teknon*." In *Qui Miscuit Utile Dulci: Festschrift Essays for Paul Lachlan MacKendrick*, edited by Gareth Schmeling and Jon D. Mikalson, 31–49. Wauconda, IL: Bolchazy-Carducci.

———. 1999. "The KAI SY Stele in the Fitzwilliam Museum, Cambridge." *Zeitschrift für Papyrologie und Epigraphik* 126:169–74.

Brögger, Jan. 1968. "The Evil Eye in a Calabrese Village." *Folk: Dansk etnografisk tidsskrift* 10:13–24.

Brown, Peter. 2009. "The Color Blue." *Scientific American* 301/93:93.

Bryen, Ari Z., and Andrzej Wypustek. 2009. "Gemellus' Evil Eyes (P.Mich. VI 423–424)." *Greek, Roman, and Byzantine Studies* 49:535–55.

Budge, E. A. Wallis. 1914. *The Literature of the Ancient Egyptians*. London: Dent.

———. 1971 [1901]. *Egyptian Magic*. Reprinted, New York: Dover.

———. 1978 [1930]. *Amulets and Superstitions*, with 22 plates and 300 Text Illustrations. Reprinted, New York: Dover.

Burkert, Walter. 1992. *The Orientalizing Revolution: Near Eastern Influence on Greek Culture in the Early Archaic Age*. Translated by Walter Burkert and Margaret E. Pinder. Cambridge: Harvard University Press.

Cahill, J. M. 1984. "'Horus Eye' Amulets." In *Excavations at the City of David: Final Report. Varia*, edited by D. Shiloh, 291–97. Qedem 35. Jerusalem: Institute of Archaeology, Hebrew University.

Campbell, John K. 1964. *Honour, Family and Patronage: A Study of Institutions and Moral Values in a Greek Mountain Community*. Oxford: Oxford University Press.

Carney, Thomas F. 1975. *The Shape of the Past: Models and Antiquity*. Lawrence, KS: Coronado.

Casson, Lionel. 1971. *Ships and Seamanship in the Ancient World*. Princeton: Princeton University Press.

Cauville, S. 1989. "La chapelle de Thot-Ibis à Dendera édifiée sous Ptolémée Ier par Hor, scribe d'Amon-Rê." *BIFAO* 89:43–56, esp. 52–54.

Cavassini, Maria Teresa. 1954. "Lettere cristiane nei papyri greci d'Egitto." *Aegyptus* 34:266–82.

Cavigneaux, A. 1996. "Notes Sumérologiques." *ASJ* 18:31–45.

Cavigneaux, A., and F. N. H. Al-Rawi. 1993. "Textes magiques de Tell Haddad (Textes de Tell Haddad II)." *ZA* 83:195–205.

———. 1994. "Charmes de Sippar et de Nippur." In *Cinquante-deux reflections sur le Proche-Orient ancien: offerts en homage à Léon De Meyer*, edited by Hermann Gasche et al., 73–89. Mesopotamian History and Environment Occasional Publications 2. Louvain: Peeters.

———. 1995a. "Textes magiques de Tell Haddad (Textes de Tell Haddad II). Deuxième partie." *ZA* 85:19–46.

———. 1995b. "Textes magiques de Tell Haddad (Textes de Tell Haddad II). Troisième partie." *ZA* 85:169–220.

Contenau, Georges. 1947. *La magie chez les Assyriens et les Babyloniens*. Paris: Payot.

Crawford, O. G. S. 1991 [1957]. *The Eye Goddess*. Reprinted, Oak Park, IL: Delphi.

Cross, Frank Moore. 1974. "Leaves from an Epigraphist's Notebook." *CBQ* 36:486–94.

Cryer, F. H., and M.-L. Thomsen. 2001. *Witchcraft and Magic in Europe: Biblical and Pagan Societies*. Philadelphia: University of Pennsylvania Press.

ed-Dairabī, A. 1940. *Kitābu muğarrabāti . . .* [Arabic Book of Magic] Cairo.

Daremberg, Charles, and Edmund Saglio, eds. 1877–1919. *Dictionnaire des antiquités grecques et romaines*. 5 vols. Paris: Hachette. Abbrev: Daremberg-Saglio.

Darnell, John Coleman. 1997. "The Apotropaic Goddess in the Eye." *Studien zur altägyptischen Kultur* 24:35–48.

De Cenival, Françoise. 1988. *Le mythe de l'oeil du soleil: Translittération et traduction avec commentaire philologique*. Demotische Studien 9. Sommerhausen: Zauzich

Delatte, A. and Derchain, P. 1964. *Les intailles magiques gréco-égyptiennes*. Paris: Bibliothèque nationale.

Deutscher, Guy. 2010. *Through the Language Glass: Why the World Looks Different in Different Languages*. New York: Metropolitan.

Devish, René. 2007. "Witchcraft and Sorcery." In *A Companion to Psychological Anthropology: Modernity and Psychocultural Change*, edited by Conerly Casey and Robert B. Edgerton, 389–416. Blackwell Companions to Anthropology 4. Malden, MA: Blackwell.

de Wit, C. 1979. "Les Valeurs du Signe de l'Oeil dans le Système Hiéroglyphique." In *Festschrift für Elmar Edel*, edited by M. Görg and E. Pusch, 1:46–55. Studien zur Geschichte, Kultur und Religion Ägyptens und des Alten Testaments. Bamberg.

Dietrich, Manfred, and Otto Loretz. 1997. "Der Charakter der Göttin 'Anat: *'nn* und weitere Schreibfehler in KTU 1.96." *UF* 29:151–60.

Dobberahn, F. E. 1976. *Fünf Äthiopische Zauberrollen: Text, Übersetzung, Kommentar*. Beiträge zur Sprach- und Kulturgeschichte des Orients, 25. Walldorf-Hessen: Verlag für Orientkunde.

Douglas, Mary Tew. 1963. "Techniques of Sorcery Control." In *Witchcraft and Sorcery in East Africa*, edited by John Middleton and E. H. Winter, 123–41. London: Routledge & Kegan Paul, 1963.

———. 1967. "Witch Beliefs in Central Africa." *Africa* 37:72–80.

———. 1970a. "Introduction. Thirty Years after *Witchcraft, Oracles and Magic*." In *Witchcraft Confessions & Accusations*, edited by Mary Douglas, xiii–xxxviii. New York: Tavistock.

———, ed. 1970b. *Witchcraft Confessions & Accusations*. New York: Tavistock.

————. 1999. "Sorcery Accusations Unleashed. The Lele revisted, 1987." In *Implicit Meanings. Essays in Anthropology*, 77–94. New ed. London: Routledge & Kegan Paul.

Drower, E. S. 1937. "Shafta d Pishra d Ainia: A Mandaean Magical Text." *JRAS* 69:589–611.

————. 1938. "Shafta d Pishra d Ainia: A Mandaean Magical Text." *JRAS* 70:1–20.

————. 1943. "A Mandaean Book of Black Magic." *JRAS* 75:149–81.

Ebeling, Erich. 1938. "Blick, Böser." In *Reallexikon der Assyriologie und Vorderasiatischen Archäologie*, 2:55.

————. 1949. "Beschwörungen gegen den Feind und den bösen Blick aus dem Zweistromlande." *Archiv Orientalni* 17/1:172–211.

Ebeling, Erich et al., eds. 1938. *Reallexikon der Assyriologie und Vorderasiatischen Archäologie*. Vol. 2. Berlin: de Gruyter.

Edwards, Dennis. 1971. "The 'Evil Eye' and Middle Eastern Culture." *Folklore Annual* (Austin, Texas) 3:33–40.

Eisen, Gustavus. 1916. "The Characteristics of Eye Beads from the Earliest Times to the Present." *American Journal of Archeology* 20:1–27.

Erman, Adolf. 1901. *Zaubersprüche für Mutter und Kind aus dem Papyrus 3207 des Berliner Museums*. Berlin: Berlin Museum.

————. 1907. *A Handbook of Egyptian Religion*. Translated by A. S. G. Johns. London: Constable.

————. 1934. *Die Religion der Ägypter*. Berlin: de Gruyter, 1934.

————, ed. 1966. *The Ancient Egyptians: A Sourcebook of Their Writings*. Translated by Aylward M. Blackman. Introduction to the Torchbook edition by William Kelly Simpson. New York: Harper & Row.

Evans-Pritchard, E. E. 1950. *Witchcraft, Oracles and Magic among the Azande*. 2nd ed. Oxford: Clarendon.

Falkenstein, Adam. 1931. *Die Haupttypen der Sumerischen Beschwörung*. Leipzig: Hinrichs.

Falkner, R. O. 1969. *The Ancient Egyptian Pyramid Texts*. 2 vols. Oxford: Oxford University Press.

————. 1973–78. *The Ancient Egyptian Coffin Texts*. 3 vols. Warminster: Aris & Phillips.

Falkner, R. O. 1985. *The Ancient Egyptian Book of the Dead*. Revised edition by C. A. R. Andrews. *London*: British Museum Press.

Faraone, C. A. 2000. "Handbooks and Anthologies. The Collection of Greek and Egyptian Incantations in Late Hellenistic Egypt." *Archiv für Religionsgeschichte* 2:195–214.

Farber, W. 1981. "Zur älteren akkadischen Beschwörungsliteratur." *ZA* 71:51–72.

————. 1984. "Early Akkadian Incantations: Addenda et Subtrahenda." *JNES* 43:69–71

————. 1989. *Schlaf, Kindchen, Schlaf! Mesopotamische Baby-Beschwörungen und Rituale*. Mesopotamian Civilizations 2. Winona Lake, IN: Eisenbrauns.

————. 1995. "Witchcraft, Magic, and Divination in Ancient Mesopotamia." In *Civilizations of the Ancient Near East*, edited by Jack M. Sasson, 3: 1895–909. New York: Scribner.

Ford, James Nathan 1998. " 'Ninety-Nine by the Evil Eye and One from Natural Causes.' KTU 1.96 in Its Near Eastern Context." *UF* 30:201–78.

———. 2000. "Additions and Corrections to 'Ninety-Nine by the Evil Eye . . .'" *UF* 32:711–15.

Fossey, Charles. 1902. *La Magie assyrienne*. Paris: Leroux.

Foster, Benjamin R. *Before the Muses: An Anthology of Akkadian Literature*. Bethesda, MD: CDL Press, 1993; 2nd edition, 2 vols., 1999; 3rd. ed., one vol., 2005.

Frachtenberg, Leo. 1918. "Allusions to Witchcraft and Other Primitive Beliefs in Zoro-astrian Literature." In *The Dastur Hoshang Memorial Volume*, 399–453. Bombay: Fort Printing Press.

Frankfurter, David. 1998. *Religion in Roman Egypt. Assimilation and Resistance*. Princeton: Princeton University Press.

———. 2006. "Fetus Magic and Sorcery Fears in Roman Egypt." *Journal of Greek, Roman, and Byzantine Studies* 46:37–62.

Gardiner, Alan H. 1916. "A Shawahti-Figure with Interesting Names, The Evil Eye in Egypt." *Proceedings of the Society of Biblical Archaeology* 38:129–30.

Gaster, Theodor H. 1989. "Amulets and Talismans." In *Encyclopedia of Religion*. New York: Macmillan, 1987; reprinted in *Hidden Truths: Magic, Alchemy, and the Occult*, Lawrence E. Sullivan, 145–50. New York: Macmillan.

Geller, Markham J. 1985. *Forerunners to Udug-hul: Sumerian Exorcistic Incantations*. Freiburger altorientalische Studien 12. Wiesbaden: Steiner, 1985.

———. 1995. "The Influence of Ancient Mesopotamia on Hellenistic Judaism." In *Civilizations of the Ancient Near East*, edited by Jack M. Sasson, 1:43–54. New York: Scribner.

———. 2003. "Paronoia, the Evil Eye, and the Face of Evil." In *Literatur, Politik und Recht in Mesopotamien*, edited by W. Sallaberger, et al., 115–34. Wiesbaden.

———. 2004. "Akkadian Evil Eye Incantations from Assur." *ZA* 94:52–58.

———. 2007. *Evil Demons: Canonical Utukkū Lemnūtu Incantations*. State Archives of Assyria Cuneiform Texts 5. Helsinki: Neo-Assyrian Text Corpus Project University of Helsinki.

Ghosh, Amitar. 1983. "The Relations of Envy in an Egyptian Village." *Ethnology* 22: 211–23.

Gollancz, Hermann. 2012 [1912]. *The Book of Protection, being a Collection of Charms Now Edited for the First Time from Syriac MSS with Translation, Introduction and Notes, with 27 Illustrations*. Reprinted, Piscataway, NJ: Gorgias, 2012.

Goodenough, E. R. 1953–65. *Jewish Symbols in the Greco-Roman World*. 12 vols. Bollingen Series 37. New York: Pantheon.

Gordon, Cyrus H. 1934. "Aramaic Magical Bowls in the Istanbul and Baghdad Museums." *ArOr* 6:324–26.

———. 1937. "Aramaic and Mandaic Magic Bowls." *ArOr* 9:84–106.

———. 1957. "A World of Demons and Liliths." In *Adventures in the Ancient Near East*, 160–84. London: Phoenix.

Green, A. R. 1983. "Neo-Assyrian Apotropaic Figures." *Iraq* 45:87–96 and plates 9–15.

Griffith, F. L., and Herbert Thompson, eds. 1904–9. *The Demotic Magical Papyrus of London and Leiden*. 3 vols. London: Grevel.

Griffiths, J. Gwynn. 1938. "A Protection against the Evil Eye in Lower Nubia and Upper Egypt." *Man* 38:68–70.

———. 1960. *The Conflict of Horus and Seth*. Liverpool: Liverpool University Press.

Grossi, Vincenzo. 1886. *Il Fascino e La Jettatura nell' Antico Oriente*. Milan-Torino: Dumolard.

Gurney, O. R. 1935. "Babylonian Prophylactic Figures and Their Rituals." *Annals of Archaeology and Anthropology* 22:21–96.

Gyory, Hedvig. 1994. "Les amulettes de l'oeil 'oudjat' ailé et le Mythe de l'OEil du Soleil." *Bulletin de la Société d'Égyptologie* 18:23–32.

Haas, Volkert. 1980. "Die Dämonisierung des Fremden und des Feindes im Alten Orient." *Roesnik Orientalistyczny* 41/2:37–44.

Hallo, William W. 2005. "Divination in Ancient Babylonia." *Biblical Archaeology Review* 31/2:32–39.

Hamp, Douglas M. 2000. "A Study of the Continuum of Hypostasis in Ancient Israel." MA thesis, Hebrew University of Jerusalem.

Hardie, Margaret M. [Mrs. F. W. Hasluck]. 1992 (1923). "The Evil Eye in Some Greek Villages of the Upper Haliakmon Valley in West Macedonia." In *The Evil Eye: A Casebook*, edited by Alan Dundes, 107–23. 2nd ed. Madison: University of Wisconsin Press, 1992. Reprinted from *Journal of the Royal Anthropological Institute* 53:160–72.

Helck, Hans Wolfgang. 1971. *Die Beziehungen Ägyptens zu Vorderasien im 3. und 2. Jahrtausend v. Chr.* 2nd ed. Wiesbaden: Harrasowitz.

———. 1979. "Horus." In *Der Kleine Pauly* 2:1231–33.

Helck, Hans Wolfgang et al., eds. *Lexikon der Ägyptologie*. 7 vols. Wiesbaden: Harrassowitz, 1975–1992.

Hermann, A., and M. Cagiano di Azevedo. 1969. "Farbe." In *RAC* 7:358–447.

Herrmann, Christian. 1994. *Ägyptische Amulette aus Palästina/Israel*. Orbis Biblicus et Orientalis 138. Göttingen: Vandenhoeck & Ruprecht.

———. 2002. *Ägyptische Amulette aus Palästina/Israel II*. Orbis Biblicus et Orientalis 184. Göttingen: Vandenhoeck & Ruprecht.

Höbl, Günther. 1986. *Ägyptisches Kulturgut im phönikischen und punischen Sardinien. I. Textteil; II. Anmerkungen, Indizes und 188 Tafeln*. Leiden: Brill.

Horsley, Richard A. 2014. *Jesus and Magic: Freeing the Gospel Stories from Modern Misconceptions*. Eugene, OR: Cascade Books.

Hunter, E. C. D. 1993. "A Scroll Amulet from Kuristan." *ARAM* 5:252.

Jahn, Otto. 1855. *Über den Aberglauben des bösen Blickes bei den Alten*. Berichte der Sächsischen Gesellschaft der Wissenschaften zu Leipzig. Philologisch-Historische Classe. Leipzig: Hirzel.

Jastrow, Marcus. 1905–12. *Die Religion Babyloniens und Assyriens*. 3 vols. Giessen: Ricker.

Johnstone, Paul. 1980. *The Sea-craft of Prehistory*. Prepared for publication by Sean McGrail. London: Routledge & Kegan Paul.

Kees, Hermann. 1923. *Horus und Seth als Götterpaar*. Leipzig: Hinrichs.

Kötting, Bernhard. 1954. "Böser Blick." In *RAC* 2:473–82.

———. 1978. "Geste und Gebärde." In *RAC* 10:895–902.

Kötzsche, Lieselotte. 1986. "Hand II (ikonographisch)." *RAC* 13:402–82, esp. 467–69.

Kotzé, Z. 2013. "The evil eye and agoraphobia in the Maqlū-series." *Tydskrif vir Semitistiek / Journal for Semitics* 22/2:268–275.

Kramer, Samuel Noah. 1960. *Two Elegies on a Pushkin Museum Tablet: A New Sumerian Literary Genre*. Moscow: Oriental Literature.

———. 1963. *The Sumerians: Their History, Culture, and Character*. Chicago: Chicago University Press.

————. 1969. "Sumerian Lamentation." In *Ancient Near Eastern Texts Relating to the Old Testament*, edited by James B. Pritchard, 611–19. 3rd ed. Princeton: Princeton University Press.

Krebernik, Manfred. 1984. *Die Beschwörungen aus Fara und Ebla: Untersuchungen zur älstesten keilsschriftlichen Beschwörungsliteratur*. Hildesheim: Olms.

Kriss, Rudolf, and Hubert Kriss-Heinrich. 1962. *Volksglaube im Bereich des Islam*. Vol. 2. *Amulette, Zauberformen und Beschwörungen*. Wiesbaden: Harrassowitz.

Kuhrt. Amélie. 1995. *The Ancient Near East, c. 3000–330 BC*. 2 vols. London: Routledge.

Lane, Edward William. 1973 [1895]. *An Account of the Manners and Customs of the Modern Egyptians*. 5th ed. Reprinted, New York: Dover, 1973.

Lenormant, F. 1878. *Die Magie und Wahrsagekunst der Chaldäer*. Jena: Costenoble.

Lenski, Gerhard, and Jean Lenski. "Agrarian Societies." In *Human Societies. An Introduction to Macrosociology*. 5th ed. New York: McGraw Hill, 1987; 7th ed. with Patrick Nolan, 1995.

Lewis, Napthali. 1983. *Life in Egypt under Roman Rule*. Oxford: Oxford University Press.

Lexa, F. 1925. *La Magie dans l'Egypte antique*. 3 vols. Paris: Geuthner.

Licht, Hans. 1971 [1932]. *Sexual Life in Ancient Greece*. London: Abbey Library.

Lichtheim, Miriam. 1973. *Ancient Egyptian Literature*. Vol. 1. *The Old and Middle Kingdoms*. 1973. Berkeley: University of California Press.

Ludwig, Theodore M. 1989 [1987]. "Incantation." In *Hidden Truths*. Selections from the *Encyclopedia of Religion*, edited by Mircea Eliade. Edited by L. E. Sullivan, 193–201. New York: Macmillan.

Lurker, M. 1980. *An Illustrated Dictionary of The Gods and Symbols of Ancient Egypt*. London: Thames & Hudson.

Lyavdansky, Alexey. 2011. "Syriac Charms in Near Eastern Context: Tracing the Origin of Formulas." In *Oral Charms in Structural and Comparative Light*, edited by T. A. Mikhailova et al., 15–21. Moscow: Probel.

Mallowan, M. E. L. 1947. "Excavations at Brak and Chagar Bazar." *Iraq* 9:1–259.

————. 1965. *Early Mesopotamia and Iran*. New York: McGraw-Hill.

Maloney, Clarence, ed. 1976. *The Evil Eye*. New York: Columbia University Press.

Meisen, Karl. 1950. "Der böse Blick und anderer Schadenzauber in Glaube und Brauch der alten Völker und in frühchristlicher Zeit." *Rheinisches Jahrbuch für Volkskunde* 1:144–77.

Mouton, Alice. 2009. "Le 'mauvais œil' d'après les textes cunéiformes hittites et mésopotamiens." In *Pensée grecque et sagesse d'Orient*, edited by M. A. Amir Moezzi et al., 425–39. Hommage à Michel Tardieu. Bibliothèque de l'École des Hautes Études—Sciences religieuses, 142. Turnhout: Brepols.

Müller-Winkler, C. 1987. *Die ägyptischen Objekt-Amulette. Mit Publikation der Sammlung des Biblischen Institutes der Universitäat Freiburg Schweiz, ehemals Sammlung Fouad S. Matouk*. OBO Series Archaeologica 5. Göttingen: Vandenhoeck & Ruprecht.

Naveh, J. 1975. "Another Mandaic Lead Roll." *JOS* 5:47–53.

————. 1998. "Fragments of an Aramaic Magic Bowl from Qumran." *IEJ* 48:252–61.

Naville, E. 1910. "Charms and Amulets (Egyptian)." In *HERE* 3:430–33.

Nowak, Troy Joseph. 2006. "Archaeological Evidence for Ship Eyes: An Analysis of Their Form and Function." M. A. thesis, Texas A &M University.

Ogden, Daniel. 2002. "The Evil Eye." In *Magic, Witchcraft, and Ghosts in the Greek and Roman Worlds: A Sourcebook.* New York: Oxford University Press, 2002.

Olmo Lete, G. del. 1992a. "Un conjuro ugarítico contra el 'mal ojo' (KTU 1.96)." *AF* 15:7–16.

————. 1992b. *La religion cananea según la liturgia de Ugarit: Estudio textual.* AOS 3. Sabadell (Barcelona): Editorial AUSA. [Pp. 255–59 is an abridged version of 1992a].

————. 1999. *Canaanite Religion: According to the Liturgical Texts of Ugarit.* Translated by W. G. E. Watson. Bethesda, MD: CDL.

————. 2010. "KTU 1.96 Once Again: De nuevo sobre KTU 1.96." *Aula Orientalis* 28:39–54.

Oppenheim, A. Leo. 1977. *Ancient Mesopotamia: Portrait of a Dead Civilization.* Rev. ed. Chicago: University of Chicago Press.

Otto, E. 1975. "Auge." In *Lexikon der Ägyptologie,* edited by Wolfgang Helck and Eberhard Otto, 1:559–661. Wiesbaden: Harrassowitz.

Oyler, D. S. 1992 [1919]. "The Shilluk's Belief in the Evil Eye: The Evil Medicine Man." In *The Evil Eye: A Casebook,* edited by Alan Dundes, 78–85. 2nd ed. Madison: University of Wisconsin Press. Reprinted from *Sudan Notes and Records,* 2:122–28.

Pardee, Dennis. 2002. "The Attack of the Evil Eye and a Counterattack. Text no. 50. RS 22.225." In *Ritual and Cult at Ugarit,* 161–66. Writings from the Ancient World 10. Atlanta: Society of Biblical Literature.

Pastoureau, Michel. 2001. *Blue: the History of a Color.* Translated by Markus I. Cruse. Princeton: Princeton University Press.

Petrie, W. M. Flinders. 1972 [1914]. *Amulets.* Reprinted, Warminster: Aries & Phillips.

Pinch, Geraldine. 1994. *Magic in Ancient Egypt.* Austin: University of Texas Press.

Pinches, T. G. 1901. "Assyriological Gleanings." *Proceedings of the Society of Biblical Archaeology* 23:188–210.

Quirke, Stephen. 1992. *Ancient Egyptian Religion.* London: British Museum Press.

Rakoczy, Thomas. 1996. *Böser Blick, Macht des Auges und Neid der Götter: Eine Untersuchung zur Kraft des Blickes in der griechischen Literatur.* Classica Monacensia 13. Tübingen: Narr.

Redford, Donald B., ed. 2001. *Oxford Encyclopedia of Ancient Egypt.* 3 vols. New York: Oxford University Press.

Reitzenstein, Richard. 1904. *Poimandres: Studien zur griechisch-ägyptischen und frühchristlichen Literatur.* Leipzig: Teubner.

Reminick, Ronald A. 1975. "The Structure and Function of Religious Belief among the Amhara of Ethiopia." In *United States Conferences on Ethiopian Studies.* 1st Proceedings, Michigan State University. 1973. East Lansing: Michigan State University Press.

————. 1976 [1974]. "The Evil Eye Belief among the Amhara of Ethiopia." *Ethnology* 13:279–91. Reprinted in *The Evil Eye,* edited by Clarence Maloney, 85–101. New York: Columbia University Press.

Riemschneider, Margarete. 1953. *Augengott und heilige Hochzeit.* Leipzig: Koehler & Amelang.

Ritner, Robert K. 1993. *The Mechanics of Ancient Egyptian Magical Practice.* Studies in Ancient Oriental Civilization 54. Chicago: Oriental Institute Press.

Ritner, Robert K. 1995. "The Religious, Social and Legal Parameters of Traditional Egyptian Magic." In *Ancient Magic and Ritual Power*, edited by Marvin Meyer and Paul Mirecki, 43–62. Religions in the Graeco-Roman World 129. Leiden: Brill.

Roberts, John M. 1976. "Belief in the Evil Eye in World Perspective." In *The Evil Eye*, edited by Clarence Maloney, 223–78. New York: Columbia University Press.

Rohrbaugh, Richard L. 1996. "Introduction." In *The Social Sciences and New Testament Interpretation*, edited by Richard L. Rohrbaugh, 1–15. Peabody, MA: Hendrickson.

Romdon, M. A. 2000. *Kitab Mujarobat: Dunia Magi Orang Islam-Jawa*. Yogyakarta: Lazuardi.

Rougé, Jean. 1981. *Ships and Fleets of the Ancient Mediterranean*. Translated by Susan Frazer. Middletown, CT: Wesleyan University Press.

Rudnitzky, Günter. 1956. *Die Aussage über 'Das Auge des Horus': Eine altägyptische Art geistiger Äußerung nach dem Zeugnis des Alten Reiches*. Analecta Aegyptica 5. Copenhagen: Munksgaard.

Rundle Clark, R. T. 1978. *Myth and Symbol in Ancient Egypt*. London: Thames & Hudson.

Rossiter, Evelyn. 1979. *The Book of the Dead: Papyri of Ani, Hunefer, Anhaï*. New York: Crown.

Sainte Fare Garnot, J. 1960. "Défis au destin." *Bulletin de l'Institut Français d'Archéologie Orientale* 56:1–28.

Sasson, Jack, ed. 1995. *Civilizations of the Ancient Near East*. 4 vols. New York: Scribner.

Sauneron, Serge. 1966. "Le monde du magicien égyptien," In *Le monde du sorcier. Égypte, Babylone, Hittites, Israël, Islam, Asie centrale, Inde, Nepal, Cambodge, Viet-nam, Japon*, edited by Serge Sauneron, 27–65. Sources orientales, 7. Paris: Seuil.

Sauneron, Serge et al. 1966. *Le monde du sorcier: Égypte, Babylone, Hittites, Israël, Islam, Asie centrale, Inde, Nepal, Cambodge, Viet-nam, Japon*. 20 vols. Sources orientales 7. Paris: Seuil, 1966.

Schmidt, Bernhard. 1913. "Der böse Blick und ähnlicher Zauber im neugreichischen Volksglauben." *Neue Jahrbücher für das klassische Altertumsgeschichte und Deutsche Literatur* 31:574–613.

Schott, Siegfried. 1931. "Ein Amulett gegen den bösen Blick." *ZÄS* 67:106–10.

Schwemer, Daniel. 2007. *Abwehrzauber und Behexung: Studien zum Schadenzauberglauben im alten Mesopotamien*. Wiesbaden: Harrassowitz.

Scurlock, Jo Ann. 1991. "Baby-Snatching Demons, Restless Souls and the Dangers of Childbirth: Medico-Magical Means of Dealing with Some of the Perils of Motherhood in Ancient Mesopotamia." *Incognita* 2:135–83.

———. 2002. "Translating Transfers in Ancient Mesopotamia." In *Magic and Ritual in the Ancient World*, edited by Marvin Meyer and Paul Mirecki, 209–23. Religions in the Graeco-Roman World 141. Leiden: Brill.

Seawright, Helen L. 1988. "The Symbolism of the Eye in Mesopotamia and Israel." MA thesis, Wilfried Laurier University. Online: http://scholars.wlu.ca/etd/94.

Seligmann, Siegfried. 1985 [1910]. *Der Böse Blick und Verwandtes: Ein Beitrag zur Geschichte des Aberglaubens aller Zeiten und Völker*. 2 vols. Reprinted Hildesheim: Olms.

Sethe, Kurt H. 1964 [1912]. *Zur altägyptischen Sage vom Sonnenauge das in der Fremde war*. Untersuchungen zur Geschichte und Altertumskunde Ägyptens 5.3. Leipzig: Hinrichs. Reprinted Hildesheim: Olms, 1964.

Shaw, Ian, ed. 2000. *The Oxford History of Ancient Egypt*. Oxford: Oxford University Press.

Spiegelberg, Wilhelm. 1915. *Der ägyptische Mythos vom Sonnenauge in einem demotischen Papyrus der römischen Kaiserzeit*. Sitzungsberichte der königlich Preussischen Akademie der Wissenschaften, Philologisch-Historische Klasse, 1915.

Spiegelberg, Wilhelm. 1917. *Der ägyptische Mythus vom Sonnenauge nach dem Leidener demotischen Papyrus I 384*. Strassburg: Strassburger Druckerei und Verlagsanstalt.

———. 1924. "Der böse Blick im altägyptischen Glauben." *ZÄS* 59:149–54.

Spooner, Brian. 1976 [1970]. "The Evil Eye in the Middle East." In *The Evil Eye*, edited by Clarence Maloney, 76–84. New York: Columbia University Press. Reprinted from *Witchcraft Confessions and Accusation*, edited by Mary Douglas, 311–19. Association of Social Anthropologists Monograph 9. London: Tavistock, 1970.

Sterman, Baruch, with Judy Taubes Sterman. 2012. *The Rarest Blue: The Remarkable Story of an Ancient Color Lost to History and Rediscovered*. Guilford, CT: Lyons.

Strommenger, Eva. 1964. *5000 Years of the Art of Mesopotamia*. Photographs by Max Hiermer. New York: Abrams.

Sullivan, Lawrence E., ed. 1989 [1987]. *Hidden Truths: Magic, Alchemy, and the Occult. Religion, History, and Culture. Selections from the Encyclopedia of Religion*, edited by Mircea Eliade (1987). New York: Macmillan, 1989.

Tamborino, Julius. 1909. *De antiquorum daemonismo*. Religionsgeschichtliche Versuche und Vorarbeiten 7.3. Giessen: Töpelmann.

Tarelko, Michael. 1999–2000. "A Magical Scroll from the Drower Collection. DC 21 Šapta d-pišra d-aina 'The Scroll of the Annihilation of the Eyes.'" *ARAM* 11–12:249–52.

Thompson, R. Campbell. 1903–4. *The Devils and Evil Spirits of Babylonia: Being Babylonian and Assyrian Incantations against the Demons, Ghouls, Vampires, Hobgoblins, Ghosts, and Kindred Evil Spirits, Which Attack Mankind*. 2 Vols. London: Luzac.

Thompson, R. Campbell. 1910. "Charms and Amulets (Assyro-Babylonian)." In *HERE* 3:409–11.

Thomsen, Marie-Louise. 1987. *Zauberdiagnose und schwarze Magie in Mesopotamien*. Carston Niebuhr Publications 2. Copenhagen: Museum Tusculanum Press.

———. 1992. "The Evil Eye in Mesopotamia." *Journal of Near Eastern Studies* 51:19–32.

Toorn, Karel van der. 1999. "Magic at the Cradle: A Reassessment." In *Mesopotamian Magic: Textual, Historical, and Interpretive Perspectives*, edited by Tzvi Abusch, and Karel van der Toorn, 139–47. Studies in Ancient Magic and Divination 1. Groningen: Styx. esp. 140–143.

Ulmer, Rivka Kern. 2003. "The Divine Eye in Ancient Egypt and in the Midrashic Interpretation of Formative Judaism." *Journal of Religion and Society* 5:1–18.

Van Buren, E. Douglas. 1945. "Amulets in Ancient Mesopotamia." *Orientalia* n.s. 14:18–23.

———. 1955 "New Evidence Concerning an Eye-Divinity." *Iraq* 17:164–75.

van Dijk, Jan J. A. 1967. "VAT 8382. Ein zweisprachiges Königsritual." In *Heidelberger Studien zum Alten Orient*, edited by D. O. Edzard, 233–68. Wiesbaden: Harrassowitz.

Virolleaud, C. 1960. "Un nouvel épisode du mythe ougaritique de Baal." *CRAIBL*. Paris: Picard, 1960.

Vittmann, G. 1984. "Ein Amulett aus der Spätzeit zum Schutz gegen Feinde." *ZÄS* 111: 164–70.

Walker, James. 1990. "The Place of Magic in the Practice of Medicine in Ancient Egypt." *Bulletin of the Australian Centre for Egyptology* 1:85–95.

———. 1993. "Egyptian Medicine and the Gods." *Bulletin of the Australian Centre for Egyptology* 4:83–101.

Ward, J. O. 1980. "Witchcraft and Sorcery in the Later Roman Empire and the Early Middle Ages." *Prudentia* 12/2:93–108.

Ward, William A. 1963. "Egypt and the East Mediterranean from Predynastic Times to the End of the Old Kingdom." *JESHO* 6:1–57.

———. 1971. *Egypt and the East Mediterranean World 2200–1900 B.C.* Beirut: American University of Beirut.

———. 1992. "Egyptian Relations with Canaan." In *ABD* 2:399–408.

Wasserman, Nathan. 1995. "'Seeing eye to eye . . . ' Concerning Two Incantations against Lamashtu's Evil Eye." *NABU* (Sept.) 61 §70.

Watterson, Barbara. 1984. *The Gods of Ancient Egypt.* London: Batsford.

Weinreich, Otto. 1909. "Helios, Augen Heiland." *Hessische Blätter für Volkskunde* 8: 168–73.

Wiedemann, Alfred. 1910. *Die Amulette der alten Ägypter.* Leipzig: Hinrichs.

Wiggermann, F. A. M. 2000. "Lamashtu, Daughter of Anu: A Profile." In *Birth in Babylonia and the Bible: Its Mediterranean Setting,* edited by M. Stol, 217–52. Cuneiform Monographs 14. Groningen: Styx.

Wilkinson, A. 1971. *Ancient Egyptian Jewelry.* London: Methuen.

Woodard, Roger, ed. 2004. *The Cambridge Encyclopedia of the World's Ancient Languages.* Cambridge: Cambridge University Press.

Worrell, W. H. 1909. "Studien zum abessinisichen Zauberwesen." *ZA* 23:149–83.

———. 1910. "Studien zum abessinisichen Zauberwesen (Fortsetzung)." *ZA* 24:59–96.

———. 1914–15. "Studien zum abessinisichen Zauberwesen (Fortsetzung und Schluss)." *ZA* 29:85–141.

———. 1935. "Coptic Magical and Medical Texts." *Orientalia* n.s. 4:1–37, 184–94.

Wyatt, N. 2002. "KTU 1.96: A Spell against the Evil Eye." In *Religious Texts from Ugarit,* 375–77. 2nd ed. Biblical Seminar 53. New York: Continuum.

INDEX

ARAMAIC SOURCES

UGARITIC & PHOENICIAN SOURCES

EGYPTIAN SOURCES

ETHIOPIAN SOURCES